FROM CODEX
To Hypertext

A VOLUME IN THE SERIES
Studies in Print Culture and the History of the Book

EDITORIAL ADVISORY BOARD
Greg Barnhisel
Robert A. Gross
Joan Shelley Rubin
Michael Winship

FROM CODEX
To Hypertext

Reading at the Turn of the Twenty-first Century

EDITED BY
ANOUK LANG

UNIVERSITY OF MASSACHUSETTS PRESS
Amherst and Boston

Copyright © 2012 by University of Massachusetts Press
All rights reserved
Printed in the United States of America

LC 2012022568
ISBN 978-1-55849-953-9 (paper); 952-2 (library cloth)

Designed by Sally Nichols
Set in Minion Pro
Printed and bound by Thomson-Shore, Inc.

Library of Congress Cataloging-in-Publication Data

From codex to hypertext : reading at the turn of the twenty-first century / edited by Anouk Lang.
   pages cm. — (Studies in print culture and the history of the book)
   Includes bibliographical references and index.
   ISBN 978-1-55849-952-2 (library cloth) — ISBN 978-1-55849-953-9 (pbk.) 1. Books and reading. 2. Reading interests. 3. Books and reading—Technological innovations. 4. Book industries and trade—Technological innovations. 5. Electronic publishing. I. Lang, Anouk, 1976–
   Z1003.F84 2012
   028'.9—dc23
                              2012022568

British Library Cataloguing in Publication data are available.

Publication of this volume has been supported by the Centre for Canadian Studies at the University of Birmingham and an Aid to Scholarly Publications Grant from Mount Saint Vincent University.

Portions of chapter 6 were previously published in *Reading Is My Window: Books and the Art of Reading in Women's Prisons,* by Megan Sweeney. Copyright © 2010 by the University of North Carolina Press. Used by permission of the publisher. www.uncpress.unc.edu.

CONTENTS

Acknowledgments — vii

INTRODUCTION
Transforming Reading
Anouk Lang — 1

PART I
COMMUNITIES AND PRACTICES

1. ZINES THEN AND NOW
What Are They? What Do You Do With Them? How Do They Work?
Janice Radway — 27

2. HAVE MOUSE, WILL TRAVEL
Consuming and Creating Chinese Popular Literature on the Web
Jin Feng — 48

3. ONLINE LITERARY COMMUNITIES
A Case Study of LibraryThing
Julian Pinder — 68

4. BUILDING A NATIONAL CULTURE OF READING IN THE "NEW" SOUTH AFRICA
Molly Abel Travis — 88

5. LITERARY TASTE AND LIST CULTURE IN A TIME OF "ENDLESS CHOICE"
David Wright — 108

6. **"KEEPIN' IT REAL"**
   Incarcerated Women's Readings of African American Urban Fiction
   Megan Sweeney — 124

7. **PRODUCING MEANING THROUGH INTERACTION**
   Book Groups and the Social Context of Reading
   Joan Bessman Taylor — 142

8. **GENRE IN THE MARKETPLACE**
   The Scene of Bookselling in Canada
   Julie Rak — 159

PART II
METHODS

9. **NEW LITERARY CULTURES**
   Mapping the Digital Networks of Toni Morrison
   Ed Finn — 177

10. **CONFOUNDING THE LITERARY**
    Temporal Problems in Hypertext
    David S. Miall — 203

11. **READING THE READING EXPERIENCE**
    An Ethnomethodological Approach to "Booktalk"
    Daniel Allington and Bethan Benwell — 217

12. **MIXING IT UP**
    Using Mixed Methods Research to Investigate Contemporary Cultures of Reading
    Danielle Fuller and DeNel Rehberg Sedo — 234

    About the Contributors — 253
    Index — 255

ACKNOWLEDGMENTS

In assembling this volume I feel fortunate to have been the beneficiary of a great deal of support and advice from many scholars from the constellation of fields surrounding literary studies, book history, and reception study. Chief among these are Danielle Fuller and DeNel Rehberg Sedo, who directed the research project which gave rise to this volume, Beyond the Book: Mass Reading Events and Contemporary Cultures of Reading in the UK, USA and Canada, funded by the Arts and Humanities Research Council in the UK (grant number 112166). I feel privileged to have worked with Danielle and DeNel on Beyond the Book, and I thank them for the many illuminating conversations about reading that we had while on the road as researchers together. I also owe a particular debt of gratitude to Jan Radway, whose exceptional generosity and encouragement has meant a great deal to me.

I am also grateful to Stephen Brown, Susan Brown, Nigel Edley, Kate Eichhorn, Dick Ellis, John Frow, Jennifer C. Greene, Caroline Hamilton, Jenny Hartley, Michel Hockx, Lynette Hunter, Deena Inghams, Belinda Leach, Ruthann Lee, Karin Littau, Anne McDermott, Adrian Miles, Sam Naidu, Dru Pagliasotti, Anna Poletti, Chris Walton, Claire Warwick, Teresa Zackodnik, and Heather Zwicker. Many thanks to Brian Halley, Carol Betsch, Sally Nichols, and Mary Bellino at University of Massachusetts Press for taking such care in bringing this volume to publication, and to Amanda Heller for her meticulous copyediting of the manuscript.

Above all, love and thanks beyond words to Andrew, and to our little son Corin, whose journey through the joys of reading has just begun.

FROM CODEX
To Hypertext

INTRODUCTION
Transforming Reading

Anouk Lang

To investigate reading practices in the decades on either side of the turn of the twenty-first century is to expose a rapidly evolving field whose inner dynamics are still in the process of being mapped and understood. Interpretive practices that previously might have been found only among a small circle of intimates can now be shared and disseminated online, and as a result are becoming visible, searchable, and, increasingly, commercially significant. The same is occurring with the digital traces left by book purchasing. A variety of technological developments are emerging as alternatives to existing systems of book production and distribution: the near-instantaneous delivery of texts to an e-book reader such as the Kindle, for example, and the arrival of technology that can print and bind a single book on demand and deliver it directly to the consumer within minutes. Interest in—and concern about—these developments registers in the popular press as well as in the academy, where a steadily rising tide of interest in the field of book history has coincided with developments in reception study, communications, and cultural studies.[1] Methodologies for the study of reading are also evolving, with ethnographic approaches being adopted for use, and critiqued, by those in fields such as literary studies within which the study of reading had in earlier decades found a home.[2] In the context of such rapid and recent change, it is an area in need of scholarly attention, and one worth braving the perils of setting down any conclusions in codex form.

Research into the nature of contemporary reading practices necessarily involves inquiring into the changing social conditions for the production and consumption of texts. The interpretations that readers take from texts are contingent on the contexts in which their reading occurs, and what readers articulate about their reading therefore needs to be understood as embedded within a network of social and interpersonal relationships.[3] As John Frow observes, texts are positioned within and are constituted by multiple frameworks of social meaning, entering into a diverse array of relations with readers, and therefore coming to signify in different and not necessarily compatible ways.[4] The work that readers do on texts—accepting or resisting interpretations presented as normative, meshing their reading with other social practices and semiotic domains—can be performed only from within these regimes of reading.[5]

Taking these insights as a starting point, this volume proceeds from a position of keen attentiveness to the constellation of social relations within which acts of reading are embedded, and seeks to situate individual instances of reading in relation to what Tony Bennett describes as "the broader fields of relations (discursive, institutional, intertextual) that organize the cultural terrain of specific text-reader encounters."[6] At the same time, however, it is important not to let an emphasis on structure and social context lead us to lose sight of acts of individual agency, creativity, resistance, and freedom within the interaction between reader and text: the task must be to grasp both realities at the same time. By exploring the sociality of an increasingly networked world of readers, this volume positions itself at the intersection of precisely these two concerns which have animated the study of reading and reception: on the one hand, the integration of reading into the lives and experiences of individuals, and on the other, the constrictions and limitations that social and ideological structures place on readers' actions and freedom. Keeping the tension between these two strands in view, the essays gathered here demonstrate how it is not resolved but reconfigured, for example, when new technologies open up spaces in which readers can generate their own constructions of texts and offer critical responses that need not adhere to the sanctioned judgments of literary experts.

Although this volume draws heavily on, and speaks to, the tradition of reception studies, it seeks also to integrate this tradition with forms of inquiry usually pursued elsewhere. For example, by approaching reading as something that is not merely being transformed but is itself a force for transformation, it aims to integrate reception study with a consideration of the ways that developments in technology and other spheres are reconstituting audiences and the reading practices they adopt. In addition, the reality of contemporary reading practices forces us to confront the artificiality of the historical divide between scholarly work on social processes around the *consumption* of texts and research that deals with textual *production*. As the essays in this volume make clear, the processes of consumption and production exist in a reciprocal relation, shaping and setting the limits for each other and inflecting the dynamic interrelations between readers and the network of social relations in which they are embedded. Acts of textual production are borne out of—and inflected by—readings of the cultural texts and contexts that precede them: as each text is itself read, it gives rise to new instances of textual generation.[7]

The essays in this volume bring together a variety of contexts in which ideas about reader tastes, interactions, and interpretive activities can be reconsidered at a moment of technological change. They have been selected to offer a range of case studies which bring different kinds of disciplinary expertise to bear on contemporary reading practices, which both attend to the impact of new technologies and do not limit themselves to it, and which account for continuities as well as transformations. Substantively, the essays in this volume traverse a number of central themes: how to account for both change and continuity with existing reading practices; the extent to which new technologies make different forms of literary knowledge accessible; the interpenetration of textuality and identity; the rising value of the trade in culture; the presence of ethnocentrism and other forms of bias in scholarship; and challenges to the disciplinary frames within which the study of reading occurs. Some treat developments brought about by new technologies, while others discuss non-technological changes, and others consider familiar institutions such as reading groups and bookshops, with all investigating how these respond to the conditions of the early twenty-first century. In bringing these contributions together, this volume makes the case for the importance of studying reading practices at a moment of significant technological upheaval by presenting a variety of angles from which to approach this task and a range of regimes in which readers are situated and by which they are shaped.

This introduction uses the notion of hybrid practices to describe contemporary transformations to reading, identifying areas of particular significance where these can be seen playing out and gesturing toward some of the theoretical and critical problems that are likely to confront reception researchers as they attend to the wider ramifications of these changes. Turning to the individual essays in the volume, it points to the ways in which these are in dialogue with one another and with existing scholarship on reading, and it demonstrates how questions that engage scholars of reception study today are also pertinent ones for the study of historical periods. By offering carefully contextualized case studies of the web of relationships between readers, texts, and reading contexts, the essays present a range of perspectives on the ways textual meanings and literary value circulate among interpretive communities at a time of rapid technological change.

Transformations as Remediations

In *Codex in Crisis*, the historian Anthony Grafton claims that the computer and the Internet have transformed reading more extensively than any other technology since the printing press.[8] Although it is clear that we are living at a time of significant changes for certain kinds of reading practices, simplistic and ahistorical characterizations of this period as one of radical discontinuity need to be resisted. In light of the high degree of interdependence among the elements at work in the encounter between text and reader, attempts to account for new developments are not best served by epistemological models that rest on radical disjunctive breaks. As Paul Duguid argues, strong claims that the book will be superseded entirely by other technologies are likely to be overstated,[9] and such assertions speak more to anxieties around the unknown impact of new technologies than to the often gradual ways in which such developments tend to be integrated into existing practices that are transformed organically rather than abruptly. Websites such as LibraryThing and BookCrossing and online book-swapping services, for example, demonstrate a variety of ways in which printed books are not marginalized but made the central focus of different ways of interacting with other readers and accessing book-related information. The resulting hybrid practices rarely present an entirely new formation but rather create a meshing of old and new technologies and established and emergent modes of interaction. Indeed, there are many points of continuity to be found between the modes of reading described in this volume and those of previous eras. Urban fiction had its origins in the 1970s, for example, while book clubs go back several centuries further. Although One Book projects have appeared more recently, at the end of the 1990s, they are still anchored for the most part in face-to-face activities rather than new media. Understanding the import of these changes, then, is as much about grasping continuities and remediations of established reader behavior as it is about charting new territory.

Conceptualizing the contemporary period as a time of hybridization of the old and the new can help us to be more attentive to complex patterns of both continuity and change. In this way, familiar reading practices that have been detailed by book historians of previous eras can be related to new ways in which texts and readers interact.[10] These connections are apparent in the use of terms such as *page*, *scroll*, and *index*, which are firmly anchored in codex publication and also central to our understanding of new technologies for reading. As the Transliteracies project points out, these terms recall historical reading technologies even as the material practices associated with their use have evolved and developed, leading to the imperative for scholars to consider "the interplay between inherited conventions and recent inventions, expectations and improvisations."[11] Geoff Hall observes that developments including audiobooks, iPods, and radio programs such as the BBC's *Book at Bedtime* recall historical practices such as reading aloud, and these echoes remind us that the process of making meaning through books has been, and continues to be, a dynamic one.[12] The move toward digitization should be seen as the most recent in a long series of efforts in human history to store and retrieve information, and one that, Grafton claims, will result "not in the infotopia that the prophets conjure up but in one more in a long series of new information ecologies."[13] The concentration of technological change in the decades spanning the third millennium may bear the hallmarks of a critical moment, but it is one that looks both backwards and forwards.

Detailed analyses of textual reception such as those in this volume make it difficult to take at face value generalized criticisms that the rise of the Internet will bring about a decline in reading and literary culture, such as Sven Birkerts's claim that the "stable hierarchies of the printed page" are being irrevocably undermined and displaced by "the rush of impulses through freshly minted circuits."[14] In fact, as Wendy Griswold shows, technological change and practices of reading have been closely connected throughout history.[15] When windows became more affordable for the middle classes in the eighteenth century, there was an upsurge in reading; when the development of the railways in the nineteenth century offered travelers long periods of time to fill, the same effect occurred. Indeed, the tendency for emergent technologies to prompt moral panics is itself a recurrent historical phenomenon, as Toby Miller points out. From film in the 1920s to radio in the 1930s, television in the 1950s, video recorders in the 1980s, and video games in the 1990s, new technologies have been seen to offer "forms of mastery and fun that threaten, however peripherally, the established order."[16]

In the twenty-first century, one of the most familiar scapegoats for the putative decline of print culture after television is the Internet, yet the available evidence suggests that spending time online does not appear to discourage print reading. A study by the National Endowment for the Arts reported that Internet users spent the same amount of time reading as individuals who did not use computers at all. Moreover, when education was held constant, those who reported the greatest amount of Internet use were also those who reported themselves to be the heaviest readers.[17] Book production, too, has been helped rather than hindered by new media technologies.[18] That the relationship between reading and the Internet should be in some respects a mutually supportive one rather than a zero-sum game is not surprising when we consider the wide range of opportunities for engaging in book-related activities; as Griswold puts it, "The imagery of dividing up a media pie misses the considerable synergy at work."[19] The analyses in this volume show how emerging technologies often act in concert with those through which print volumes are disseminated and instrumentalized. They also demonstrate the utility of the concept of hybridity in drawing attention to the complex patterns of continuity and discontinuity that characterize the contemporary moment of transformation, and in expressly avoiding the nostalgia and hyperbolism of claims of radical newness.

Hybrid Practices

It is possible to identify at least four key themes around which discussions of various hybrid reading practices coalesce: the democratizing effects of the Internet; the challenges that new reading practices pose to existing ways of establishing literary value; the role played by textuality in subject formation in Internet-mediated contexts; and questions around the identity-work that readers can be observed to be doing through book-related technologies. One change invoked with some regularity in relation to digital technology is its capacity to open up access to information. Where the availability of books is at issue, however, debates over the merits of the Internet as a democratizing space play out with particular sharpness, serving as a reminder that books are no ordinary commodity but are heavily invested with symbolic value and deeply embedded in systems of social and educational stratification. On the one hand, the Internet is seen to have increased openness on a global scale by making it easier to access knowledge previously kept behind the walls of gatekeeping institutions such as research libraries. Yet on the other, not all texts are affected in the same way, and not all circulate everywhere equally. A text file of an out-of-copyright novel downloaded for free from an online repository such as Project Gutenberg is quite a different object from an error-free edition of the same novel, with critical apparatus on whose accuracy the reputation and livelihood of the editor and publisher depend. While the first is available to anyone with an Internet connection, the audience for the second is likely to be restricted to those who can afford to buy it or who have access to a research library, and who speak the language in which it is printed. Where the texts being digitized are freely available and have passed through editorial filters, such as peer-reviewed articles in open-access journals or published print volumes available for public viewing through Google, other logics of accessibility and inaccessibility are engaged to delimit their readership, for example, the social distribution of sufficient levels of print and Web literacy needed to know how to distinguish between more and less authoritative textual provenance.

A further consideration is raised by Robert Darnton, who cautions that the utopian possibilities of mass digitization should not obscure the problems that can arise when corporate entities become gatekeepers of digital texts. Google's project to scan the entire holdings of major research libraries offers the possibility of making Enlightenment ideals of free access to the world's knowledge a reality, yet the cost of accessing these data in future years—and perhaps the hidden costs of centralized control over the accessibility of such data by one company—is not yet clear. Darnton draws attention in this respect to some troubling examples in which library users become dependent on electronic journal subscription services only to have the prices ramped up by publishers with a monopoly on the content.[20]

The Internet is also said to democratize the production side of the textual equation, offering individuals—who may lack the required cultural capital to have much influence in matters of taste and canon formation—platforms where they can voice their own interpretations and critiques. This may occur either in individualized formats such as blogs, or in relatively depersonalized forms such as the aggregated statistics of Amazon book reviews. Michel de Certeau's reflections on reading in *The Practice of Everyday Life* predate the mainstream adoption of Internet technology by over a decade, but they are apropos here. De Certeau situates reading at the intersection of class relationships and interpretive operations: as readers construct their readings of a text, "social hierarchization seeks to make the reader conform to the 'information' distributed by an elite (or semi-elite)."[21] While it is tempting to think of the Internet as destabilizing and disrupting de Certeau's social hierarchies, these processes are not as unidirectional or untrammeled as popularly conceived. It is not that the gates of knowledge have been thrown wide open but rather that new forms of expertise are valorized, such as the ability to manipulate and analyze algorithms. It is also interesting that concurrent with initiatives such as the BBC's Big Read—which offer nonprofessional readers the chance to register their own taste preferences and canonical choices through the mass media—we have seen the rise of state-sponsored One Book projects, in which public institutions such as libraries and local governments decide on one book which members of their community are then encouraged to read.

As alternative models of canon construction—such as sales-based lists and blogs—become possible outside institutions where cultural authority conventionally accrues, spaces open up in which readers need no longer be bound by the evaluative frameworks set down by elites. Readers have, of course, always resisted the prescriptions and proscriptions of cultural elites. My argument here is that the Internet offers a hitherto unprecedented number of opportunities for such unruly readers to find one another, and to create spaces where they have the freedom to construct evaluative taxonomies of their own. How often and in what contexts readers will exercise this freedom, however, is another question. Scholars of reception study have shown that print-based literacies conveyed through mass education continue to be powerful in shaping the way readers interpret texts. Janet Staiger has indicated how online fan discussions of David Lynch films model interpretive behaviors that can be traced to the U.S. film education movement which began in the 1920s.[22] Rhiannon Bury's work on another kind of text, the television show *Six Feet Under*, demonstrates that its fans are firmly steeped in the reading practices of bourgeois aesthetics. Far from "uncritical dupes of the culture industry" or "rebellious poachers who hijack authorial meaning," most of the fans she studied were aware of, and respected, the distinction between legitimate conjecture anchored in close analysis and wild speculation unsupported by textual evidence.[23] Although this volume is primarily concerned with readers of print-based texts rather than those of moving images, Bury's study has implications beyond media fandom. In the face of concerns that those who are habituated to retrieving information from the Internet rather than from books will lose crucial critical functions and the ability to follow a sustained narrative, she suggests that the future of the books and the reading practices that coalesce around them are secure "as long as mass literacy and cultural reproduction remain the foundational focus of classroom instruction."[24] The far-reaching influence of institutional education is not to be undone overnight. What is perhaps less clear is what will happen when instructional practices and educational policy are developed by those who are not so firmly steeped in print culture.

The interconnections between reading and emerging technologies elaborated in this introduction and in the rest of the volume bring into focus the textuality of experience: the way texts mediate between individuals, their histories and memories, and the social world. If, as the Canadian critic Frank Davey argues, all experience is social and textual, books take their place alongside other social texts in constructing the semiotic landscape that individuals inhabit. In this view, literary texts are a "sinuous and ultimately inextricable part of the general social text, both leaving their marks 'outside' themselves and containing marks which refer 'beyond' themselves."[25] The interpenetration of reading experiences with other dimensions of life is one reason why the analysis of reading practices is simultaneously difficult and important. As Davey observes, readers bring meanings, materials, and motivations to a book in ways that the book itself neither signals nor invites.

An example of this interpenetration may be seen in the modes of textual performativity that arise in digitally mediated encounters. In online communities in which communication is distinct from the body of the speaker, readers author themselves as characters, fashioning their gender, identity, and behavior, and using only text to enact what Mark Poster describes as "an unprecedented type of performative self-constitution" which occurs entirely on screen.[26] Inventing themselves textually solely by means of words entered through the keyboard, participants are aware that others are likewise inventing themselves, and thus "the process of interpellation becomes an explicit question in the communication."[27] In a different digital context, danah boyd outlines how those participating in social network sites write their communities into existence by defining themselves and the context in which they operate solely by manipulating text.[28] As individuals perform their online personae and interpret those of others purely through textual activity, understanding the reception of online language becomes increasingly important in order to grasp how subjectivity is constructed in these mediated contexts.

Similarly, reading can itself be regarded as a performance that mobilizes the words of others, which, as Janice Radway elaborates, are themselves the product of prior performances: "acts of languaging that are part of an ongoing, fluid, social process."[29] This is a productive way to conceptualize reading in light of debates over subjectivity, in which insights from postmodernism and poststructuralism have dismantled notions of the subject as unified, coherent, and reflective, and have instead proposed a view of constructed subjectivity that is fractured, decentered, and diffuse. As Andrea Press and Elizabeth Cole observe, this shift poses less of a challenge to theorists than it does to those undertaking empirical and ethnographic work requiring "a level of faith in the possibility of creative activity at the level of the subject and in the potential of ethnographers to come to understand their subjects."[30] Considering this problem in the context of reception study, Radway proposes a new approach to ethnography, one that does not seek to freeze dynamic subjects mid-motion for ease of classification, but instead, by grounding itself in the everyday, turns its attention to the fluid processes—the collision and the confluence of multiple discourses, practices, and actions—by which historical individuals are constituted, and through which the multiple subjectivities within them interact.

In this view, the act of reading can be seen as an osmotic process whereby a reader and a book, and a reader and an interpretive practice, dissolve into each other. This fluidity between text and reader is illustrated by Kimberly Chabot Davis's work with the readers and viewers of postmodern melodramas, which offers compelling evidence that readers' encounters with the subjectivities of others on the page or the screen can have a transformative effect. Davis found that these texts encouraged "cross-over identifications in cultural space," connections that fostered affective identifications which crossed gender, sexuality, and minority-majority lines, and went some way toward diminishing the difference between readers' selves and the textual subjects they encountered.[31] As Alison Light observes, if subjectivity is recognized as a primary site where "the operations of power and the possibilities of resistance are also played out," the ways in which individuals express and define themselves will continue to be important to the analysis of reading.[32] The challenge lies in finding methods capable of investigating and representing these fluid processes which render them intelligible but do not ossify them into fixed arrangements in which agency is granted to some and not others.[33]

Other developments in the digital realm, including the sale of books on sites such as Amazon and AbeBooks, contribute to the identity-work done by reading. On these retail sites, readers are offered an enticing menu of interactive resources which interpellate them not as consumers but rather as literary critics and discerning members of an imagined community of other readers. The reviews, lists, and prior purchasing history of these unseen other readers signal that they, too, appreciate the books that the potential customer is considering purchasing, and offer affirmation that this book purchase is a socially validated action. As Caroline Hamilton argues, these tools exploit the cultural capital of books by enabling readers to redefine their consumption habits as critical practices and expressions of individual taste. The linking of commodities such as Diet Coke or MasterCard to book culture is emblematic of "the cultural power that books represent as tools for idealistic self fashioning,"[34] as these brands take on an aura of prestige and high culture by their association with the literary.

Challenges for the Field

One of the features of reception study which can make it simultaneously appealing yet fraught is that it demands forms of knowledge that cut across received disciplinary traditions. Those accustomed to delving into the meaning of literary texts, for example, may find their work intersecting with scholarship in fields such as the visual arts and psychology as they seek to understand the cognitive processes that occur when readers engage with hypertext fiction, a form of text that demands very different skills from those required for a codex book, which is conventionally read from the front cover to the back. Scholarship that marries sociohistorical awareness with interpretive sensitivity is comparatively rare, as Leah Price remarks in her review essay on the state of the discipline.[35] Where tools from more than one discipline are successfully combined, however, such interdisciplinary work has the capacity to be generative, contributing to a variety of areas including the history of generic conventions, the constitution of readerships, analyses of political events, the workings of nationalism, the demographics of literacy, and the definition of knowledge.[36]

In addition, interdisciplinary work gives impetus to the important task of rethinking the intellectual conventions that underlie discourses and disciplines. Given that a reader is, to paraphrase James Anderson, not a fact but a set of pragmatics invoked in the eye of the researcher,[37] it is as important to contextualize the fields from which an investigative perspective derives as it is to contextualize the act of reading itself. In this way, interdisciplinary research can be generative as well as critical, involving "the constant invention of new tools for working a changing landscape and making do with what is available in a given context."[38] As well as new tools and methods, new knowledge can also be generated. Davis's conjoining of literary theory and ethnography revealed to her aspects of reading that disciplinary schisms had obscured, made visible new avenues of inquiry, and nuanced existing theory. She found that her theoretical understandings of subjectivity and identification were enriched by bringing them into dialogue with actual spectators and readers, and by considering what her subjects' narratives had to say about the semiotic and political significance of particular texts.[39] What also became clear to Davis was the tendency for critics of cultural production to focus on close analysis while ignoring the moment of interpretation, and for those studying audience responses to go to the opposite extreme, underestimating the role of the text in directing or limiting interpretations.[40] Given Ien Ang's caution that curiosity about audiences is not innocent, it is important to account for these disciplinary divergences.[41] The perspective from which we see readers is highly dependent on our own interests and disciplinary orientation, and inevitably shape the form, content, and scope of the information we set out to obtain.

One way in which the use of methods from different disciplines makes clear its value for reception study is in offering a variety of tools with which to interpret the acts and articulations that are the outward signs of the interior processes of reading. Pierre Bourdieu cautions against taking these accounts of individuals' own reading practices at face value because of what he terms the "legitimacy effect." He notes: "As soon as people are asked what they read, they hear, 'What have I read that is worth mentioning?' That is, 'What have I read that is considered literature?' ... The answer they give is not what they actually listen to or actually read, but what seems respectable among what they happen to have read or listened to."[42] In *Reading the Romance*, to which many of the essays in this collection make plain their debt, Radway also addresses this problem, making explicit her methodological decision to juxtapose multiple viewpoints in order to capture as many aspects as possible of the complex interaction between text and reader.[43] Listening to the women of Smithton, Radway heard them giving their reasons for reading romance novels and elaborating on the functions these books fulfilled for them. Yet she also observed them to be acting "on cultural assumptions and corollaries not consciously available to them precisely because those givens constitute[d] the very foundation of their social selves, the very possibility of their social action."[44] Neither of these two perspectives was capable of fully capturing these reading experiences and their significance in the lives of the Smithton women, which Radway attributed in part to the way that culture is simultaneously perceptible and explicit yet also implicit and covert. Her solution was to present these two views alongside each other in the attempt to understand the significance of the women's reading in the terms in which they themselves articulated it, while also revealing the unintended effects and hidden implications of that reading. Similarly, this volume seeks also to grasp the double nature of reception study: to preserve the integrity of an individual's own articulated reading experience on the one hand, and on the other to pursue the structural forces and constraints that act to shape it.

As we think about the challenges for the field that will emerge out of the changing conditions of reading that have arisen around the turn of the twenty-first century, then, it seems likely that it will only become harder to disambiguate the elements of reading on which humanists have tended to focus—those centered on the text and textual interpretation—and those that have more conventionally fallen within the purview of social scientists, that is, the human response to texts and the social structures surrounding these encounters. Much about reading remains undocumented and understudied, not only because obtaining evidence is difficult, but also because when it is obtained, it is made contestable by the multiple disciplinary approaches that the study of reading imbricates. A central task, then, will be to find ways for scholars in these areas to work together to recognize, and overcome, the differences that stand in the way of mutual understanding and collaboration. The fields of reception studies and gender studies provide good models in this respect.

Another challenge will be finding ways to preserve and record bibliographic data for born-digital texts, especially where these are in a state of flux, for example, as a result of ongoing interactions between authors and readers. It is too soon to say whether the take-up of e-books and devices such as the Kindle will create a tipping point for reading practices, but as the data on reader preferences made available by such technologies grow, so too will the ways publishers and booksellers will find to track reader behavior, shape purchasing choices, and offer book recommendations ever more closely tailored to the individual. This information—paratextual information browsed, other books purchased, even the rate at which screens are scrolled and pages turned—will only increase in volume and granularity, making it especially important that the limitations of these data, including the difficulty of connecting reading practices to meaningful demographic information, need to be kept in view.

The essays gathered in this volume have been selected because they connect to core questions that have defined reception study and book history across a range of historical periods. These include how context, format, production, and circulation inflect textual interpretation; how to understand the tension between readers' integration of texts into their individual lives and the structural and ideological forces that constrain them; to what extent texts shape readers or readers shape texts; and how we come by our knowledge of the ways readers respond to texts. Taken together, the chapters range over some of the central components of a reshaped research agenda for reading studies as it seeks to understand the technological reconstitution of the spheres of authorship, reading, and publishing. Communities and practices are the two organizing concepts around which the essays in Part I of the book are grouped, and among them they attempt to capture the cognitive, affective, social, hermeneutic, economic, and taste-related dimensions of "the regimes of reading that constitute texts, readers, and the manner of their encounter as a historically specific assemblage."[45] Reading communities are understood as gatherings both virtual and face-to-face, ranging from an intimate knot of people who know one another well to a vast crowd of anonymous and invisible strangers who are brought together partly or primarily by their shared focus on a text. Interpretive processes are central to the work of community-making done at and through these gatherings, but so too are other acts, including buying, selling, collecting, sharing, and evaluating books. "Reading practices" refer broadly to what individuals do in the process of engaging with books. Under this heading are gathered not only intellectual and affective responses but also the strategies by which readers negotiate the temporal and physical demands made on them by texts; the paratextual and extratextual baggage texts bring with them, such as their position in a bookstore or their location in taste hierarchies; and the efforts of institutions such as book clubs, libraries, or governments to influence readers to use texts in particular ways.

The essays grouped under the Part I heading, "Communities and Practices," focus on the ways social contexts and regimes of reading shape the textual encounter, producing the kinds of rigorously contextualized analyses that are called for by Duguid so that we may better comprehend the transitions that are occurring.[46] Molly Abel Travis explores how reading in the postimperial nation of South Africa is affected by the existence of multiple languages and differing socioeconomic levels among its population, while Julie Rak shows how Canadian independent bookstores respond to the needs of their local communities in the effort to stay afloat in the face of competition from big-box bookstores and their globalized business models. Examining the conditions in which the need to read is produced, as Bourdieu urges, is another task necessary for understanding the regimes of reading in which individual acts of reading are located. In Travis's investigation, these conditions include the need to promote nation-building on a large scale, and to find ways for groups within the nation to access textual materials that are relevant to their linguistic and cultural heritage. Megan Sweeney's exploration of urban fiction and its uses by incarcerated women, meanwhile, demonstrates how these readers utilize narratives both to access the pleasurable elements of stories about street crime and to make sense of the choices they have made so far and that they may face in the future. These incarcerated women readers exemplify the richness and diversity of textual interpretation found beyond the boundaries of academic literary criticism. Demonstrating the way texts can function as technologies with which to process experiences and work out affiliations and identity, these readers show how books serve as a ground for reflection and critique as well as a means by which readers may be co-opted into various social groups or ideological positions. By challenging our understanding of urban fiction and how it signifies to its readers, this chapter and others bring us closer to the critical task of reworking what Radway terms "taken-for-granted notions about books, texts, authors, readers, and reading," which need to be complicated by reimagining them as "the contingent effects of particular social relations and social activity." Other chapters in the "Communities and Practices" section connect to scholarship of previous eras through their attention to the formatting, production, and circulation of texts, illustrating as they do that the term "book" is no longer adequate to account for the variety of artifacts—for example, zines, hypertext narratives, and serialized romances published online—now available to readers. Radway's exploration of zine culture demonstrates how these handmade publications came into being through networks of young women who learned the ropes of production from one another's artifacts, and reveals how a low-tech model in which informal networks of zinesters circulated zines among themselves was able to bypass not only the structures through which mainstream publications such as magazines are distributed but also the gendered ideologies disseminated by these magazines. Geoffrey Nunberg has challenged scholars to reconsider ideas of authorship and access models by rethinking established notions about how information is circulated, accessed, and stored.[47] Radway's essay is particularly valuable for pursuing zines into their "afterlives" in library and archive collections, and thereby throwing light on another set of circulation, access, and storage models.

Jin Feng's work on time travel romances published on the Chinese website Jinjiang showcases a very different set of formatting, production, and circulation questions, showing how transformations in new media make it possible for authors to respond to the market more directly than before. With no significant financial barriers to publication, authors whose work has found success in this online space have been able to move on to print publication, a modern-day analogue of sorts to the process of "sounding the market" which Darnton points to among eighteenth-century publishing houses trying to determine which books would turn out to be best-sellers.[48] Other chapters illustrate how the structures through which books are purchased are changing as booksellers and other agents of distribution operate in different ways and in collaboration with new technologies. Julian Pinder's analysis of LibraryThing, for instance, shows how the website connects different agents in the chain of book distribution. Readers can be linked to library catalogues, online booksellers, and book-swapping services, while publishers such as Random House, which distribute books to bloggers in return for reviews, can use the site to match bloggers algorithmically to the books they will be most likely to enjoy and hence to review favorably. Large booksellers and publishers are able to work such developments to their advantage, then, but so too are smaller players, who can find means to resist the forces of global capital and respond to them in imaginative ways. The strategy that Rak finds in Canadian independent bookstores of "cross-shelving" books in order to subvert centrally mandated generic descriptions is one example.

The tension between individual agency and structural determination is apparent in many of the essays, including those by David Wright and Joan Bessman Taylor. Wright explores the insights into reader behavior that new technologies can yield in the form of algorithm-generated information about the purchasing choices of substantial numbers of readers, and the growing role of mass media–facilitated lists in understanding taste preferences on a large scale. His study of digital zones of canon formation demonstrates that while readers are in principle free to make their own choices about which books to read and purchase, structures such as "best books" lists and Amazon recommendations limit the selection from which they can choose. In a different context, Taylor's research subjects also traversed this tension, themselves recognizing the importance of the text in the production of meaning but also acknowledging that identifying and resolving semiotic gaps was part of their own responsibility. Taylor's five-year study of book club readers—which would have been equally appropriate in the "Methods" section of this volume as a carefully observed example of participant observation—reveals some of the ways that readers both shape and are shaped by texts, as they evaluated and recreated the texts that they considered an author should have written.

The essays in Part II, the "Methods" section of the book, have been selected to illustrate the disciplinary diversity that characterizes contemporary scholarship in the field. These contributions approach their readers—Amazon customers and reviewers, hypertext readers, book club members, and participants in community reading projects—from the perspective of digital humanities, literary theory, linguistics, and mixed methods, as they engage another problematic that resonates with research across all centuries, not just the twenty-first: How do we construct our knowledge of what, and how, people read? Ed Finn's analysis of Amazon reviews and recommendations demonstrates how methodologies such as network visualization and text mining can uncover patterns in large amounts of aggregated data such as book purchasing patterns, which in turn shed light on the different canons and critical conversations in which texts, authors, and readers take part. If the growing body of information about reading habits generated through the Internet is an enticing one, it is evidently crucial to scrutinize the methods by which it is gathered, analyzed, represented, and preserved. Similarly, as an increasing number of encounters between readers and texts occur in, or in close proximity to, a networked universe of paratextual information, it is correspondingly important to theorize what happens when readers move from link to link, as David Miall does in using Henri Bergson's theories of temporality to consider how the temporal and spatial aspects of hypertext reconfigure the processes through which readers apprehend textual meaning, and how the responses hypertext engenders differ from those of print-based texts. Daniel Allington and Bethan Benwell also address how readers come to their understanding of a text, employing methods from linguistics and discursive psychology to examine the way individuals verbalize their interpretations in the context of a book club discussion. Their approach is particularly valuable for demonstrating that readers can be observed to change their interpretation as part of the process of entering into conversation with others about it. Danielle Fuller and DeNel Rehberg Sedo provide a fitting close to the volume, as they address the very problem of bringing multiple disciplinary perspectives to bear on the study of reading and chart some of the disciplinary crossings researchers do as part of that process. Proposing various methodological approaches through which a One Book community reading project can be grasped, they show that evidence obtained via qualitative methods offers a productive challenge to results gleaned from quantitative methods, and vice versa.

In addition to the points of convergence already mentioned, a number of other threads connect the essays. Finn, Pinder, and Wright trace the overlapping networks of prestige through which critical and commercial approbation circulate, while also demonstrating how online technologies make more accessible the word-of-mouth recommendations that predate the Internet. The question of what constitutes literary reading is another strand that runs through the essays. Miall proposes a distinction between hypertext reading and literary reading based on the different experiences that readers undergo while moving through different kinds of text. Wright points out that readers in fan communities resist and challenge established ideas of the literary in pursuit of their own preferences for particular forms of genre fiction, while Travis demonstrates that in the context of nation-building, the "literary" dimensions of texts can be perceived as disruptive to nationalist obligations, as complexity and ambiguity get in the way of stipulations such as the need for a satisfying ending and the affirmation of democratic values. The essays by Feng and Radway illustrate how the roles of producer and consumer have become increasingly difficult to extricate from each other, and they explore the political ramifications of that intertwining. For Radway, creating a zine can be a politically liberating act for individuals, while for Feng the blurring of the line between producer and consumer opens a different set of political possibilities. The affective realm of reading is addressed in the chapters by Miall and by Allington and Benwell, who attest to its value as a vehicle for personal reflection. Sweeney and Wright use different contexts to show how consumer culture has limited readers' choices even as it creates the illusion that those choices are endless. Rak, Taylor, and Allington and Benwell reaffirm the importance of physical spaces, and physical presence, when readers come together to share or access books. Many of the essays—among them those by Travis, Pinder, and Fuller and Rehberg Sedo—also invoke different imagined reading communities, from citizens of the "new" South Africa, to those who join together in a virtual space devoted to recording their book collections, to readers taking part in One Book projects.

Another point of commonality for many of the essays is that they point to changes in the ways literary value and authority accrue in the twenty-first-century world. As different constituencies of readers find avenues to make their critiques of books and authors public, and the boundaries between private musings and public discourse are redrawn by interactive technologies, so too the locus of cultural authority changes. Birkerts articulates the unease felt by some at the dissolution of the once clear distinction between armchair critic and professional:

> The implicit immediacy and ephemerality of "post" and "update," the deeply embedded assumptions of referentiality (linkage being part of the point of blogging), not to mention a new of-the-moment ethos among so many of the bloggers (especially the younger ones) favors a less formal, less linear, and essentially unedited mode of argument. While more traditional print-based standards are still in place on sites like Slate and the online offerings of numerous print magazines, many of the blogs venture a more idiosyncratic, off-the-cuff style, a kind of "I've been thinking . . . " approach. At some level it's the difference between amateur and professional. What we gain in independence and freshness we lose in authority and accountability.[49]

Among the features singled out here are the capacity to update, the ability to link, a high degree of immediacy, a move away from linearity, and an informality of style, which do not in themselves seem to threaten literary quality but which Birkerts implicitly opposes to "print-based standards." Value still needs to be determined, and the caliber and accuracy of critique assessed—making authorship available to anyone is not a guarantee of quality—but the validity of the criticism is not the central issue. The problem, it seems, is that these offerings do not pass through an editor or other filter in the institutional machinery of conventional publication required to transform them from subjective opinion to authoritative pronouncement. In fact, however, a number of the essays in this volume make clear that filtering mechanisms are frequently in place, although they may look very different from those within print culture. The complicated systems described by Feng for "validating" reviewers on the Jinjiang website, for example, are one illustration of editorial mechanisms in place. A conventional literary critic or reviewer would in fact be of little use within this particular reading community. The Jinjiang reader-reviewers have their own form of authority and accountability: they are experts in the culture of the site and in the genre they are helping to construct, and their criteria are more transparent than those of editors, critics, and publishers working within conventional structures of publication. Arjun Appadurai employs the concept of "regimes of value" to describe the paths by means of which a particular commodity circulates. Institutional networks maintain the value cohesiveness of these regimes, so when institutional channels of dissemination are challenged, so too are the strength and cohesiveness of the value regimes called into question.[50] This, it seems to me, is what underlies Birkerts's critique: concern about the formation of new channels by which literary opinion can be disseminated, and which subvert or bypass established regimes through which value is habitually determined. Examples of such alternative channels are given throughout this book. Pinder, for example, explores the ramifications of making visible the personal libraries in which a particular text is likely to be located, which LibraryThing aggregates and brings into public view, while Sweeney investigates the ways incarcerated women obtain and use works of urban fiction, a genre often forbidden by prison authorities and all but ignored by literary critics.

What is observable within the constantly evolving online spaces for book buying and its associated activities discussed in this volume is the adroitness with which online book retailers have devised activities to draw readers into book consumption and to interpellate them as particular types of readers on the basis of their past purchasing history or the purchasing habits of others. As Hamilton observes, trading in culture is profitable, and this is particularly the case for retailers who are able to recognize, and capitalize on, the uses readers make of literary culture, particularly in terms of what reading means for their idealized identities. Sites for literary engagement such as Amazon and LibraryThing "are not simply taking advantage of the individual's desire for self improvement or authority but, rather, demonstrate that the operations and systems of consumerism (exchange, markets, etc.) are a perfect complement to the operations and systems of culture. They exemplify Bourdieu's observation that, 'one reads when one has a reason: a "market" in which to "trade" readings.'"[51] These processes, it should be noted, do not derive their impetus solely from new technology. This is a transformation that has been occurring offline as well as online but has found the Internet a particularly fertile medium for expression. One function performed by book retail sites is that they enable the economic elements of the exchange to be displaced or sublimated by its symbolic elements: interpersonal engagement with other readers, cultural affiliation, identity-work, and the exploration and expression of one's own tastes.[52] These activities, however—whether online or offline—are not always reducible to the displacing of economic exchange. LibraryThing and Jinjiang both provide examples of book-centered interactions that are not driven directly by transactions and that provide a forum in which readers can do identity-work.

In addition to these transformations in the realm of technology, there are broader geopolitical and demographic changes occurring in the contemporary global moment to which the volume is attentive. In 2008 China overtook the United States as the country with the largest number of Internet users. The existing scholarship in English on online reading rarely yields a sense of this fact, however, reflecting instead the prevailing ethnocentrism of the Anglophone academy. Feng's study of the Chinese website Jinjiang is an important corrective, serving as a reminder that while the place from which much Anglophone scholarship on reading comes may be the West, vast audiences and uncharted reading practices lie largely outside its current purview in the countries of the developing and newly developed world. Bourdieu is among those who caution against this kind of selective blindness, observing that critics are themselves "lectores" who bring their own presuppositions to their analysis of the reading experiences of others.[53] In order for scholars from the industrialized West to guard against misconstruing the reading practices of those beyond their own borders, it is necessary to recognize that the divergence between literary cultures in their own nation and others may be considerable. In China, for example, online literature is accorded a much higher status than in the West, and is more closely linked to print culture. Established authors publish their work online, while websites such as Rongshu and Qidian publish some of their content in hard copy. The scale on which these sites operate is also considerable, with Rongshu boasting 2 million registered users and containing over 1.9 million works of literature.[54]

The other end of the technological scale is equally important for scholars of reading to bear in mind, particularly as the utopian horizon of digitization is limited by the inequities of underdevelopment. As Grafton notes, digitizing books from poorer nations is a less attractive proposition for companies that rely on subscriptions or advertising to sustain themselves commercially. While online publication means that some texts from wealthy nations may become accessible to those in the developing world, such cultural flows are much less likely to run in the opposite direction.[55] Travis's discussion of the efforts to promote reading in post-apartheid South Africa illustrates the extent to which national development influences individuals' access to books. An important function of her essay is that it makes visible the specificity and contingency of the reading practices analyzed in other chapters, demonstrating the extent to which literacy and reading habits in the developed world depend on wealth and positions of global cultural dominance and indicating some of the difficulties that arise when a nation's citizens do not all share the same language. These are challenges that are all but invisible from a position of global privilege. While many of the chapters in this volume center on reading practices and developments in English-speaking nations of the industrialized West, the analyses by Feng and Travis are a crucial reminder of their historical and geographical contingency.

As a whole, the volume aims to explore changing notions of literary value, recontextualize denigrated genres such as urban fiction and romance, and bring into visibility less prominent interpretive communities such as book club members and readers of hypertext. The reading formations gathered here are not immutable—many may disappear and all will change, perhaps even in the time between the writing and the publication of this book—but in recording them, the essays contribute to the important work of historicizing different kinds of reading carried out by a range of individuals in a variety of times and places. Given that our understanding of others' reading practices is colored by our own, as researchers we are always at risk of distorting our analyses of other readers with the presuppositions we bring from our own reading. It is to an extent possible to guard against this by historicizing the reading regimes of ourselves and others and thereby helping, as Bourdieu suggests, to "free ourselves of the unconscious presuppositions that history imposes on us. Contrary to what is commonly thought, rather than relativizing history, this is a means of relativizing one's own practice, and therefore of escaping relativism altogether. If what I am saying about reading is true, that it is the product of the conditions in which I have been produced as a reader, then becoming aware of that is perhaps the only chance of escaping the effects of those conditions. That is what gives an epistemological purpose to any historical reflection on reading."[56] In offering a window onto a diverse array of reading practices and communities at the turn of the twenty-first century, the essays gathered here offer a multidimensional picture of reading at a moment of transition. In this way, they demonstrate continuities with the regimes of reading that have preceded ours, and they offer ways to improve our understanding of those that will follow.

Notes

1. Examples of historical studies of reading include Barbara Hochman, *Getting at the Author: Reimagining Books and Reading in the Age of American Realism* (Amherst: University of Massachusetts Press, 2001); Elizabeth McHenry, *Forgotten Readers: Recovering the Lost History of African American Literary Societies* (Durham: Duke University Press, 2002); Barbara Ryan and Amy M. Thomas, eds., *Reading Acts: U.S. Readers' Interactions with Literature, 1800–1950* (Knoxville: University of Tennessee Press, 2002); and David Vincent, *The Rise of Mass Literacy: Reading and Writing in Modern Europe* (Cambridge: Polity, 2000). Three anthologies in the field of reception study that give a sense of the field's disciplinary eclecticism are Jon Cruz and Justin Lewis, eds., *Viewing, Reading, Listening: Audiences and Cultural Reception* (Boulder: Westview Press, 1994); Philip Goldstein and James L. Machor, eds., *New Directions in American Reception Study* (New York: Oxford University Press, 2008); and James Hay, Lawrence Grossberg, and Ellen Wartella, eds., *The Audience and Its Landscape* (Boulder: Westview Press, 1996). Leah Price provides a survey of the scholarship in her review essay "Reading: The State of the Discipline," *Book History* 7 (2004): 303–20. For some examples of the way anxieties about changes to books and reading are registering in the popular press, see Naomi Alderman, "How the Web Is Undermining Reading," *Guardian*, January 20, 2009; Nicholas Carr, "Is Google Making Us Stupid?" *Atlantic Monthly* 302.1 (July–August 2008): 56–63; Nicholas Clee, "The Decline and Fall of Books," *The Times*, May 7, 2009; Steven Johnson, "How the E-Book Will Change the Way We Read and Write," *Wall Street Journal*, April 20, 2009; and Sramana Mitra, "How Amazon Could Change Publishing," *Forbes.com*, May 16, 2008, www.forbes.com/2008/05/16/mitra-amazon-books-tech-enter-cx_sm_0516mitra.html.
2. For examples of critical adoptions of ethnography, see Janice Radway, "Reception Study: Ethnography and the Problems of Dispersed Audiences and Nomadic Subjects," *Cultural Studies* 2.3 (1988): 359–76; and Kimberly Chabot Davis, *Postmodern Texts and Emotional Audiences* (West Lafayette, Ind.: Purdue University Press, 2007).
3. Joan Swann and Daniel Allington, "Reading Groups and the Language of Literary Texts: A Case Study in Social Reading," *Language and Literature* 18.3 (2009): 250.
4. John Frow, "Afterlife: Texts as Usage," *Reception: Texts, Readers, Audiences, History* 1 (Fall 2008): 17.
5. John Frow, *Marxism and Literary History* (Cambridge: Harvard University Press, 1986), 185–86.
6. Tony Bennett, "Figuring Audiences and Readers," in Hay, Grossberg, and Wartella, *The Audience and Its Landscape*, 153.
7. Frow, "Afterlife," 18–19.
8. Anthony Grafton, *Codex in Crisis* (New York: Crumpled Press, 2008), 2.
9. Paul Duguid, "Material Matters: The Past and Futurology of the Book," in *The Book History Reader*, ed. David Finkelstein and Alistair McCleery, 2nd ed. (Abingdon, UK: Routledge, 2006), 495. For an example of the view that books will be superseded, see Jeff Gomez, *Print Is Dead: Books in Our Digital Age* (London: Macmillan, 2008).
10. See Karin Littau, *Theories of Reading: Books, Bodies and Bibliomania* (Cambridge: Polity, 2006), 6–7.
11. Alan Liu, "Transliteracies » Definition of Online Reading," http://transliteracies.english.ucsb.edu/category/research-project/definition-of-online-reading/.

12. Geoff Hall, "Texts, Readers—and Real Readers," *Language and Literature* 18.3 (2009): 335.
13. Grafton, *Codex in Crisis*, 9.
14. Sven Birkerts, *The Gutenberg Elegies: The Fate of Reading in an Electronic Age* (Boston: Faber & Faber, 1994), 3.
15. Wendy Griswold, *Regionalism and the Reading Class* (Chicago: University of Chicago Press, 2008).
16. Toby Miller, "The Reception Deception," in Goldstein and Machor, *New Directions in American Reception Study*, 356–57.
17. Griswold, *Regionalism and the Reading Class*, 62–63.
18. Price, "Reading," 308.
19. Griswold, *Regionalism and the Reading Class*, 64.
20. Robert Darnton, "Google & the Future of Books," *New York Review of Books* 56.2, February 12, 2009, 82–84.
21. Michel de Certeau, *The Practice of Everyday Life* (Berkeley: University of California Press, 1984), 172.
22. Janet Staiger, "The Revenge of the Film Education Movement: Cult Movies and Fan Interpretive Behaviors," *Reception: Texts, Readers, Audiences, History* 1 (Fall 2008): 43–69.
23. Rhiannon Bury, "Textual Poaching or Gamekeeping? A Comparative Study of Two *Six Feet Under* Internet Fan Forums," in Goldstein and Machor, *New Directions in American Reception Study*, 303.
24. Ibid., 303–4.
25. Frank Davey, *Post-national Arguments: The Politics of the Anglophone-Canadian Novel since 1967* (Toronto: University of Toronto Press, 1993), 19.
26. Mark Poster, "The Digital Subject and Cultural Theory," in Finkelstein and McCleery, *The Book History Reader*, 491.
27. Ibid.
28. danah boyd, "Friends, Friendsters, and Top 8: Writing Community into Being on Social Network Sites," *First Monday* 11.12 (December 2006), http://firstmonday.org/issues/issue11_12/boyd/index.html. See also Jenny Sundén, *Material Virtualities: Approaching Online Textual Embodiment* (New York: Peter Lang, 2003), 3.
29. Janice Radway, "What's the Matter with Reception Study? Some Thoughts on the Disciplinary Origins, Conceptual Constraints, and Persistent Viability of a Paradigm," in Goldstein and Machor, *New Directions in American Reception Study*, 343.
30. Andrea Press and Elizabeth Cole, "Women Like Us: Working-Class Women Respond to Television Representations of Abortion," in Cruz and Lewis, *Viewing, Reading, Listening*, 56.
31. Davis, *Postmodern Texts and Emotional Audiences*, 6.
32. Alison Light, "'Returning to Manderley': Romance Fiction, Female Sexuality, and Class," in *Feminism and Cultural Studies*, ed. Morag Shiach (Oxford: Oxford University Press, 1999), 372–73.
33. Janice Radway, "The Hegemony of 'Specificity' and the Impasse in Audience Research: Cultural Studies and the Problem of Ethnography," in Hay, Grossberg, and Wartella, *The Audience and Its Landscape*, 245; and Radway, "What's the Matter with Reception Study?" 343.
34. Caroline Hamilton, "Culture™: Consuming Culture and the Construction of an Amazon 'I,'" *New Media Poetics* (May 2004), www.newcastle.edu.au/group/poetics/issue-03/hamilton.htm.

35. Price, "Reading," 305.
36. Bill Bell, "Symposium: What Was the History of the Book? Introduction," *Modern Intellectual History* 4.3 (2007): 494. See also chapter 1 by Janice Radway in this volume.
37. James A. Anderson, "The Pragmatics of Audience in Research and Theory," in Hay, Grossberg, and Wartella, *The Audience and Its Landscape*, 75.
38. James Hay, Lawrence Grossberg and Ellen Wartella, introduction, ibid., 4. For more on the interdisciplinary nature of audience studies, see Jon Cruz and Justin Lewis, introduction to Cruz and Lewis, *Viewing, Reading, Listening*, 1–3.
39. Davis, *Postmodern Texts and Emotional Audiences*, 32, 173.
40. Ibid., 3.
41. Ien Ang, "Ethnography and Radical Contextualism in Audience Studies," in Hay, Grossberg, and Wartella, *The Audience and Its Landscape*, 247.
42. Pierre Bourdieu and Roger Chartier, "Reading Literature/Culture: A Translation of 'Reading as a Cultural Practice,'" trans. and intro. Todd W. Reeser and Steven D. Spalding, *Style* 36.4 (2002): 667.
43. Janice Radway, *Reading the Romance: Women, Patriarchy, and Popular Literature* (Chapel Hill: University of North Carolina Press, 1984), 210.
44. Ibid.
45. Frow, "Afterlife," 15.
46. Duguid, "Material Matters," 498.
47. Geoffrey Nunberg, "Farewell to the Information Age," in Finkelstein and McCleery, *The Book History Reader*, 511.
48. Robert Darnton, "'What Is the History of Books?' Revisited," *Modern Intellectual History* 4.3 (2007): 501.
49. Sven Birkerts, "Lost in the Blogosphere: Why Literary Blogging Won't Save Our Literary Culture," *Boston Globe*, July 29, 2007.
50. See Jim Collins, "High-Pop: An Introduction," in *High-Pop: Making Culture into Popular Entertainment*, ed. Jim Collins (Oxford: Blackwell, 2002), 24.
51. Hamilton, "Culture™." The Bourdieu quote is from Bourdieu and Chartier, "Reading Literature/Culture," 668.
52. Hamilton, "Culture™."
53. Bourdieu and Chartier, "Reading Literature/Culture," 664.
54. Richard Lea, "A New Cultural Revolution," *Guardian*, January 16, 2008.
55. Grafton, *Codex in Crisis*, 33–34.
56. Bourdieu and Chartier, "Reading Literature/Culture," 665.

1
COMMUNITIES AND PRACTICES

1

ZINES THEN AND NOW
What Are They? What Do You Do With Them? How Do They Work?

Janice Radway

Zines are peculiar.[1] There's no way around that fact. They are well known enough to have been the subject of a number of compilations, anthologies, books, and films devoted to their analysis, most issued since 1990.[2] They are considered significant enough to be archived at a number of university, state, and big city libraries in the United States.[3] Collections have also been developed in Europe, the UK, Canada, and New Zealand.[4] The wealth of online material relating to zines includes an alternative online encyclopedia dedicated to zines in general, known as Zinewiki, as well as an elaborate site, Grrrl Zine Network, providing access to a huge amount of material about girl zines, the Riot Grrrl movement, and third wave feminism.[5] Yet more often than not, if you explain to someone that you are researching girl zines, the immediate response is to ask, "What's a zine?" This is as true for me as it was for Stephen Duncombe in 1997, when he began the first full-length academic book about the recent zine explosion, *Notes from Underground: Zines and the Politics of Alternative Culture*, with the sentence "But what are they?"[6] A more recent how-to book on the subject even underscores the familiarity of the question with its zine-speak title, *Whatcha Mean, What's a Zine?*[7]

The ubiquity of this question even in the face of the increasing legitimacy enjoyed by zines has meant that the initial gesture on almost all the websites and in nearly every published discussion is to venture some kind of a definition while acknowledging how difficult a task that is. Most agree with Duncombe and Julie Bartel, both of whom suggest that it is difficult to convey the true essence of zines "without a show-and-tell session."[8] Indeed, after agreeing that "zines are not easily defined," the Duke University Library's website for the Sarah Dyer Zine Collection nonetheless ventures a definition by foregrounding their distinctive physical characteristics and by highlighting their do-it-yourself production and circulation beyond the mainstream: "They can be a messy hodgepodge of personal thoughts or an expertly designed political treatise. They can fit easily into a pocket or take up an entire 8 1/2 x 11 sheet of paper. They can be heavily collaged or minimalist; colored or black-and-white; handwritten or typed; stapled, sewn, or loose. The unifying thread is their outside-of-the-mainstream existence as independently written, produced, and distributed media that value freedom of expression and freedom from rules above all else."[9] Defining zines abstractly is difficult, nearly everyone agrees. Better to invoke their materiality, their particularity, and their modes of production, distribution, and circulation.

And yet, however often definitions like these focus on zines as unique forms of material culture that circulate socially through do-it-yourself distribution and informal social networks, those offering the definition more often than not move quickly past materiality and sociality to focus intensively on their textuality and therefore on the content of zines.[10] They do so by likening them to magazines and books and by highlighting their status as part of the underground or alternative press. As a result, most accounts move on to analyze the politically and ideologically alternative nature of what is contained within them. In doing so, such studies designate zines as booklike texts. What you do with zines, they suggest, is read them.

Library-based zine collections underscore this move by providing topical finding aids that direct zinesters, fans, and researchers alike to the subjects covered in zines. This practice assumes that all of these groups are interested principally in what zines "say." A number of the compilations assume the same thing by organizing their zine excerpts, which are rendered in the uniformity of print, according to the topics they take up. Though several of the compilations reproduce actual pages from zines in an attempt to convey their material specificity and in exemplification of their graphic creativity, none of them insists on the aesthetic integrity of the zines themselves by reproducing them in toto.[11] Even the book *Zine Scene* by Francesca Lia Block and Hillary Carlip, which was designed to encourage young people to produce their own zines and therefore highlights the materials and *practices* involved in making them, begins by discussing what zines are *about*.[12] Whatever else they might be, it seems, zines end up being construed as texts to be read.

If you have ever held a zine in your hands, you might well be tempted to say: "What's the problem here? This looks like a pamphlet or a little magazine. It seems to have a title, an apparent editorial page, and a back cover with a space for the address of a hoped-for reader. Its interior pages, therefore, must be addressed to putative readers with whom the zine's 'author' wants to communicate. How else would you approach zines except by analogy to books and magazines? Aren't they part of the alternative press? What else could you do with them but read them?"

Indeed. The status of the zine as text-to-be-read appears self-evident. Yet it is that very self-evidentness I want to complicate by invoking the rich interdisciplinarity of the field of book history, whose practitioners have insisted for some time that taken-for-granted notions about books, texts, authors, readers, and reading must be complicated by reimagining them as the contingent effects of particular social relations and social activity.[13] Book historians have taught us that books are more than texts and that people do more with their books than read them. And even the practice of reading itself, they have argued, is far more complex and contingent *as a practice* than it is sometimes portrayed. Even as they read their books, people engage with them, too, as material objects. At the same time, they treat them as occasions for participating in different kinds of activities or performances, including the solitary work of meditation and the more social, intersubjective activities of conversation, discussion, recommendation, and evaluation. They also treat books as tools for generating subsequent activities, including writing.

Book historians have taught us, then, that books and other forms of mediated communication must be approached at once as signifying texts, as materially crafted objects, as occasions of and for social exchange, and as incitements to reading and writing and a host of other activities. In order to manage such a capacious and inclusive approach to book production and use, book historians call on the full array of knowledge practices associated with a range of disciplines including literary studies; art history; material culture studies; social, economic, and cultural history; communication studies; and the history of technology. The interdisciplinary mode of apprehension they employ directs our attention to the way book-related activities have been articulated together at particular historical moments through specific constellations of social relations. In effect, book history suggests that the now familiar question "What's a zine?" ought to be reformulated in both a more social and a more performative way. We ought to ask not what a zine is but what zinesters do with them, how, and in what contexts. At the same time, we ought to ask how the practices of zine-ing reciprocally act upon all those who engage in them. We need to know how zine-ing works and how the forms it generates exert their multiple effects.

What I am suggesting here is that the constant posing of the definitional question "What's a zine" is not simply a function of zines' obscurity or their position on the cultural periphery. Rather, the question recurs because we haven't yet adequately attended to zines as the critical yet always wholly integral element in complex and socially specific forms of cultural activity. This performative and socially oriented mode of apprehension is hampered by the lingering effects of discipline-bound knowledge practices that direct attention and focus analysis on only one or two aspects of zine-ing at a time, usually the textual forms that result from the activity of zine production, thereby reifying and simplifying the activity significantly and missing its distinct playfulness and investment in defying familiar categories. In my view, knowledge practices that are too discipline bound hinder our capacity to understand the significance of the fact that zines are actively created by individuals who also circulate them and use them deliberately to trouble all sorts of familiar categorical distinctions to quite powerful effect.[14]

Zines deliberately confound the boundary between the particular and the generic, for example, between the unique and the formulaic. They prompt us to wonder, Are they unique art objects or ritualized forms of communication? Zines also disrupt the boundary between the materialities of writing and typeface and the signifying capacities of language. Should they be considered forms of material culture, then, or texts demanding to be read? Zines play, too, with the dividing line between orality and print as well as that between affect and reason. Should we attend to their rhetorical effects or primarily to their ideological content? Zines also disturb the categorical distinction between production and consumption, between writing and reading. As a consequence, they trouble the too easy dichotomy between author and reader. Most significantly perhaps, zines worry the distinction between object and event, between text and the activities it sets in motion.

It is not enough to focus on what zines *are*, therefore. We need to pursue more resolutely not only how individuals and groups act in and through zine-ing but also how they mobilize zines as dynamic, unsettling forms in order to challenge familiar distinctions that traditionally separate art from life, politics from the everyday, the individual from the social, and the self from the world. We need to understand not only how zines work on those who initially created them, exchanged them, mailed them, and read them, but also how they *continue* to work on those who now engage zines in different contexts and considerably after the moment of their major efflorescence in the 1980s and 1990s.

I introduce this last point into the larger methodological discussion because my preliminary investigation of the practice of girl zine-ing has demonstrated to me that although many of the girls who engaged so assiduously in this activity in the 1990s gave up zine-ing as they moved into their twenties and thirties—and although zine-ing has waned somewhat in popularity as a new cohort of girl cultural producers has gravitated to other forms of writing and reading, including cell phone texting, blogging, and communicating through online tools such as MySpace, Friendster, and Facebook—zines actually live on. They have not simply disappeared into boxes of stored teen memorabilia. In fact, girl zines now live complex afterlives in the library archives I have already mentioned, in popular and academic essays about zines like this one, in university course syllabi, in high school classrooms, in films, on the Web, and even in art exhibits. And they do so, I have discovered, in part because of the efforts of former zinesters who have played a critical role in perpetuating the life of zines by preserving their collections, by writing about zines in a number of different contexts, by persuading others to investigate zines, and by building on the effects of zine-ing in their own present-day lives. Indeed the contemporary activities of former zinesters—as well as the activities of the many others who have been inspired by their earlier zine work—testify to the extended impact that zines and zine-ing have had since the first moment of their creation.[15]

In my view, we will begin to understand zines and the full extent of their impact only by taking both a resolutely interdisciplinary and a longitudinal approach to zines and zine-ing. It seems especially imperative—given the fact that zines have not disappeared as ephemeral, subcultural forms—to avoid the assumption that the political effect of zines can be judged in the short term according to whether they propelled their original creators into radical politics in the conventional public sphere. This mistake has been made by Stephen Duncombe, Chris Atton, and a number of other commentators on zines, whose work is otherwise excellent.[16] Instead, a longitudinal approach enables us to understand how zines have functioned over time as aesthetic, rhetorical, and social technologies for making an array of things happen. It allows us to take the measure of zines as historically specific forms of social practice that have continued to involve, inspire, influence, and affect not only their initial creators and their immediate interlocutors but also a panoply of subsequent students, fans, and proponents of the genre who, through their own subsequent labor, ensure that zines live on as a cultural force with an articulated range of sometimes delayed effects.

I have been led to these assertions, and to the insights about the practice of zine-ing on which they are based, through a now extended interaction with a small collection of zines in my possession lent to me by the daughter of a colleague, a young woman I have known since she was born. Jess is close to my own daughter in age, and for a time they were friends until we moved to another city. They have seen each other only briefly since we moved, usually during summers when our families visited. I first discovered zines during one of those summer visits when I happened upon a basket of obviously handmade pamphlets that varied tremendously in size, length, aesthetic sophistication, and even in the topics they covered. At the time, several things struck me about them. They were visually exuberant and written in a highly emotional, rhetorically intense mode. Most seemed to be created by girls, and many of them made explicit reference to the way girls were treated in high school and beyond. Some even evoked the term "feminism." I was intrigued by the juxtaposition of high political awareness with the familiar affective exuberance of adolescence figured through exaggerated punctuation, especially exclamation marks, and through the use of in-group abbreviations and teen jargon.

Like everyone else who happens upon zines, I asked immediately, "What are these?" "Zines," Jess told me. Although I knew the term and was familiar with the field of fan studies that took the world of popular culture–inspired fanzines as its proper subject, I knew little about the punk-related explosion of zine-ing in the 1980s and 1990s. In fact, I don't recall much of what Jess said in response to my initial question, but I do remember learning that for her, zines were associated with punk music, especially that created by girl bands, and that they were connected to a movement called Riot Grrrl, which she followed with friends from school and beyond.[17] In fact I was surprised by how the form took Jess and her friends significantly beyond the confines of the suburban community in which they lived to engage with other Riot Grrrls and fans of bands such as Bikini Kill and Bratmobile at gatherings in a number of different cities.

Eventually, when Jess graduated from high school and moved on to college, she allowed me to borrow her small collection as the basis for an emergent research project on zines, which had begun to take shape, albeit inchoately at first, as I engaged in conversation with a few graduate students about the subject of girls and the changing nature of cultural forms targeting them.[18] Indeed at the time I first discovered zines, we were discussing the magazine *Sassy*, the television shows *Beverly Hills 90210* and *My So-Called Life*, films like *The Breakfast Club* and *Sixteen Candles*, and celebrity artists like Madonna and the Spice Girls. Although I didn't introduce zines into my cultural studies classes until much later as evidence of how some girls wrote themselves into a media and cultural environment they found alienating, I continued to read around in Jess's collection, and began to look tentatively into the history of Riot Grrrl and the place of girls bands and the fanzines they generated in the lives of young women in the United States during the 1990s.[19]

I have now begun to explore more systematically the nature and extent of the girl zine universe in the United States by examining zines held in archives at Duke, Smith, Barnard, and elsewhere. I can tentatively say at this point that Jess's small collection seems fairly representative of what can be found in those much larger archives. It contains Riot Grrrl zines—some well known, others not (*Bikini Kill, Riot Grrrl [nyc], Queer Punk Issue 7*); a host of explicitly feminist zines (*Bitch* 1, no. 2; *Princess Charming* 2; *sourpuss* 8 and 9); an important, much-cited zine focused on questions of race and ethnicity (*Bamboo Girl* 7); a range of zines preoccupied with questions of sex and gender identity (*One Mint Julep* 2; *Tales from the Clit* 2); a small number of what are known as perzines, that is, highly idiosyncratic and personal meditations on an individual's interests, problems, and daily life (*snarla* 2; *Silver Rocket* 3); a range of obviously local, exuberant, but inexperienced zines (*Restroom* 1; *being real and getting clean*) apparently generated in imitation of better-known Riot Grrrl titles; and a number of zines focused intently on aspects of the alternative music scene (*Teeter Totter* 5).

As soon as I venture this categorization scheme for Jess's collection, however, I am immediately dissatisfied not only with the categories themselves but also with the assignment of individual zines to them.[20] Although some zines stress feminist politics, while others focus on alternative music or the exploration of alternative sex and gender identities, many of them combine these interests in idiosyncratic ways. Like everyone else, then, I find it nearly impossible to define zines abstractly, to distinguish among them according to a set of relatively fixed criteria, especially when those criteria are pegged to reading them for their content. Indeed it was the difficulty of specifying the topical range of the zines contained in Jess's small collection for an early paper on the subject that first suggested the importance of attending instead to the material and formal properties they shared as well as to the modes of address they adopted in common. And attention to those qualities in the context of discussions about changing gender norms and forms of sexuality in the nineties prompted interest in how zines functioned internally as mechanisms of gendered subject formation and how they circulated socially as occasions for and technologies of network construction.

This last topic had been on my mind since I first marveled at the way zineing expanded Jess's social world beyond her local relations with her family, friends, and high school classmates. Indeed it was when I began to see that there was a distinct connection between the practices of subject construction rendered textually through writing, drawing, and collaging in zines and the actual networking activities through which zines were circulated that I began to see the importance of thinking about zines as a constellation of linked practices that undoubtedly had complex effects, individually and collectively, in the short and long term. Ultimately the process of conceptualizing zine-ing as a concatenation of practices with mutually intersecting effects pushed me to define my project as an oral history and a kind of longitudinally focused ethnography, aiming to understand not only how zinesters functioned in the nineties but also how some of them recall their zine activities now and integrate their effects into their present-day lives, thereby influencing others and drawing them into the orbit of the zine universe. Because I am only now embarking on this larger project, what I aim to do here is to articulate a few preliminary formulations I have developed by working closely with Jess's collection. These formulations seek to specify how zines may have functioned internally and externally for their young fans and to hypothesize about why such activity might have continued to generate subsequent zine work within a range of different contexts.[21]

When first encountering the girl-produced zines in Jess's collection, one can't help but notice that they mobilize a range of aesthetic and rhetorical strategies, as if deliberately to escape the condition of being inert. They display a wild mixture of handwriting and print, nearly all of which refuses to stay put within the lines. They sport images that overlap and bleed into one another. In many cases those images strain to burst from the page, and sometimes narratives do not follow serially, page by page. Indeed zines are nothing if not motley. Ordered reading is constantly disrupted, as a result, by jagged, nervous, zigzaggy motion, by the sense that one is encountering random miscellany rather than ordered sequence. Zines display a protean energy that refuses to be circumscribed within the decorous confines of print form or the ordered circuits through which print and books usually circulate. As handcrafted material objects, therefore, they constantly call attention to the conventional limits of the handwriting, print, and paper out of which they are fabricated. As much as they demand to be read, they also foreground their status as "not books."[22]

Indeed zines always gesture beyond the codex form of the book they evoke to the uncontainable actions and affective complexities of the zine artist(s) responsible for their creation. At the same time, they call attention to the fractured, layered, and contradictory subjects generated *within* their pages through the use of the aesthetic practices of collage and the adoption of a range of rhetorical styles and strategies that call attention to their display of a kind of uncontainable, ecstatic generativity.[23] They also highlight the densities and dynamism of the social relations that course through them and around them by calling attention to the words of others within their pages and by referring constantly to the imagined readers for whom they are destined. Zines foreground their porousness, therefore, their radical openness to, and dependence on, social activities that permeate them, extend beyond them, and actively set them in motion.

Zines gesture insistently toward the rich densities of the social world not simply through indexical reference and representation but, literally, by incorporating bits and pieces of that world within their pages. This is done through practices of collage, bricolage, citation, and cultural recycling. Indeed zines almost always incorporate the words and images of multiple others into their miscellaneous mix. Zine artists constitute themselves, then, in and through constant conversation with others. Virtually every utterance and every representation is staged as a response. Nothing appears sui generis as if originating in a single writer. Rather, every speech act is called forth as part of a dialogue, at least, and more often as part of an extended conversation.[24] Zines are not, in any simple way, then, expressions of preexisting selves. Nor are they authored in the usual sense. Though they call attention to themselves as singular creations and often claim that expressive authenticity is their foremost reason for being, they also foreground their status as the work of a collective process, almost as the utterance of a chorus. Zines are performances, it seems to me, and performances of a particular type. They haul onto the stage a range of shape-shifting actors who play with multiple roles, ventriloquize through a range of voices, and experiment with an especially protean form of thoroughly socialized subjectivity. Not for nothing do zinesters continually refer to their involvement in zine-ing as being part of the zine *scene*. As performances, zines are transformative, productive, and socially generative, which is to say, they propagate new ways of inhabiting the world.

Even zines that apparently foreground familiar discourses of self-expression and stress how much their creators are giving authentic voice to ideas and affects usually proscribed by gendered standards of propriety evidence a propensity for trying out a range of points of view and a number of different identities. In fact, far from elaborating a coherent viewpoint and therefore a unified, cohesive, and internally consistent subjectivity, zines incorporate the views of others within their own textual representations. The self constructed within a zine is therefore an intersubjective self, a self in active, quite literal relation to another. At the same time, the subjectivity constructed in zines is highly fluid and always changing. Indeed zines careen from subject position to subject position as zine artists experiment with what it feels like to speak from a number of different positions. Sometimes zines are even retitled or discontinued altogether to reflect felt changes in the zine artist's self.

Significantly, these fluid, intersubjective forms of self-presentation crafted within zines apparently extend beyond the pages of individual zines themselves and even beyond any single act of writing or reading. Indeed in the 1990s, as soon as girls created their zines and sent them out into the world, they called into being a whole range of additional, decidedly intersubjective activities in the extratextual world as well. In addition to generating reading of their zines, they also sparked exchanging, mailing, bartering, distributing, networking, letter writing, face-to-face meeting, and even the production of new zines. Zines, it would seem, had multiple and extended effects not only for the zine artist herself but also for those who received and witnessed her performance, reflected it back to her, responded to it, changed it, or passed it on. Passing it on was done by reviewing a zine, by giving it to another, by incorporating bits of it into one's own zine, by circulating it through a zine distro. Zines proliferated then, and in multiple ways. They generated other zines; they called into being new zinesters; they expanded the zine scene; they generated new friendships. In effect, they constructed new social networks.

It seems clear, in fact, from perusing Jess's collection and comparing it with the larger collections found in the major zine archives that the social networking at the heart of zine-ing was of critical importance to young girl zinesters of the 1990s. Evidence for such a claim emerges quickly, in fact, almost from the first moment one takes up a single zine. Indeed it's impossible to avoid getting caught up in the latticework of citation and counter-citation that zines build together. Because every zine makes reference to other zines, one quickly gets a sense of an emergent zine network drawing girls out of their local situations and into connection with other like-minded girls united not by proximity but by interest. It becomes evident very quickly that zinesters actively sought to transmute their hoped-for readers into friends and, in quite utopian fashion, to transform those friends into an ever-expanding network of empowered girl zinesters.

Take *Velvet Grass* 14, a relatively sophisticated zine found in Jess's collection. Created by a zinester who identified herself only as "Grasshopper," *Velvet Grass* is composed of Grasshopper's own writings, clip art culled from a range of sources including books and popular magazines, excerpts from others' zines, and constant apostrophes to her imagined and hoped-for readers.[25] As is true for most other zines in Jess's collection, its back page incorporates a blank space under the heading "DELIVER TO: . . ." This open-ended gesture inscribes the intense hope that generates and underwrites all zine-ing, that is, the longing to find an addressee for this handcrafted composition, a like-minded reader. In this case the addressee's name is not filled in, suggesting that Jess may have acquired this particular zine at a Riot Grrrl event, club performance, or workshop rather than through the mail. Others in her collection, however, are specifically addressed to her and include special handwritten notes to her both on the back page and tucked into the middle somewhere, hailing her individually.[26]

Clearly, zinesters desired more than the typical anonymous reader who might pick up a mass-market paperback at the supermarket. Their textual and extratextual activities suggest that what they really desired was direct communication with identifiable others who shared their interests, attitudes, and views. Apparently what they longed for most was communication that might be pursued through letter writing, at the gigs of favorite bands, at girl-centered workshops and symposia, even at zine fests designed to bring zinesters together to promote zine-ing.

Among the many apostrophes to her imagined, not yet named readers included in one issue of *Velvet Grass* is a selection that has been titled by Grasshopper "Do You Know Who Lauren Martin Is?" Apparently designed to introduce her readers to Lauren Martin's zines, this page does not feature, as one might expect, Grasshopper's own description and assessment of Lauren Martin. Rather, it reprints the text of a fan letter Lauren Martin herself wrote to Grasshopper about an earlier number of *Velvet Grass*. This rhetorical move joins Grasshopper to Martin socially and textually, interposes Martin's characterization of an earlier Grasshopper zine into this particular issue, enables Grasshopper to represent herself through Martin's evocation of her, and enables her to let Martin speak for herself under Grasshopper's own aegis. In effect these two young women are thoroughly interposed, which is to say, made present intersubjectively through this representational strategy. Finally, at the conclusion of Martin's letter, Grasshopper seeks to duplicate, even multiply, her relation to Martin by connecting her readers to Martin herself. She does so by instructing her readers on how to order Martin's five different zines, including one titled *Princess Charming*. Whether it was this recommendation that moved Jess to order Martin's zine is unclear. Nevertheless, there *is* a copy of *Princess Charming* in her collection.

One coincidence like this certainly doesn't amount to much. But when single ties like this one multiply, the zine network begins to emerge more strongly. Another mini-zine in Jess's collection, issue eight of *sourpuss*, includes the usual clip art and refers constantly to other zines. Despite the fact that it is only three by three inches in size and only twenty-two pages in length, it devotes an entire page to reviewing and recommending other zines. At the end of the page, there is a recommendation for Villa Villa Kula, not a zine but rather a "collection of gerl labels done by nice, nice Tinuviel." I didn't make too much of this reference initially until I discovered, while working in the Smith zine collection, that a significant portion of that collection is composed of zines collected by Tinuviel herself, a former business partner of Slim Moon, who was one of the founders of the alternative label Kill Rock Stars and the original producer of the Riot Grrrl bands Bikini Kill, Bratmobile, and Heavens to Betsy. Not only did Tinuviel donate her zines to Smith, but also she sent a large collection of correspondence that includes many letters and notes from the girl zinesters who were ordering music from her and sending her their zines in exchange. As we have seen with Jess's collection, this kind of correspondence was widespread among girl zinesters in the 1990s. Indeed as zines crisscrossed the United States as well as oceans and continents accompanied by notes of introduction penned on all manner of postcards, colorful stationery, and Hello Kitty notes, they stitched their young creators together into a loose network of like-minded girls and young women who not only amassed their own zine collections as a result but also formed widely scattered extralocal friendship groups based not on proximity but on shared, incipiently feminist interests and on a critical orientation to the world.

It would seem, then, that the pleasures of zine-ing for girls in the nineties were distinctly intersubjective and bound up with the exploration of new ways of being in the world. Significantly, the act of forging new subject formations was pursued in concert and in collaboration with others who functioned as witnesses, co-conspirators, and co-creators of alternative ways of being a girl. In a world where girls felt hemmed in by the gender discourses of others and divided from one another by competition and by the corporate interests of teen magazines and the cosmetics and fashion industries, girl zinesters sought to forge their own social networks, which they hoped might function as substitutes for the geo-spatial and local relations that situated them, in their view, so conventionally and problematically within their families, high schools, college dorms, and workplaces.[27]

That this network and the political commitments that developed within it have had long-term effects is testified to by Tinuviel's apparent desire to make her zine collection available to more, different, and later readers. Indeed her activism on behalf of zines has been repeated by others. In addition to Tinuviel's zines, the Smith Collection harbors those donated by Tristan Taormino. Taormino assembled her collection during her own activities as a zinester and during the process of producing one of the first mainstream books about zines, the 1997 anthology *A Girl's Guide to Taking Over the World: Writings from the Girl Zine Revolution,* which was designed to get more girls reading and writing zines. This book samples many Riot Grrrl zines and amply demonstrates that body issues, feminism, sexuality, and alternative gender presentations figure centrally in girl zines. Although Taormino hasn't formally explained why she donated her collection to Smith or what she thought the collection might enable, it does at least seem clear that, like Tinuviel, she hoped her donation would preserve her collection of zines and make them available to new readers. Her subsequent activities also suggest that the political commitments she developed and realized through zine-ing have continued to animate her life. She is the creator of *Pucker Up,* a pornographic website that bills itself as "smart, sexy, anal, kinky, and fun," where Taormino herself declares: "My mission is to educate people of all genders and sexual orientations in their pursuit of healthy, empowering, and transformative sex and relationships. I spread my pleasure-positive message through my books, videos, writing, teaching, and coaching."[28]

Tinuviel and Taormino are not alone in helping to expand access to zines nor in seeking to extend their political views and orientation into new arenas. Former zinesters Sara Dyer, Julie Bartel, and Jenna Freedman, for instance, have been instrumental in helping to create the Duke University zine collection (named after Dyer in response to her founding donation), the Salt Lake City Public Library zine collection, and the one at Barnard. As Barnard's zine librarian, Freedman also maintains an elaborate website devoted to the collection that allows people interested in zines to network with one another, to pursue a range of bibliographic references, and to link to a wide range of writing about zines. Her site indicates that Lauren Martin's own zine collection is now housed at Barnard, as is that of Yumi Lee, another zinester and one of Jess's closest friends from her time in college. Additionally, Freedman is active in the Radical Reference movement within the library profession, which seeks to broaden and diversify the kinds of materials, including zines, collected at libraries, in order to ensure that they collect things other than the conventional and the mainstream. So many do, in fact, that a zine has been published targeting zine librarians.[29]

Jenna Freedman's website connects students, zine fans, and interested researchers to a number of other zine sites, including the aforementioned Grrrl Zine Network, which is the creation of Elke Zobl, who wrote her dissertation on the international girl zine network for the Academy of Fine Arts in Vienna. Her website is even more extensive than Freedman's, with links to other writings on zines, both popular and academic, and it includes many references to academic papers by former zinesters, including one crafted by Sabrina Margarita Alcantara-Tan, the creator of *Bamboo Girl,* that well-regarded zine devoted to race, ethnicity, and the hybrid nature of identity in the contemporary world, found in Jess's collection.

I could continue for some time listing the names of former zinesters who have established zine archives or written university papers, master theses, dissertations, and academic articles about zines. There are also many secondary school teachers who hold zine workshops in their classes and use zines to interest their students in the practices of writing and reading as activities directly relevant to their daily lives. All of these young women are involved in sustaining the afterlives of zines, and as they do so, they testify again and again to the impact of zine-ing on their self-understanding and on the kinds of later work they have taken up in the world.

Zine-ing, it would seem, has been nothing if not generative, bringing into being additional zines and zinesters while also transforming zinesters themselves, thereby begetting new friendship networks, new ways of acting in the world, and subsequent modes of cultural production, a significant portion of which deliberately seeks to ensure that zines and zine-making continue to live on after the moment of their first flourishing. All of this is significant because it calls attention to what may have been the most important impulse generating zine-making, that is, the driving desire to create new social networks through a web of citation, connection, reprinting, and circulation. What zinesters were apparently circulating when they mailed off their creations was hope—hope for a new kind of community, hope for a different future. Zines were engaged—quite literally, I think—in the practice of utopian social construction, an attempt to bring into being an elsewhere where lives might be different. They were also attempting to transform not simply contemporary girlhood but the very future of girls themselves. The challenge facing individuals interested in the fate of girls must be to understand not only how they tried to do this but also how successful they were, what the limits of their imagined communities may have been, and where and why they may have failed.

I hope this exploratory account of zine-ing as a practice has made clear that more than anything else, zine-ing is a *social* phenomenon, a form of social action driven by desires for new forms of sociability and new ways of being in the world. Yet it is important to note that zine-ing is not just any kind of social action. It is both a communicative practice *and* an aesthetic one, an activity that draws people into conversation with one another and one that results not only in the creation of an aesthetic object but also in the execution of an aesthetic performance. By drawing attention to the modes of connection, conversation, and dialogue mobilized by zinesters as well as to the particular ways in which they engaged with and deformed the technologies of print and the codex form, we might be able to identify why at the precise moment of the waning decades of the twentieth century, when new technologies were emerging everywhere and at warp speed, some young people seized on older modes of literary production—the typewriter, the pen, paper, paste, twine, and staples—and sought to play with them in new ways, turning them to their own ends.

It is significant, I think, that zinesters seized on older technologies of book production at the very moment when they were being superseded by the explosion of electronic and digital forms of communication. Reclaiming print materials and publication practices that for three hundred years at least had served as the material basis for the commercially organized production and reproduction of legitimate knowledge as well as virtually all literary communication, they insisted on the viability of do-it-yourself publication. They insisted as well on their right and ability to engage in DIY publication precisely so as to develop ideas that ordinarily would be ruled out of hand by corporate, commercial culture. At the same time, they reveled in the specificities of old typewriters, outmoded and highly variable typefaces, the individuated nature of handwriting, and the materialities of reproduction, folding, binding, stapling, and distribution. Thus they doubly refused corporately produced mass culture by defying its ideological strictures and by insisting on the materiality of the actual and quite varied forms of labor involved in publication. Indeed, as Stephen Duncombe has pointed out, despite the expense of DIY publication and the claims it made on their time, zinesters actually testified again and again to how much they enjoyed developing a very different relationship to their own labor. In fact, their zines often called attention to the difference between the labor they invested in creating their zines, which they did for themselves, and what they did for others, whether at school or as a job. Zine labor, they stressed, was a form of pleasure, not an onerous, alienating burden.

Additionally, by insisting on the tight relationship between their reading and writing, girl zinesters refused the typical position offered to them by contemporary culture, that is, the position of champion consumer. Girl zinesters insisted again and again on the fact that they were not consumers of others' ideas but rather producers of their own. They called attention to themselves, therefore, as thinkers, as vernacular intellectuals—although most would not have used that language—as people with active capacities for reflection and a desire to think critically about the conditions of their everyday lives. At the same time, by using zines as a way to network, they also moved vigorously to create a space in which to debate their ideas, to compare them with those of others, to think collectively about the immediate world surrounding them.

They sought, in effect, to create a more responsive, more girl-positive form of communication than the professionalized, mass-produced, commercial system of the still patriarchal mainstream. Through their production, as a result, they modeled a different politics, one potentially more mutual and communal in structure than the hierarchical and gendered social relations that troubled them at school, at work, and in their families.[30]

Although it will take careful ethnographic research and oral history to be sure, it is worth assessing whether this vision of different forms of sociality and sociability produced changes in the lives of the girls who took up zines so passionately. This will be a challenge especially because the work will be retrospective. Whatever its difficulties, though, it seems worth attempting in order to assess whether girls' activities as zinesters might have changed their way of being in the world and their capacities to act on that world. Indeed it seems clear even now that zine-ing transformed some of them at least into cultural producers and into advocates dedicated to ensuring that the zines they created so enthusiastically not only would not disappear but also would continue to have an impact on others in the future. The zines they created functioned in the end as incitements to social change, as rickety handcrafted bridges to a future not yet imagined but dimly discerned just past the horizon. What was powerful about girl zines, it seems to me, was their capacity to generate hope and a determined willingness to act on that hope, even modestly, with only an old typewriter, a marker, scissors, paste, and a few stamps.

Notes

    The author would like to thank Anouk Lang and two anonymous readers for their helpful comments on an earlier version of this chapter.
1. The word "zine" is a contraction of the word "fanzine," itself a neologism generated to refer to amateur publications produced by fans of various popular cultural forms—initially science fiction, later comics, television shows, then music and musicians.
2. See, for instance, Pagan Kennedy, *Zine: How I Spent Six Years of My Life in the Underground and Finally . . . Found Myself . . . I Think* (New York: St. Martin's Griffin, 1995); R. Seth Friedman, *The Factsheet Five Zine Reader: The Best Writing from the Underground World of Zines* (New York: Three Rivers Press, 1997); V. Vale, *Zines!* vol. 1 (San Francisco: RE/Search, 1996), and *Zines!* vol. 2 (San Francisco: RE/Search, 1997); Karen Green and Tristan Taormino, *A Girl's Guide to Taking Over the World: Writings from the Girl Zine Revolution* (New York: St. Martin's Griffin, 1997); Francesca Lia Block and Hillary Carlip, *Zine Scene: The Do It Yourself Guide to Zines* (Los Angeles: Girl Press, 1998); and *$100 and a T-Shirt: A Documentary about Zines in Portland*, DVD, directed by Joe Biel (2004, Microcosm Publishing).

3. There are major zine collections at Barnard College, Bowling Green State University, DePaul University, Duke University, Michigan State University, San Diego State University, Smith College, the University of Michigan (the Labadie Collection), the Salt Lake City Public Library, and the New York State Library. In addition, there are a number of private zine libraries including the ABC No Rio Library in New York, the Denver Zine Library, and the Olympia Zine Library in Olympia, Wash.
4. See Elke Zobl, "Persephone Is Pissed! Grrrl Zine Reading, Making, and Distributing across the Globe," *Hecate: An Interdisciplinary Journal of Women's Liberation* 30.2 (2004): 156–74.
5. See http://zinewiki.com. Zinewiki describes itself as "the zine encyclopedia that anyone can edit" and notes that it "is an open-source encyclopedia devoted to zines and independent media. It covers the history, production, distribution, and culture of the small press." The site includes useful lists of distros (zine distribution services), zine events, zine libraries, and even zinesters themselves.
6. Stephen Duncombe, *Notes from Underground: Zines and the Politics of Alternative Culture* (London: Verso, 1997). Duncombe's book was one of the first academic books to treat zines seriously. It is still the single best account of the zine phenomenon and should be consulted by anyone interested in the history and significance of zine-ing.
7. Mark Todd and Esther Pearl Watson, *Whatcha Mean, What's a Zine? The Art of Making Zines and Minicomics* (Boston: Graphia, 2006).
8. Stephen Duncombe quoted in Julie Bartel, *From A to Zine: Building a Winning Zine Collection in Your Library* (Chicago: American Library Association, 2004), 1.
9. http://library.duke.edu/specialcollections/bingham/zines/index.html.
10. Stephen Duncombe's book *Notes from Underground* and Chris Atton's *Alternative Media* (London: Sage, 2002) are notable exceptions in that they treat the modes of production involved in zine-ing as well as common methods of distribution and circulation as alternative political forms, that is, as social activities designed as a refusal of the traditional social relations prescribed by a capitalist system of mass production and consumption. Still, because both are heavily invested in judging the effectiveness of zine politics, they spend a substantial amount of time discussing the coherence and consistency of the ideas conveyed in zines. At the same time, because Duncombe and Atton retain the traditional distinction between the cultural realm and a separate realm of the political, they judge the political effectiveness of zines wanting because they did not propel their creators to full-blown political activism in the public sphere. It should become clear through the course of this essay that I find this approach somewhat myopic in its focus on the short term and in its failure to assess the way zines might have functioned as practices of subject formation with gradual, extended, long-term effects. It is also worth pointing out here that because much of the early work on girl zines connected them to Riot Grrrl (a movement originating among girls bands within the punk music scene) and placed them in the context of third wave feminism, that work tended to focus most intensively on the nature of girl zines' *ideological* resistance to the dominant culture despite the fact that early scholars did acknowledge the political significance of zinesters' alternative modes of production and distribution. As a result, this scholarship tended to foreground zine content and the way zines took up questions about sex and gender, body image, eating disorders, rape, and physical abuse. See, for instance, the following early writings about girls and zines: Joanne Gottlieb and Gayle Wald, "Smells Like Teen Spirit: Riot Grrrls, Revolution, and Women in

Independent Rock," in *Microphone Fiends: Youth Music and Youth Culture,* ed. Andrew Ross and Tricia Rose (New York: Routledge, 1994), 250–74; Catherine Driscoll, "Girl Culture, Revenge and Global Capitalism: Cybergirls, Riot Grrls, Spice Girls," *Australian Feminist Studies* 14.29 (1999): 173–93; Ednie Kaeh Garrison, "U.S. Feminism—Grrrl Style! Youth (Sub)Cultures and the Technologies of the Third Wave," *Feminist Studies* 26.1 (Spring 2000): 141–69; Melanie Ferris, "Resisting Mainstream Media: Girls and the Art of Making Zines," *Canadian Woman Studies* 20.4/21.1 (2001): 51–55; Anita Harris, "gURL Scenes and Grrrl Zines: The Regulation and Resistance of Girls in Late Modernity," *Feminist Review* 75.1 (2003): 38–56. Although I, too, am interested in the feminist politics of girl zines and the zinesters who created them, I think it imperative to pay close attention to the practices of subject formation and community building at the heart of girl zine-ing. It then becomes possible to see that girl zine-ing was generated not solely by anger, rage, disappointment, or depression but also by profound hope that alternative ways of being in the world might be created through zine-ing.

11. See, for instance, Friedman, *The Factsheet Five Zine Reader,* 42–44, where he reproduces two comics-like pages from *babysue* but then transposes a long piece from *Celluloid All* into the regularity and uniformity of print. Similarly, although V. Vale acknowledges the importance of the aesthetic act of zine creation in his compilations *Zines,* vols. 1 and 2, and closely questions the zinesters whose work he features there about their aims and aesthetic decision-making process, he rarely reproduces more than a single page of a zine at a time. More often than not, he illustrates the printed interview with small images taken from larger zine pages.

12. Despite the early focus on zine content, attention to the aesthetics and formal qualities of zines has been increasing. Indeed, Liz Farrelly, *Zines* (London: Booth-Clibborn, 2001), a large art-book type compilation, reproduces images from selected zines on heavy, high-quality paper. The editor and book designers comment: "The main body of this book is visual. We want you to see just how graphically innovative these publications are, so we've pulled out favourite images and played with them. Up at the front of the book is information about the zines; dimensions, materials, and dates. We've selected writings from the publications and printed taster samples; sadly there just isn't space for complete articles, but many of the existing books on zines present written content very comprehensively" (unpaginated). Similarly, Todd and Watson, *Whatcha Mean, What's a Zine?* and Alex Wrekk, *Stolen Sharpie Revolution: A DIY Zine Resource* (Portland, Ore.: Microcosm, 2003), both volumes aimed at would-be zine creators, emphasize the material process of producing a zine. Again, though, because of space, they do not reproduce zines or even zine pages in toto.

13. For an introduction to the field, see David Finkelstein and Alistair McCleery, *An Introduction to Book History* (New York: Routledge, 2005). For a sampling of work done in the field, see their companion volume *The Book History Reader,* 2nd ed. (Abingdon, UK: Routledge, 2006).

14. A significant historical question needs to be posed about why zinesters engaged in boundary defiance of all sorts during the 1980s and 1990s. What prompted their desire to blur the boundaries between texts and the world, writing and reading, affect and reason, culture and politics? Although this will take further investigation, it seems possible that their efforts in promoting category confusion had something to do with the fact that they were working at a moment of rapid technological change as computers and digital communication promoted economic integration and further extension of consumer

society as well as the passive forms of attendance that have accompanied it. Zine practice may have developed as an exploratory effort to construct forms of subjectivity and sociality capable of negotiating this world without capitulating totally to it.

15. I am one of those who has been thus inspired. In fact zines live on in my work in this essay. They therefore continue to exert their manifold effects even on someone who has never created a zine. My work here has been inspired by the hundreds of zines I have now read but most especially by the young women who created them and forged the social connections, friendships, and networks that enabled them to contest dominant representations of girlhood, and thus to suggest that a girl might have a future other than simply becoming a woman, that is, a subject defined wholly by her gender. See my account later in this chapter of how my interest in zines and zine-ing developed.

16. See note 10 for a discussion of this point.

17. The body of work on Riot Grrrl seems to grow every day. I have found the book *Riot Grrrl: Revolution Girl Style Now!* edited by Nadine Monem (London: Black Dog Publishing, 2007) especially helpful. Because the volume includes wonderful photographs of the bands, their performances, and their fans, as well as commentaries written by the young women who participated in the movement, it does a fine job of capturing the intense energy and complicated affects infusing the Riot Grrrl phenomenon.

18. I especially thank Katie Kent, Mandy Berry, Jennifer Doyle, Jonathan Flatley, Melissa Solomon, and Jessica Blaustein for the many conversations that have inspired my work here, albeit at some temporal distance. Although they may not be aware of it, their thinking has had an enormous impact on my interests and ongoing work.

19. It is important to point out that although my work concentrates on the zine-ing generated by Riot Grrrl in the United States, the Riot Grrrl phenomenon was international in scope, as demonstrated by the previously mentioned volume *Riot Grrrl: Revolution Girl Style Now!* and by Elke Zobl's website *grrrl zine network*.

20. Julie Bartel discusses the problem of zine categorization at length in Bartel, *From A to Zine*, 77–91, where she observes: "Subject categories can be problematic (though not impossible) to define in any classification scheme, and zines take the difficulties to a whole new level. A zine may include numerous topics in a single issue; a title may change topics completely from issue to issue; and certain categories such as 'perzines' or 'compilation' zines are likely to properly contain so many zines as to become unwieldy all on their own" (78).

21. Jennifer Sinor's excellent article "Another Form of Crying: Girl Zines as Life Writing," *Prose Studies* 26.1–2 (April–August 2003): 240–64, conceptualizes zine-ing as a practice of life writing. I have found Sinor's important essay enormously helpful and believe it to be congruent with the performative approach I am recommending here. Indeed there is significant overlap between the account of zine-ing I develop based on Jess's zine collection and the account Sinor gives, especially of the way the zine network is constructed both textually and extratextually. I should note, however, that despite her recognition of the centrality of community to zine writers, I think Sinor individualizes zinesters too much as singular life writers or as authors—the very idea of writing a life is bound up with the novel form and the way it develops in tandem with the emergence of bourgeois subjectivity—and thus risks placing too much stress on the expressive nature of their practice. As a result, although Sinor discusses the fluid nature of the subjectivities constructed in zines, she misses their highly social and intersubjective nature, which I believe was probably key to the attraction zines and zine-ing held for the many girls who

involved themselves with them and tied them to the form just as it tied the form to its historical moment (ibid., 248). Thus, although I agree with her that the act of writing a zine was crucially important to zinesters, I do not agree that the act of being read was of less significance. Ibid., 248.

22. I have come across a number of zines that graphically insist they are not at all like traditional books. *one night stand,* for instance, which can be found in box 6 of the Tinuviel Papers in the Sophia Smith Collection at Smith College, appears to be a two-by-three-inch mini-zine, constructed from a single sheet of carefully folded paper. It is designed to open like a triptych, and the cover image is drawn across the folds. When the cover is opened, however, an internal triptych is revealed, and the potential reader must begin reading not on the extreme right but on the left. The reader must proceed down the extreme left, cross over to the center reading from top to bottom, and then move on to the right fold to follow the comments of the zine's creators. Then the folded triptych page lifts up, and the reader must turn it around and over to keep reading. Eventually the zine must be refolded so one can finish reading on the back of the left-facing page of the tri-folded triptych. For an introduction to the most common fold and format strategies, see Todd and Watson, *Whatcha Mean, What's a Zine?* 45–57, where directions for the micro-mini, the no staples zine, the stack-n-wrap, and the fold-n-bind can be found. The authors also make suggestions about how to "Breakout! Of the Format." Because zinesters played so creatively with the familiar codex form, their zines defied conventional strategies for making them give way simply to parsable content. As a result, they never arrived "already read," as Jennifer Sinor has argued ("Another Form of Crying," 242). They highlighted, then, the fact that a quite different practice of reading had to be forged in order to make any kind of sense of zines.

23. A number of commentators on the DIY (do it yourself) ethos that has underwritten the larger punk music scene and zine production have connected it to the aesthetic practices of situationism, to anarchism, and to the concerns of French Left intellectuals in the 1950s and 1960s. See, for instance, Greil Marcus, *Lipstick Traces: A Secret History of the Twentieth Century* (Cambridge: Harvard University Press, 1989). See also Duncombe, *Notes from Underground,* 17–43; and Mary Celeste Kearney, "The Missing Links: Riot Grrrl—Feminism—Lesbian Culture," in *Sexing the Groove: Popular Music and Gender,* ed. Sheila Whiteley (London: Routledge, 1997), 215, 227.

24. Stephen Duncombe (*Notes from Underground*) places great emphasis on the search for originality, individuality, and authenticity among zinesters. In my view, though girl zines do mobilize languages of self-expression and self-exploration and insist on the importance of individuality and giving vent to "authentic" emotions such as anger, rage, and frustration, their actual aesthetic practices—as well as distribution procedures—function in considerable tension with such ideologies. In my view, the strength of the political critique embedded in zines rests upon the collaborative, collective, and conversational practices that characterize nearly all girl zines and not on their search for individual forms of "authentic" critique.

25. *Velvet Grass* 14, Jess's zine collection, in author's possession. All quotations come from this issue.

26. One such message, handwritten on the back of a flyer addressed "To the Young Women [of] Orange County Riot Grrrl," notes: "Hello. I hope you enjoy #2. #3 will be out in a month (probably). This is a flier for the RG chapter I wanna start. I know that you don't

live around here (takes a genius to figure that out) but if you have contacts w/anyone in So. Cal I'd be super grateful if you could let 'em know about it!"
27. On the "international communication network" that has grown up around girl zineing, see Elke Zobl's dissertation "The Global Grrrl Zine Network: A DIY Feminist Revolution for Social Change" (Academy of Fine Arts, Vienna, 2004). I have not yet been able to find a copy of this dissertation, although there is an abstract of it on her website. The article mentioned in note 4 apparently summarizes some of the work in her dissertation.
28. www.puckerup.com.
29. The zine is known as *Zine Librarian Zine*. There is also a Library Workers Zine Collection at the School of Library and Information Studies Library at the University of Wisconsin.
30. As is undoubtedly true of all political practice, at times these activities proved more constraining than enabling for some. For a discussion of the ways in which the girl zine community could be rigid and as censorious about certain behaviors as even the most traditional of communities, see Sinor, "Another Form of Crying," 260–62.

2

HAVE MOUSE, WILL TRAVEL
Consuming and Creating Chinese Popular
Literature on the Web

JIN FENG

The democratizing power of the World Wide Web in China, a favorite topic of both Chinese and Western scholars,[1] seems to have been borne out by official statistics. According to the state-run China Internet Network Information Centre (CNNIC),[2] by December 2009 more than 384 million people had accessed the Internet in mainland China. A survey by CNNIC released in January 2009 claims that 22.6 percent of the Chinese population accessed the Internet, higher than the global average. Although Chinese users still tend to be young, urban, and well educated, statistics reveal some distinct changes from previous years. As of 2009, rural users had increased by 60.8 percent from 2007, faster than urban users (35.6 percent); growth in use in China's traditionally underdeveloped western region (52 percent) was higher than that in the more industrialized eastern (39.3 percent) and central (40.6 percent) regions; and the difference between the numbers of male and female users due to different levels of formal education has been decreasing since 1997. All these statistics seem to indicate that in terms of Internet usage, gaps of class, education, and gender have diminished in contemporary China.

With the increasing popularity of Internet use in China, many individuals spend considerable time reading and writing online literature. According to Michel Hockx, by the end of 2004 there were 668,900 websites on the Chinese World Wide Web, with a significant number of these publishing literature.[3] Moreover, by 2000, Web literature consisting mainly of unedited items also surpassed the volume of published printed matter.[4] As of 2009, 162 million people were writing blogs on the Chinese Web.[5] Chinese and English-language scholarship on Chinese cyberspace, however, rarely explores the kind of reader and author behavior that Web literature has inculcated. English-language scholarship focuses on issues of state censorship and civil liberties while ignoring "cultural production" on the Chinese Web.[6] Mainland Chinese scholars, by contrast, usually engage in theoretical discussions of the ontology, aesthetics, and sociology of Web literature rather than in case studies.[7]

In order to fill in this lacuna and scrutinize the dynamic cultural production and consumption happening on the Chinese Web, in this chapter I investigate one Chinese literature website by the name of Jinjiang. I focus on serialized time travel romances published on this website to explore how the consciousness of gender and society among contemporary Chinese women shapes and is in turn shaped by their reading and writing practices. I show that Jinjiang's interactive features transform the experience of both authors and readers, helping to instantiate a kind of "reader-oriented" form of writing. The text is transformed from a single, closed-up entity into a continual process of becoming, thanks to the collective contributions of multiple agents. Furthermore, since textual meanings and significances are subjected to constant negotiations between different users, author and reader have turned into fluid and mutually constitutive categories. In other words, users not only readily shift between the identities of author and reader but also use rewriting as a tool to access power granted by the production of meaning, and thereby to carve out their virtual identity and a communal life on Jinjiang.

By facilitating direct and emotive communications, Jinjiang makes it possible for users to establish among themselves a community that is "imagined" and imaginary in the sense outlined by Benedict Anderson: "in the minds of each lives the image of their communion" because they consume the same fictional text.[8] Furthermore, users utilize the platform available at Jinjiang to appropriate from existing cultural products in order to address their own immediate interests and needs. Jinjiang thus cultivates a community of readers and authors who foster emotional nurturance, explore gender identities, and test their creative voices beyond any particular text. I begin with a brief description of the history of Jinjiang. Then I examine the highest-ranked time travel romances and summarize their similarities. Finally, I look at the three groups of human players in the creation and consumption of Jinjiang texts—webmasters, authors, and readers—and examine how interactive features of the website shape their relations.

What's Hot?

Though not the earliest or the largest Chinese literature website,[9] Jinjiang Literature City has established an enthusiastic, faithful, and largely female readership. Launched in Jinjiang, Fujian province, in 1998,[10] it has since developed into an elaborate organization consisting of an online e-bookstore, a discussion forum, a users' feedback forum, as well as a website for publishing unedited works, called Yuanchuang wang (Creative Work Net, hereafter the Net). To judge by self-identifications, the majority of authors and readers are fairly well educated women who range in age from their late teens to their late thirties.[11] Only a few are full-time Web writers. Most have other occupations such as student, teacher, or accountant. The majority reside in mainland China, but a significant number of them appear to be studying or working abroad.[12] The age, education, and occupation of Jinjiang users fit the national profile of users of Chinese literature websites. As described by the CEO of Qidian (Starting Point), one of the largest Chinese-language literature websites, they possess the "three highs" (*sangao*): high salary, high level of education, and high social status.[13]

Jinjiang experienced several financial and legal crises and changes of ownership before finding an investor in the Shanghai Shengda Internet Development Cooperation in November 2007. Shortly afterward it followed the example of other Chinese literature websites and charged a fee for access to certain "VIP" works. This practice, albeit controversial, reflects the increasing influence of the market economy in the publishing industry in China.[14] So far only a small percentage of Jinjiang works have been published, and mostly by more recently established houses known for their lists of popular literature rather than by large state-run houses specializing in serious literature.[15] But more and more Chinese publications have joined in the sale of popular fiction, and they have especially targeted female readers of time travel romances as a profit-generating consumer base.[16]

This reader enthusiasm about time travel romances also reigns at Jinjiang. Rank lists at Jinjiang identify novels by four descriptors: whether they are fan fiction (*tongren*)[17] or "original" work (*yuanchuang*); whether they feature heterosexual (*yanqing*), male-male (*danmei*), or female-female (*baihe*) sexual relationships; whether they are set in modern (*jindai xiandai*), premodern (*guse guxiang*), or fictionalized historical (*jiakong lishi*) periods; and finally, whether they belong to the genre of romance (*yanqing*) fiction, martial arts (*wuxia*) fiction, horror (*kongbu*) fiction, legend (*chuanqi*), fantasy (*xuanhuan*), fiction based on film and TV (*yingshi*), or fiction based on *manga* (comic strips) and animation (*dongman*). Despite the evolution of its categorization systems since its inception, including the addition of nontraditional genres such as animation and the elimination of time travel as a descriptor (probably because it is so commonplace in all Jinjiang romances nowadays), various rank lists at Jinjiang still show the continual popularity of romances that feature the trope of time travel.[18]

Both Jinjiang's traditional privileging of the romance genre and the upsurge of the time travel genre in popular Chinese culture can shed some light on the dominance of time travel romances on Jinjiang.[19] Jinjiang writers do list many popular culture products in print, on the Web, and on TV as sources of inspiration for them.[20] Interestingly, they also express a deep dissatisfaction with blatant male fantasies in existing works even as they acknowledge them as predecessors. They unflatteringly call many Web-based works "stud [zhongma] fiction" because they depict male protagonists who, endowed with superhuman prowess, change history and acquire numerous beautiful women at the same time.[21] Consequently, in their own fictions they often showcase self-conscious differences from male-authored works. Furthermore, because the Internet enables fast dissemination and ready imitation of any high-ranked Web fiction, Jinjiang readers and authors also exhibit the typical Web user's "fickleness" in tastes. That is to say, as popular tropes and plots quickly become passé, users begin to expose and criticize what they consider clichés and absurdities in time travel romances. Moreover, they continue to seek new ways to reinvent the conventions of popular romance and to depart from precedents set by earlier female authors. A good case in point is the recent rise in popularity of "farming" (zhongtian) fiction, that is, time travel romances that privilege "realistic" depictions of a heroine's ascent from obscurity to power through hard work and discretion rather than heaven-endowed prowess or ostentatious "modern" airs. It can thus be seen that, as in the case of time travel popular romance, Web-based popular literature often breeds its own destruction, correction, or antithesis even as it is in the process of being widely disseminated and imitated.

From "Stud" to "Farming" Fiction: Characteristics and Trends in Time Travel Romance on Jinjiang

It is perhaps inevitable that Jinjiang works feature female rather than male protagonists, since they have been written by women and are mainly for women's consumption. In terms of characterization, the heroine is endowed with traditionally masculine characteristics of intelligence, public prominence, sexual promiscuity, and moral ambiguity. Granted, heroines in contemporary English-language print romances have also evolved from the type prevalent in romances published in the 1980s and analyzed in Janice Radway's groundbreaking study.[22] It is, however, perhaps more surprising to see an individualist Chinese heroine boldly pursuing sexual gratification and social position in light of both a cultural tradition that censures individualism and promotes women's chastity, modesty, and selfless devotion to collective interests, and tight state control of speech in China.

Other than characterization, Jinjiang authors have added surprising twists to the well-established conventions of time travel. The four most popular time travel plots on Jinjiang are the following: a woman travels back to the past in her own body, sometimes cross-dresses, and becomes the object of passion and devotion of multiple powerful masculine figures; a woman's soul travels back to the past, inhabits the body of another man or woman, and also receives ardent romantic interest from the aforementioned male figures; a woman travels back either in her own body or by inhabiting another female body, becomes a dominant public figure in a matriarchal society, and sets up a seraglio of attractive men; and, more recently, the plot of "rebirth" (*chongsheng*), in which a woman travels back in her own life, (re)awakens in early childhood, and sets about changing her destiny and that of her family.

These plots, especially the first type, may seem formulaic and redundant at first sight, a mere rehashing of traditional heterosexual romances that play out the typical female reader's fantasy of finding the perfect combination of power and nurturance in emblems of traditional masculinity. Readers of time travel novels on Jinjiang do seem to expect a degree of similarity, and even demand the familiarity of conventions of popular romance. For example, they would express dissatisfaction if the "coupling" of the hero and heroine still remained murky after they had read several chapters of the romance, or if the work ended in any way other than "happily ever after" for the romantic couple. Nevertheless, time travel romances published on Jinjiang all feature some degree of transgression even while focusing on women's romantic relationships.

All in all, Jinjiang authors do not appear enthusiastic about either disseminating the myth that women's ultimate fulfillment is possible only through marriage and domesticity, or promoting the role model of Chinese *guixiu*: women who not only possess poetic talent but also hold "higher standards of behavior when it [comes] to piety, chastity, or other forms of self-sacrifice."[23] In fact, they often celebrate not just the female time traveler's achievements in traditionally masculine occupations such as commerce, politics, and the military but her sexual peccadilloes as well, including simultaneous (and at times incestuous) relationships with multiple partners. Readers also share this desire for a powerful heroine. In their comments, they tend to criticize female characters who seem to have forsaken notions of gender equality after traveling back to the past, and demand from them a modern or even feminist consciousness, even while acknowledging such behavior as anachronistic and improbable under the circumstances.[24]

Yet these romances generate more complex pleasures than a complete subversion of the patriarchy, as illustrated by the unique way in which they provide "compensation." Above all, they all embody the basic plot of redemption. The heroine leaves "real" times as a result of a variety of traumas including physical and emotional abuse from others. Her time travel, in contrast, provides her with the opportunity to redress the wrongs of her current world and to put things right, if only often at another, fantastic time and locale. Having traveled back to premodern China, she typically uses her modern knowledge, skills, and progressive ideas to establish herself in a patriarchal society: gaining fame and wealth, winning adoration from multiple successful men, and generally exerting power over history. If granted a second chance through "rebirth" into contemporary Chinese society, she not only has the "foresight" to invest in the stock market and the IT industry and thereby make a fortune, but also identifies a good marriage prospect in early childhood and brings him up according to her model of the ideal man. By identifying with such a morally ambiguous yet powerful female time traveler, Jinjiang users can imaginatively—albeit temporarily—suspend the social and moral constraints placed on their lives and claim sexual and political power through acts of reading and writing.

Nevertheless, these romances all start with the heroine's yearning to escape from her current dull or miserable circumstances in exchange for a past that promises a more authentic and satisfying emotional life. Moreover, while the time traveler enjoys the best of both worlds because of her dual perspective, the opportunity for her restoration and transformation, especially the change of her sex, initially occurs by accident rather than through individual will or endeavor. She is shown to be ultimately at the mercy of fate, even while struggling against the unsatisfying reality of modern life. It can thus be seen that authors' and readers' insistence on the theme of redemption and a happy ending is at odds with their urges to subvert patriarchy and disrupt current patriarchal norms, while at the same time they strive for a precarious balance between keeping and unsettling the status quo.

This dilemma faced by the protagonist is equally, albeit somewhat singularly, revealed in the two seemingly innovative plot patterns that Jinjiang romances adopt. These are *danmei* (*tanbi* in Japanese), male-male homoerotic fiction, and *nüzun*, narratives of matriarchy. I have discussed *danmei* and *nüzun* narratives in more depth elsewhere.[25] It is, however, worth touching briefly on the way these two plot patterns enact gender identities and relations that seem advantageous to women in and through their narration.

Of the two, *nüzun,* or matriarchal narratives, have an original model in the Chinese novel *Jing Hua Yuan* (Flowers in the Mirror), written by Li Ruzhen (1763–1830), in which a group of men encounter various kingdoms in their travels overseas, including a matriarchy where women serve in public roles, while men have bound feet, wear cosmetics, are confined to domestic space, and generally have to behave according to gender norms commonly assigned to women in a patriarchy. The *nüzun* romances at Jinjiang go a step further than this model in that they not only reverse women's and men's gender roles but also dole out to male characters physiological and psychological traits traditionally seen as feminine and negative. They often describe men as vain and jealous, and even have them experience menses, childbirth, and breastfeeding.[26] Although the more sophisticated Jinjiang readers point out that such narratives only reverse patriarchal gender hierarchy without eliminating gender inequality,[27] matriarchal narratives attract faithful followers at Jinjiang, who see such works as entertaining and empowering.[28]

In comparison to matriarchal narratives, *danmei* romances command attention for their conspicuous lack of positive representations of women. It should be noted from the start that *danmei* encompasses a variety of subgenres at Jinjiang, but I focus here on its deployment of time travel. Originally an anti-naturalism literary movement in early-twentieth-century Japan which promoted "aesthetic" representations of sensory impressions,[29] *danmei* has evolved to mean *manga* and adult literature for consumption by Japanese women. *Danmei* works differ from other kinds of queer texts in that they usually depict idealized love between attractive male figures for women's consumption.[30] In fact, *danmei* fans, those at Jinjiang included, often characterize themselves as heterosexual women who have no interest in real-life homosexuality.[31]

Because homosexuality is still stigmatized in contemporary China,[32] and also because *danmei* works often contain explicit sexual content, *danmei* fans sometimes incur severe criticisms from Chinese society, which accuses them of selling pornography, promoting incest, and "poisoning" young minds.[33] Yet for young Chinese women whose school curriculum includes little effective sex education, *danmei* works not only satisfy their curiosity about sex but also promise a "pure" love that transcends class, gender, ethics, and even species.[34] As relatively young women, *danmei* fans appear receptive to unconventional sexual relationships and the higher proportion of graphic sex in *danmei* novels compared to the more strictly censored heterosexual romances.[35] *Danmei* time travel romances attract Jinjiang women, however, not just because of their sexual curiosity or because they can "permanently possess a man [they] love because there is no other woman to compete with [them] in this world without women."[36] Comments left by both authors and readers reveal more sides to the story.

A survey on Jinjiang's discussion forum yields a considerable number of respondents who would wish to inhabit the bodies of powerful men in history if they could time travel.[37] This can be partly explained by their belief that the primitive hygiene conditions of ancient times posed great danger with regard to menses and childbirth.[38] Another reason behind their interest in inhabiting a male body lies in their disenchantment with heterosexual relationships. As one author remarks through the mouth of a female time traveler, heterosexual love is too often spoiled by "money, reputation, house, family, children, and parents," and only love between men can "transcend worldly concerns."[39] But most compelling to Jinjiang women is their shared conviction that only by becoming a strong man can a woman survive in a male-dominated world. According to the author of *Xieyang Ruoying* (Slanting Sun Like Shadows), a popular *danmei* romance that tells the story of a woman changing into a man through time travel, a woman "needs to become strong and independent to survive in a ruthless patriarchal society."[40] To Jinjiang women, sex change matters only because it enables women to shed disadvantageous gender identities and seize power. Its function is not so dissimilar to that of cross-dressing, another familiar trope in time travel romances.

Danmei romances thus embody and satisfy Jinjiang women's yearning for "pure" love, independence, and power in patriarchy. Like other time travel romances, however, they reveal an irresolvable dilemma. In relating how a woman gains agency only after fate grants her a miraculous metamorphosis, they suggest Jinjiang women's disenchantment with reality, their uncertainty about their own destiny, and their longing for autonomy in a rapidly changing yet still male-dominated society. It can, of course, be argued that the compensation generated through reading and writing romances only accentuates the inability of these women to raise substantial challenges to patriarchal rule. Nevertheless, users clearly do not see Jinjiang as a tool of social engineering but rather identify it as a place to find entertainment, satisfy creative impulses, and derive emotional nurturance.[41] Therefore, instead of denouncing Jinjiang for what it fails to do, we will find it more productive to investigate what it *does* do for users.

Recent trends in time travel romances reveal not only the inherent contradictions in contemporary Chinese women's desires and expectations but also the facility of the Internet as a tool to attend to their immediate needs and aspirations. As we have seen, recent Jinjiang users showed more interest in romances that portrayed a female time traveler succeeding by working hard and keeping a low profile than in earlier works that included more fantastic and improbable plots. For instance, *Wan Qingsi* (*Coiling Up Black Hair*), a high-ranked Jinjiang romance later published in multiple volumes in print form (Huashan Wenyi, 2007–8), portrays a modern woman who travels back in time to inhabit the body of another woman, survives abduction and rape, and achieves amazing feats in her turbulent career: she becomes a much-sought-after courtesan, a successful business owner, a mistress and manager of a prominent family and clan, and a political player in court conspiracy and a coup. At one point in the story she even enters the underworld in pursuit of her lover.[42] As Jun Suiyuan, author of a high-ranked matriarchal romance, comments derisively, absurdities abound in existing time travel romances that feature plots such as these: "The heroine becomes a superstar [in the other world] just by singing a modern song and performing an erotic dance, becomes a millionaire by opening a hot pot restaurant and frying a few pieces of chicken, and becomes a 'Talented Woman' by reciting [plagiarizing] a few classical poems."[43] Such charges ring true for time travel "classics" such as *Coiling Up Black Hair*.

In contrast to earlier time travel romances published on Jinjiang, which portray larger-than-life female protagonists, Jun Suiyuan depicts an ordinary modern-day Chinese woman who is frequently exposed as ignorant, timid, and generally muddle-headed in the matriarchal world to which her soul has been transposed. Her only redeeming feature seems to lie in her sincere love of her twelve husbands, who include, among others, two princes, a prime minister, a powerful businessman, a knight-errant adept with a sword, and a leader of organized crime, whose intellectual capacity, martial prowess, social status, and political clout all overshadow her. Rather than portraying a natural-born all-powerful matriarch, the author relates that the female protagonist will "meet many people, experience a lot of things, eat a lot of bitterness, make a lot of mistakes, and eventually live up to her title 'General Phoenix' after many years of trials and tribulations."[44] Yet by emphasizing the heroine's "love" and feminine nurturance, Jun Suiyuan does not diverge widely from traditional expectations of femininity. Indeed, the protagonist can be seen as the supreme mother figure of benevolence and nurturance, who eventually wins over her husbands through love.

Sometimes authors of more recent time travel romances also debunk clichés prevalent in earlier works by juxtaposing and contrasting two female time travelers in the same work. For example, in *Luohong Ru Zhou* (*Fallen Flowers Like Wrinkles*),[45] author Douyun depicts a female protagonist who possesses a surprising "conservative" streak despite her secret identity as a modern time traveler. The other female time traveler in the same novel displays all the "typical" characteristics, such as boldness in relationships between the sexes, curiosity about brothels, and self-exhibitionism, shown by her singing contemporary popular songs and plagiarizing classical poems. In contrast, the protagonist apparently adapts to her upbringing as a modest upper-class maiden and conforms to all the gender prescriptions that befit her position. Although "the other woman" succeeds in first seducing her fiancé (also her cousin) and later her husband, an idiot emperor, the protagonist shows great poise and clear-sightedness, and gradually gains power in court after giving birth to a son. While some readers complain that this protagonist does not resemble their idea of a modern time traveler at all, others support the author's more "realistic" and authentic portrayal of a complex imperial society.[46] Furthermore, even though the female protagonist apparently upholds traditional gender norms in a patriarchal society, she also exploits them to her own advantage. Her lack of romantic illusions and independence from men provoke one reader to remark: "She does not need a man. She can live very comfortably by herself."[47] Thus it can be seen that recent trends in time travel romances on Jinjiang, which feature less flamboyant heroines and more realistic depictions, also subvert the patriarchal norms and conventions of heterosexual popular romances even as they register Chinese women's ambivalence toward these time-honored precedents.

Readers/Authors, Consumers/Producers

As discussed earlier, time travel romances on Jinjiang allow readers and authors to express and experience transgressions and claim power through reading and writing, even while such acts simultaneously reveal their uncertainty about their gender identities and discontent about reality. Furthermore, in most cases only the Internet can enable and enhance such experiences. Jinjiang grants its users anonymity and the opportunity not only to produce and consume popular literature but also to exchange ideas and comments at no cost. It does not require users to register before they post comments. Although theoretically IP addresses can be traced, in practice users can assume as many Web identities as they wish. Not only do they sport numerous outlandish Web names, but also they feel free to express their interest in taboo topics more frankly than would otherwise be possible or acceptable. Moreover, Web versions of Jinjiang works can contain more explicit sex and *danmei* content, while in print versions authors have to make severe cuts before passing censorship and getting published.[48] In this section

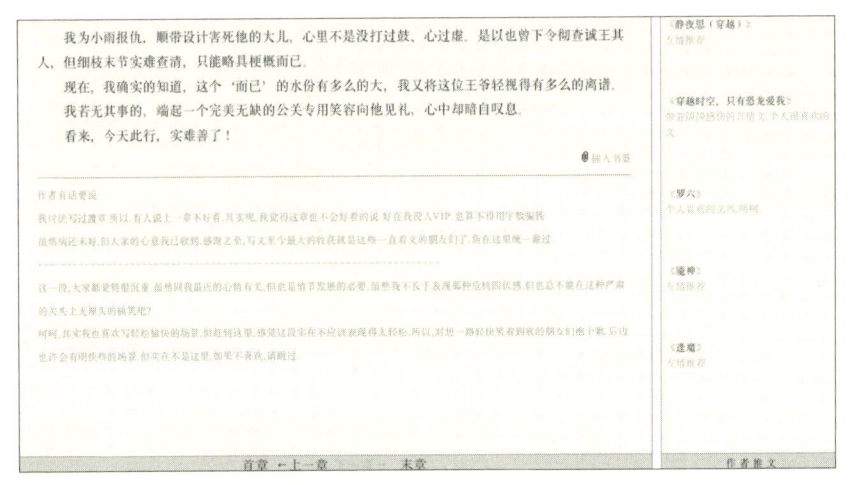

Figure 2.1. Text, author's words, and author's recommendations

I turn my attention to the interactive features of Jinjiang in order to show how they shape reading and writing behavior and create a unique kind of user experience.

After undergoing a series of improvements and upgrading, the Net settled on a layout in which each Web page is vertically divided into two large "blocks," and each block further divided into two columns, with one wider than the other. In the upper block the text occupies the wider, left-hand column and is prominently displayed in black font. Also occupying this column is a row labeled "Author's Words," which is demarcated from the text by a black line and displays authors' comments and responses to readers' remarks in a distinctive smaller green font. Side by side and to the right of this text column lies a narrower column, also divided vertically into two parts. The upper block of this narrower column displays chapter titles of the whole work, while the bottom, labeled "Author's Recommendations," allows authors to recommend other works at Jinjiang in a small gray font (figure 2.1).

The upper block, mostly featuring authors' activities, is divided by advertisements from the bottom block of the page, which showcases readers' activities. Readers can grade each installment and leave comments in a space located in a wide column positioned on the left-hand side of the bottom block and also right underneath the text column above. To the right of this column of reader comments is a narrower column of "Author's Choice of Comments," where authors highlight the reader comments that they found most appealing and profound (figure 2.2).

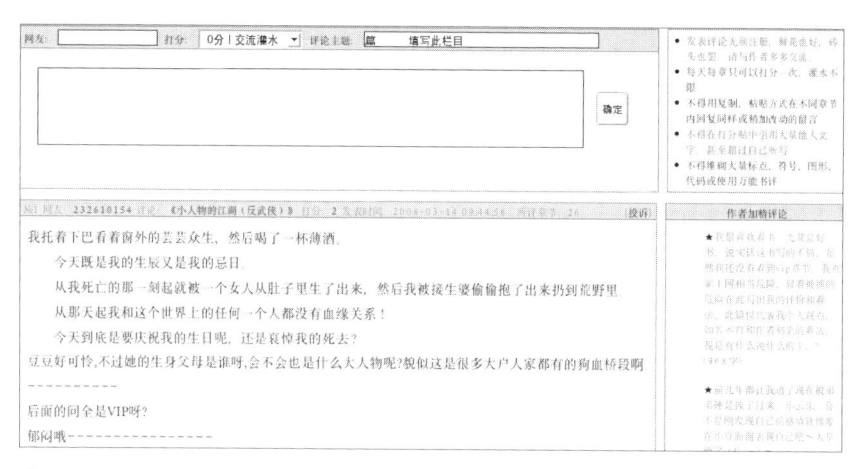

Figure 2.2. Commentary space

Thus, three major players shape the text: authors, readers, and, less obvious but equally essential, webmasters. Webmasters work as both the original architects and maintenance crew of the website. They offer a variety of services and forms of tutelage to users, such as instructing prospective authors on how to create tight-knit plots, how to display text in a more attractive format, and even how to approach publishers.[49] But more important, they not only have established the interactive devices and rules of the Net but also continually moderate the roles of author, reader, and text. In this regard, the commentary space they have set up warrants particular attention. Its basic function is to record points made by readers, and thereby to serve as a barometer of the popularity of the work and the author. The webmasters, however, emphasize the quality of readers' comments and especially encourage textual remarks that are produced by the commentators themselves. They not only display regulations prominently alongside each commentary space but also waste no time issuing warnings to violators and adjusting cumulative point totals accordingly.

The commentary space forms the basis of Jinjiang's well-regulated ranking system. Using a mathematical formula to calculate the points accrued by each work,[50] webmasters produce three lists that rank, variously, total cumulative points, half-year cumulative points, and monthly cumulative points for works, in addition to four other lists that showcase and encourage newly joined authors, authors who update their texts most frequently, and works recommended by Jinjiang webmasters and readers, respectively. These lists do not just reflect the tastes of Jinjiang readers but also help to attract readers to particular themes, genres, and authors, adding to the existing followings of certain authors and works. In this light, the ranking system works not only to represent but also to form communities of readers and authors.

Apart from generating authoritative lists of rankings, the commentary space also plays a crucial role in shaping reader and author behavior by facilitating the free exchange of information, opinions, and (positive) feelings. Because of the serialized nature of the novels, readers' comments and authors' responses often involve negotiations over plot and characterization. But the commentary space further combines the functions of a writers' workshop, an opinion column, and a social space. Here the authors and readers discuss novel writing in general. They also express their opinions on a variety of controversial topics such as homosexuality, rape, and polygamy, occasionally branching out into political parodies with their wordplay on current political slogans. Perhaps because it is more important than acquiring new knowledge and ideas, readers and authors navigate to this space for the social energy and emotional support it offers. They often exchange greetings and tell one another about changes and problems in their lives. In return, they receive not only consolation and congratulations but sometimes also practical help.[51] For instance, when one popular author told readers about her recent job loss, they posted numerous comments to comfort her.[52] Readers even post calls for Japan to apologize for forcing Asian women into sexual slavery during World War II,[53] assuming some degree of homogeneity in ideology with their peers.

While the commentary space allows readers to make their voices heard and heeded, other interactive tools help authors seek out readers. Authors often post under "Author's Words" in response to readers' questions and comments. An author's *wen'an* (the summary of a work on the first page, above its table of contents) demonstrates especially well this gesture of reaching out to readers. In addition to providing some clues to the plot, authors often use this space for a variety of other purposes: to describe the inspiration for their text; to state their opinion on sexual matters; to introduce other websites that concurrently publish their novels as a backup in case Jinjiang encounters technical problems; to inform their readers of their frequency of updating; and to paste images and links to particular music that they regard as appropriate accompaniment to the text (figure 2.3).

We can see that this summary space at the top of the page not only helps authors create their authorial personae but also allows them to manipulate reader responses. They make their texts user friendly by providing information about content and ideological bent, and in so doing they also actively seek readers who share similar values, or who are at least attracted to their work by

HAVE MOUSE, WILL TRAVEL [61]

我从重生之后，发现自己依然是个不起眼的小人物。
没有美貌，没有家世，没有聪明的脑袋。
家里只有两个老实到可怜的父母和一个聪明到可恶的弟弟。
长大后为了照顾一心想要学武的弟弟，被追跑到一个没听说过的小派别里打闲工。
这个小派别的名字叫点苍派。

Figure 2.3. Author's *wen'an*

the setting, the plot, the protagonist, or other cultural products such as texts, films, images, and music that their work invokes. Furthermore, authors also use this space to solicit feedback and thus extend to readers a virtual invitation to participate in the creation of the work. Oftentimes authors also play the role of webmasters by reiterating the rules of commenting and grading so they can receive points successfully. As with the commentary space, *wen'an* can be seen to allow authors to form supportive cohorts and communities by making the text more "reader oriented," that is, more responsive to the plethora of readers' comments.

Despite authors' attentive "courtship," however, Jinjiang readers show remarkable independence as a group. Although they willingly collaborate with authors in the creation of the text, they sometimes also defy authorial intentions and authority. Some point out mistakes or inconsistencies in the plot for the author to correct. Others request that the author move the plot in certain directions. Still others bring in external textual sources to argue for their own interpretation of the work and make demands of the author. At times readers also recommend other Web-based works to their fellow readers. This apparently directs readers' attention and commitment to other works, but it also strengthens the bond among readers still further, as it acknowledges shared tastes and enforces ideological homogeneity among them while also demonstrating readers' collective independence from any particular author or text. Discussions in the commentary space sometimes also lead to the creation of other texts as spin-offs or parodies of the original, creating a unique type of fan fiction.[54] Thus, readers have come to take up not only the traditional task of the author in producing texts but also that of the webmasters in regulating user behavior and enforcing social norms on the Web.

As a result of the lively conversations among webmasters, authors, and readers, texts published on the Net display extraordinary fluidity. This can be seen, first, in the different kinds of border crossing that it makes possible. As mentioned earlier, Jinjiang works often describe and even celebrate moral and sexual transgressions not otherwise condoned by society. The popularity of *danmei* works, and hence the prominent display of homoeroticism, is a case in point. Moreover, the reader and author behavior generated by these romances challenges traditional theories about the process of fiction writing and the demarcation between author and reader.

Since most works published on Jinjiang utilize multimedia functions and incorporate elements of music, cartoons, and cinema, the boundaries between text and other media become increasingly blurred. Furthermore, each work is in a perpetual state of flux, as it undergoes endless editing, modification, and even deletion. Because authors aspire to high ranking and positive reception, they take pains to respond to comments left by webmasters and readers. The reading community of any work is thus able to produce almost concurrent "interlinear"[55] commentary that can change the shape of the text precisely because of the speed of response and the instantaneity of results. Given that the popular novels on Jinjiang often catch the eye of publishers of print materials, this malleability on the author's part is not just a goodwill gesture to attract a greater following but also something that makes financial sense, as it is an effective way to make manuscripts more publishable.[56]

Perhaps most interesting for researchers of fiction writing, Jinjiang authors and readers also experiment with innovative devices that considerably change the form of traditional popular romances. A perfect case in point is their use of *fanwai* (*bangai* in Japanese) to insert a chapter that tells the story from the perspective of a character other than the first-person narrator of the work, usually the heroine. *Fanwai*—"special features" in cinematic terms—includes scenes that have been shot but edited out of the final version of the film. By using this device, the author creates an interstice in the narrative and generates unique reading effects. Although the flow of the plot seems to be interrupted, *fanwai* allows readers to see the other side of the story. This device can be used to provide a glimpse into male psychology and so correct a fatal flaw in traditional print romances whereby the transformation of the hero from a sadistic antagonist to a gentle and caring lover remains unexplained at the time the transformation occurs.[57] But more important, by using *fanwai* the author can induce affective identification by letting the reader see the gentler side of the masculine figure and thus understand, even if not approve of, the female protagonist's relationship with him. Oftentimes, *fanwai* becomes not only a teaser to attract readers but also a bargaining chip for authors to appease readers' insatiable appetite for reading the main story as quickly as possible, for in *fanwai* authors can recap the plot to date and hint at future developments without actually delivering new chapters of the main story. Yet *fanwai* also encourages readers to participate in the writing of the novel. Some readers post *fanwai* chapters in their commentaries, while others individually or collaboratively turn their *fanwai* into fan fiction in a different space,[58] thereby turning from readers into authors.

Jinjiang thus inculcates an interactive and reader-oriented style of writing and a community of writers and readers. It makes the boundaries between webmasters, authors, and readers increasingly fluid and their identities mutually constitutive.

By examining Jinjiang's modus operandi and the kind of reader and author behavior that it accommodates and inculcates, we can see that Jinjiang allows users to suspend their particular geographic locations temporarily and play out their conscious or unconscious aspirations, fantasies, and desires with relatively little danger of exposure and penalty. Furthermore, Jinjiang does more than provide texts that both satisfy and challenge traditional reader expectations of popular romances; through its interactive features it also effectively creates social interactions about and around those texts. Perhaps the pleasures of accessing Jinjiang boil down essentially to this: it offers readers and writers an opportunity to reinvent themselves, to transcend geographical, ideological, gender, and class boundaries, and to imagine themselves roaming the Internet initiating nurturing encounters with fellow users at will.

Of course, it is never wise to exaggerate the subversive power of Web-based popular literature. As shown earlier, readers and authors at Jinjiang are not wholly or always resistant to or complicitous with mainstream patriarchal culture; rather, they are continuously reevaluating their relationship to the text and reconstructing its meanings according to more immediate interests. By continually appropriating from popular Chinese culture, Web-based time travel romance on Jinjiang embodies what John Fiske in another context calls "a peculiar mix of cultural determinations," in that "on the one hand it is an intensification of popular culture which is formed outside and often against official culture, on the other it expropriates and reworks certain values and characteristics of that official culture to which it is opposed."[59]

Yet Jinjiang women inhabit a contemporary reality in which gender discrimination in education and employment is still rampant, and family burdens fall on women's shoulders whether or not they have a career outside the home. Web-based time travel romance establishes a new platform for them to explore their subjectivity, challenge dominant cultural norms, and cross gender and generic boundaries. Their experience on Jinjiang thus illustrates the democratic potential of Chinese online communities through the nurturance of "moral sentiment" and a utopian impulse.[60] In its critique of reality and its yearning for a better world, this impulse originates in the social, cultural, and political upheavals brought about by the market transformation of contemporary China. More important, it ushers in possibilities of reorientation and empowerment for those disenfranchised and marginalized by the traumatic processes of Chinese modernization.

Ultimately, Jinjiang demonstrates how the text in the age of the Internet can become the focus of divergent groups, because it is able to reconcile their geographical and cultural differences, to be intelligible and interesting to them on its own terms, and to fashion them into an imagined and imaginary community. This community is "imaginary" in that its members are operating in a digital world apparently free of the constraints of identity and consistency. It is also imagined and utopian in that it is called into being by the anticipation that a community of readers will be created around the text who share interest, consensus, and communion.

Notes

1. See, for example, Ouyang Youquan, "Wangluo Wenxue: Minjian Huayuquan De Huigui," *Huaiying Shifan Xueyuan Xuebao* 25.3 (2003): 335–40.
2. www.cnnic.net.cn/en/index/0O/index.htm.

3. Michel Hockx, "Virtual Chinese Literature: A Comparative Case Study of Online Poetry Communities," in *Culture in the Contemporary PRC*, ed. Michel Hockx and Julia C. Strauss (Cambridge: Cambridge University Press, 2005), 148.
4. Birgit Linder, "Web Literature," in *Encyclopedia of Contemporary Chinese Culture*, ed. Edward L. Davis (London: Routledge, 2005), 647.
5. This statistic is also from the report issued by CNNIC in January 2009.
6. Hockx, "Virtual Chinese Literature," 150.
7. A search by the keyword *wangluo wenxue* (Web literature) in CNKI, a database of full-text Chinese sources, yields more than a thousand entries, most of them theoretical constructions.
8. Benedict Anderson, *Imagined Communities: Reflections on the Origin and Spread of Nationalism* (London: Verso, 1983), 6.
9. Yin Pumin, "Web Writing," *Beijing Review* (Beijing Zhoubao) 48.34 (August 25, 2005): 31.
10. http://bbs.jjwxc.com/showmsg.php?board=3&id=56296.
11. http://bbs.jjwxc.net/showmsg.php?board=18&id=12579; see also Linder, "Web Literature," 647.
12. See also Xu Wenwu, "Lun Zhongguo Wangluo Wenxue De Qiyuan Yu Fazhan," *Journal of Jianghan Petroleum Institute* 4.1 (March 2002): 71–74.
13. Yang Ou, "Wangluo, Gaibian De Bujinjin Shi Yuedu" (Internet, It Changes Not Only Reading), *Renmin Ribao* (Haiwaiban), June 12, 2009.
14. http://bbs.jjwxc.net/showmsg.php?board=2&id=121844.
15. http://bbs.jjwxc.com/showmsg.php?board=18.
16. Qin Yuchun, "Chuanyue Xiaoshuo: Benxiang A'ge Huangdi," www.fawan.com/articleview/2007-7-23/article_view_115744.htm.
17. This refers to fictional works that lift characters, settings, or plots from existing works and usually add new twists to the canonic universe of the original.
18. For example, a quick glance at the rank list of overall most popular works at Jinjiang shows that time travel works dominate. See www.jjwxc.net/topten.php?orderstr=7.
19. Some have ascribed the popularity of time travel fiction to *Xun Qin Ji* (Tale of Seeking Qin, ca. 1991), a fantasy written by Hong Kong writer Huang Yi and adapted into a popular TV series in 2001. This novel tells the story of a Special Forces soldier who travels back to the Warring States period (475–221 BCE) in Chinese history and helps the Duke of Qin to reunify China and establish the first Chinese dynasty. The hero's sexual conquests as well as his miraculous deployment of modern knowledge have spurred widespread imitations on the Chinese Web. Others have credited Xi Juan, a popular female writer from Taiwan, whose novel *Jiaocuo Shiguang De Ailian* (Love That Crosses Time, 1993) describes the romantic adventure of a young woman traveling back to the Song dynasty (960–1279 CE).
20. For example, http://blog.sina.com.cn/u/4a6d1fd0010009jg.
21. See, for example, www.jjwxc.net/onebook.php?novelid=173864&chapterid=63 and www.jjwxc.net/onebook.php?novelid=228479&chapterid=25.
22. Radway describes the classic romance heroine as known for her "sexual innocence, unselfconscious beauty, and desire for love" in *Reading the Romance: Women, Patriarchy, and Popular Literature* (Chapel Hill: University of North Carolina Press, 1984), 131. This stereotype has changed in more recent romance works. See, for example, Jayne Ann Krentz, ed., *Dangerous Men and Adventurous Women: Writers on the Appeal of the Romance* (Philadelphia: University of Pennsylvania Press, 1992).

23. Ellen Widmer, *The Beauty and the Book: Women and Fiction in Nineteenth-Century China* (Cambridge: Harvard University Press, 2006), 229.
24. http://bbs.jjwxc.com/showmsg.php?board=25&id=5785.
25. See Jin Feng, "Addicted to Beauty: Web-Based *Danmei* Popular Romance," *Modern Chinese Literature and Culture* 21.2 (Fall 2009): 1–41.
26. For example, *Sishi Huakai* by Gongteng Shenxiu, www.jjwxc.net/onebook.php?novelid =91786.
27. http://bbs.jjwxc.com/showmsg.php?board=25&id=5706.
28. http://bbs.jjwxc.com/showmsg.php?board=25&id=5960.
29. Pi Junjun, "Tanizaki Jun'ichiro De 'Mei Yishi' Mengya Zhi Chutan," *Tianjing Waiguoyu Xueyuan Xuebao* 3 (2002): 64–67.
30. http://bbs.jjwxc.com/showmsg.php?board=9&id=276.
31. Ibid.
32. Yang Tianhua, "Tongxinglian Qunti De Meijie Xinxiang Jiangou," www.sexstudy.org/article.php?id=3767.
33. For example, "Jixing Lianqing Rangren Zuo'ou, Nüxingxiang Danmei Bu Zhide Tichang," *Jinling Wanbao* (April 2, 2004), www.njnews.cn/h/ca439904.htm and http://hi.baidu.com/inland/blog/item/59216b3ecff3b23d71cf6c55.html.
34. Yang Ya, "Tongrennü Qunti: Danmei Xianxiang Beihou," *Zhongguo Qingnian Yanjiu* (July 2006): 63–66.
35. http://bbs.jjwxc.net/showmsg.php?board=18&id=5382.
36. www.jjwxc.net/onebook.php?novelid=270152&chapterid=36 and www.jjwxc.net/onebook.php?novelid=270152&chapterid=38.
37. http://bbs.jjwxc.com/showmsg.php?board=18&id=15780.
38. www.jjwxc.net/onebook.php?novelid=97910&chapterid=1.
39. www.jjwxc.net/onebook.php?novelid=270152&chapterid=35.
40. www.jjwxc.net/onebook.php?novelid=141437&chapterid=26.
41. http://bbs.jjwxc.com/showmsg.php?board=25&id=5785.
42. www.jjwxc.net/onebook.php?novelid=130145 and www.du8.com/books/oututxt33086/66.shtml.
43. www.jjwxc.net/onebook.php?novelid=144848.
44. Ibid.
45. www.jjwxc.net/onebook.php?novelid=314891.
46. www.jjwxc.net/onebook.php?novelid=314891&chapterid=12.
47. www.jjwxc.net/onebook.php?novelid=314891&chapterid=52.
48. www.jjwxc.net/onebook.php?novelid=50785&chapterid=55.
49. For example, http://bbs.jjwxc.net/board.php?board=18&page=1.
50. According to the formula: points = number of hits/number of chapters x Ln (total number of characters in the text) x average points + Ln (total number of characters in commentaries of over one thousand characters) x grades on commentaries) + additional points given to quality commentaries.
51. For example, www.jjwxc.net/onebook.php?novelid=141437&chapterid=86.
52. www.jjwxc.net/onebook.php?novelid=245091&chapterid=64.
53. www.jjwxc.net/comment.php?novelid=92363&chapterid=27&page=2.
54. For example, the popular time-travel romance *Bubu Jingxin* (Suspense at Every Step, www.jjwxc.net/onebook.php?novelid=38029) generated not only numerous comments

and reviews but also several "sequels" at Jinjiang, including this one: www.jjwxc.net/onebook.php?novelid=181060.
55. David L. Rolston, *Traditional Chinese Fiction and Fiction Commentary: Reading and Writing between the Lines* (Stanford: Stanford University Press, 1997).
56. Yin Pumin, "Web Writing," 30–31.
57. Radway, *Reading the Romance,* 147.
58. www.jjwxc.net/onebook.php?novelid=154277.
59. John Fiske, "The Cultural Economy of Fandom," in *The Adoring Audience: Fan Culture and Popular Media,* ed. Lisa Lewis (London: Routledge, 1992), 43.
60. Guobin Yang, *The Power of the Internet in China: Citizen Activism Online* (New York: Columbia University Press, 2009), 156.

3

ONLINE LITERARY COMMUNITIES
A Case Study of LibraryThing

Julian Pinder

At first glance, the website LibraryThing (www.librarything.com) offers a means for readers to catalogue their book collections online. When a user enters a title, author, or ISBN into LibraryThing, the site retrieves the book's bibliographic data from Amazon.com, the Library of Congress, or one of over 690 libraries around the world.[1] The book can be added to an online catalogue of the user's collection, which can then be displayed on screen and searched or shared with others.

While this in itself is a useful tool for anyone with a large or unwieldy library, the site also utilizes this information for a second, social function. As the website states in its site tour for prospective members, "because everyone catalogs online, they also catalog together. LibraryThing connects people based on the books they share." In the years since its launch on August 29, 2005, LibraryThing had grown to encompass over 1.3 million members and over 63 million books by April 2011.[2] and it is through its social, connective element that LibraryThing demonstrates the potential for the Internet to offer an entirely new culture (or cultures) of reading and new forms of reading community.[3] This chapter examines LibraryThing's features in order to reflect on the nature and potential of an emerging form of literary community, of which LibraryThing is both an element and an example—a form of literary community that is global, multiple, and dynamic, and that brings into visibility an entirely new social dimension to reading.

Of course, LibraryThing is not the only—nor is it the first—online technology that gestures toward a form of online community. Indeed, LibraryThing utilizes, or is built out of, a number of quite popular existing practices and technologies, most notably online personal information management, social bookmarking, blogging (and specifically "litblogging"), online and other mass-mediated book clubs, and, more generally, social networking. What is significant about LibraryThing, however, is the way in which it utilizes and combines these technologies in pursuit of a communitarian, literary goal.[4]

Interrogating the way in which LibraryThing seeks to achieve this goal—and its success in doing so—raises a number of questions about how communities function online, as well as the ways in which technology and users interrelate. This chapter focuses on three specific questions. First, how does LibraryThing connect or converge with other reading or literary practices? Second, if this technology potentially brings together a diverse global community of readers, how do they connect with one another? And third, what are the implications for reading, literature, and literary study that arise from this literary networking paradigm?

Connection and Convergence with Other Literary Practices

LibraryThing is designed to be highly integrated with a number of practices of reading, and also to connect a number of those practices. The starting point of the site is "Your Library," an online catalogue of the user's collection. Selecting a book from Your Library brings up an entry for that book, which displays not only bibliographic information but also a list of tags used by LibraryThing users to describe the book, weighted by frequency of use, and displayed in the form of a tag cloud (figure 3.1).

LibraryThing also interfaces with a number of external websites and applications. For example, an unofficial application allows users to link their libraries to their Facebook accounts (although Facebook has its own application to monitor books owned, read, and being read). A similar application allows users to link their LibraryThing and Twitter accounts for the purpose of tweeting reviews. A "Local Books" application for iPhone and Android devices allows users to locate nearby (public) libraries and bookstores. LibraryThing also links to several "swap sites" to facilitate the exchange of books. Finally, "LibraryThing APIs" (application programming interfaces) allow users to create their own programs and applications to utilize LibraryThing's various data sets for new and creative purposes.

Each individual book entry in LibraryThing also provides external links, trading information, member reviews, and links to conversations about that book, as well as a "Common Knowledge" wiki, whereby users can add their personal knowledge to the growing body of information about the book. Additionally, member profiles and reviews often link to individual blogs (external

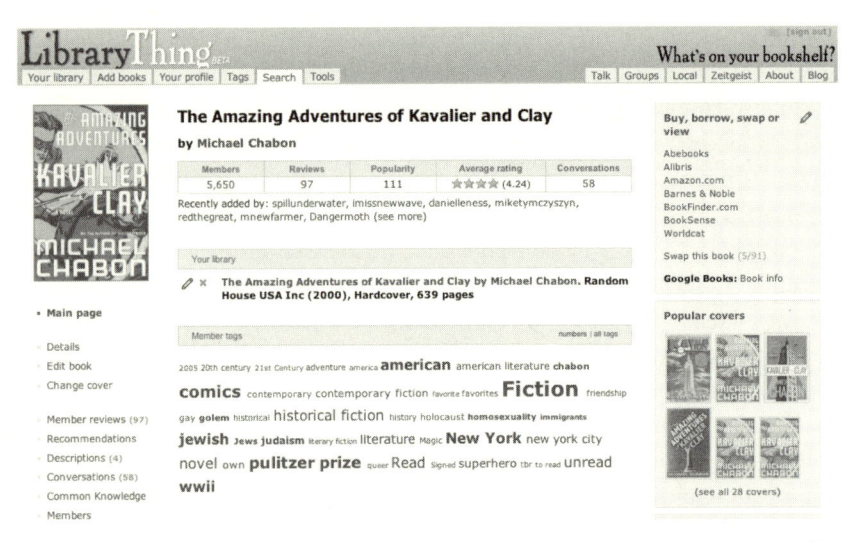

Figure 3.1. Screen showing tag cloud and links to online vendors and libraries for Michael Chabon, *The Amazing Adventures of Kavalier and Clay*

to the site), and discussion threads link to bibliographic details of specific key works, which in turn link to online vendors and libraries stocking those works. LibraryThing is thus both its own online reading space *and* a hub that mediates and links a series of other online reading spaces (shown in figure 3.1).

Perhaps the most notable venture in this regard is the "LibraryThing for Libraries" project (http://librarything.com/forlibraries/), aimed at interfacing LibraryThing with libraries by integrating LibraryThing data into library catalogues. At the time of writing, this project is still in its relative infancy, and its success is difficult to evaluate. Nonetheless, the project does show promise as a way of connecting reading communities with libraries and, indeed, libraries to one another. Similarly, LibraryThing has made efforts toward bookstore integration, which would allow users to locate retailers currently stocking a particular title by searching and cross-referencing their databases.

But LibraryThing also attempts to go beyond just linking existing online resources and institutions, for example, by forging new connections between bloggers and book publishers. One such initiative is the "LibraryThing Early Reviewers" program, which offers a number of advance readers' editions of upcoming titles to LibraryThing members on the condition that those members post reviews of the books on their blogs. The books are distributed to members who apply, who are matched algorithmically to the particular book. That is, the books are sent to the members judged most likely to enjoy them on the basis of their existing libraries. Theoretically, the publishers benefit from the (relatively) inexpensive advertising while reducing the chance of sending out books only to have them go unreviewed, while readers get free books and fodder for their blogs. Supposedly the content of a review does not affect a reviewer's chances of receiving future books, which suggests at least a hope of impartiality.[5]

This initiative appears to reflect a general trend toward transmedia marketing, and the recruitment of consumers by media producers to market their products to tailored communities, a form of marketing that is attractive not only because it is inexpensive but also because, when successful, it imbues that marketing with an aura of authenticity generally associated with a personal recommendation from a trusted friend or acquaintance. This form of global niche marketing points to a conflation of the commercial and the personal, raising some interesting moral questions, as the interests and motivations behind a (highly mediated) marketing exercise and a more conventional spontaneous recommendation are certainly not identical. It ought to be noted in counterpoint, however, that LibraryThing is involved only as an intermediary. It does not publish or sell books itself, nor does it endorse specific books or vendors. In fact, contrary to any direct commercial imputations that may be made, it links to public library holdings and other users willing to swap books for free.

Nonetheless, it is possible to trace this tension between—and conflation of—commercial, community, and individual interests across LibraryThing. The site clearly consists of libraries belonging to individuals, for-profit institutions, and nonprofit institutions, but their interrelationship is not always readily discernible, particularly insofar as recommendations and connections are determined algorithmically, and users cannot exclude certain data sets from those algorithmic calculations. While the majority of user accounts appear to belong to private individuals, as with much of the Internet, there is no way to be certain of the extent to which commercial interests are at play (particularly as accounts are tied to an account name and not a real-world identity).

This blurring of boundaries between the personal and the commercial, as well as between the public and the private, is also evident in questions that are opened up by the almost commodity-fetishistic undercurrent associated with displaying one's collection. Conversely, users are not required to own the works in their library; a library can function as a wish list or a record of books read, irrespective of ownership. Users are therefore able to use their libraries—and LibraryThing more generally—in a number of different ways to suit their purposes. What is inescapable on the site, however, is the process of associating books with an online identity or profile, and thus the performative element of consumption that this association implies.

If LibraryThing is seen as a vehicle for a kind of performative consumption constituted by the desire to proclaim one's social identity through commodities, then the fact that books tend to be privileged above other commodities because of their imputed intellectual, aesthetic, and even *moral* value sets this kind of exhibitionism on a different level from the performative consumption of commodities such as designer clothing or prestige cars. LibraryThing's high level of connectivity with other systems also foregrounds certain questions around commodity-based identity construction. Do you want your Facebook friends (and potential employers) to see all the books in your book collection and from them draw inferences about the type of person you are? Do you list only certain of your books to maintain a specific image? Do you declare books you do not own, have not read, and will not read in order to cultivate a particular persona? And if so, for what purposes? Certainly it is not only commercial players who are presented with a range of options for utilizing and flouting the online environment's structures and codes to further their purposes. LibraryThing's flexibility in this respect underscores how the Internet era marks not the simple or complete usurpation of the personal by the commercial but rather a complex intermingling of the two.

In addition to demonstrating the Internet's potential to offer new modes for the distribution and dissemination of literature, LibraryThing's early reviewers venture also gestures toward a (further) deinstitutionalization of literary criticism and taste. In bypassing traditional reviewers and critics in favor of members of a reading community, it suggests a move toward a more community-customized sense of taste, in that books are directed to particular people with an interest in certain kinds of books, determined according to their libraries. But this is not to suggest that LibraryThing is a completely deinstitutionalized space. Rather, it can be located within a process of the reconfiguration of relationships between and among institutions, the media, and participants—an example of what Henry Jenkins calls "convergence culture," which he sees as a shift in these relationships with respect to "media convergence, participatory culture, and collective intelligence."[6]

Just as LibraryThing's connection with and integration of different institutions, technologies, and modes of reception provide an interesting example of Jenkins's convergence culture model, so too do LibraryThing's mechanisms for connecting users with books—and with one another—which provide an excellent example of what Chris Anderson calls the "long tail."[7]

Anderson describes the long tail as the product of a "culture unfiltered by scarcity,"[8] and it is his thesis that we are undergoing a profound cultural and economic shift, from a culture that is dominated by "hits" (that is, a few highly successful cultural products with wide appeal) to one dominated by "niches" (that is, products of more limited, specific appeal): "The era of one-size-fits-all is ending, and in its place is something new, a market of multitudes."[9] Given that the long tail posits an abundance of (niche) works for consumers to choose from, the issue of how people will be able to find just what they want is central to this model. In other words, the important question becomes how to link consumers with these niche titles.

The key mechanism driving the long tail is a system of efficient customer *recommendation*. Anderson writes: "The other thing that happens when consumers talk amongst themselves is that they discover that, collectively, their tastes are far more diverse than the marketing plans being fired at them suggest. Their interests splinter into narrower and narrower communities of affinity, going deeper and deeper into their chosen subject matter, as is always the case when like minds gather. Encouraged by the company, virtual or not, they explore the unknown together, venturing farther from the beaten path."[10] He concludes: "The new tastemakers are us. Word of mouth is now a public conversation, carried in blog comments and customer reviews, exhaustively collated and measured."[11]

This process of recommendation, and specifically of linking users to (often obscure) works according to algorithmic assessments of highly personalized tastes, is at the heart of both LibraryThing and Anderson's long tail model. Where LibraryThing offers to expand the long tail model, however, is in the way in which it also attempts to link *users* in much the same way, that is, to forge communities in and out of the niches. This mechanism of connection between individuals (and thus the mechanism of connection between individuals and creative works) on the basis of common patterns of taste and preferences might be termed *affinity*, and it becomes the driving model for choice in the Internet era, in contrast to more traditional mechanisms of social connection or artistic taste and value. (Indeed, we can also see affinity as the underlying mechanism of other popular Web 2.0 applications such as YouTube and commercial sites such as Amazon.com.)

This reconfiguration has certainly not been met enthusiastically by all critics. Andrew Keen, for example, claims that the Internet is "really delivering . . . superficial observations of the world rather than deep analysis, shrill opinion rather than considered judgement. The information business is being transformed by the Internet into the sheer noise of a hundred million bloggers talking about themselves."[12] Keen also laments the marginalization (or disempowerment) of traditional institutional cultural gatekeepers, expressing concern about the relatively anonymous nature of online participation, and about the way the Internet places those with little experience or cultivated skill on an equal footing with those who have spent years acquiring in-depth knowledge.[13]

It is possible to respond to Keen's concerns—at least as they pertain to LibraryThing and similar environments—in a number of ways. First, according to Jenkins and other proponents of convergence culture, convergence allows for and encourages an amalgamation of different *types* of knowledge. In their account of participatory culture, John Seely Brown and Paul Duguid offer a compelling example of how participatory culture recognizes that knowledge can be socially dispersed when they recount a (possibly apocryphal) story of a typesetter working on a Greek text for Oxford University Press. Despite being unable to read Greek, the typesetter discovered a mistake because he had never come across a particular letter combination in all his years of hand-picking letters while typesetting. Brown and Duguid suggest that the story illustrates "the diverse sorts of knowledge, including the 'embodied' knowledge, which people in different roles possess."[14] In the context of LibraryThing, particularly the site's forums and reviews, this diversity of knowledge is evident in the different contributions made by users with different reading backgrounds and experiences, be they academics and teachers, students, authors, librarians, or casual readers. LibraryThing, as with much of participatory culture, recognizes that there is no single way of acquiring in-depth knowledge. Convergence culture, then, is not about ignoring expertise but rather about the productive convergence of different types of experience and expertise.

Second, Keen's argument appears to contain a contradiction when he deprecates online environments because they lack (for example) "deeply knowledgeable" store clerks who "act as cultural tastemaker[s]."[15] If Keen is willing to posit a retail store clerk as a privileged expert, it is not clear where his imagined line between expert and amateur is to be drawn, or what types of experience are sufficient to surmount the divide. Certainly it is possible to encounter experts (whatever criteria one may use to define the term) online, but it appears that Keen is concerned that the online environment is dangerous in that multiple amateur viewpoints produce only noise, and distort or drown out the valuable (expert) opinions.[16] Keen's analysis, however, appears to rest on an assumption that all information is the same and is used in the same way. A fan of a particular book may be more interested in which other books are enjoyed by fans of its author, and less interested in how the book was critically received or academically situated. Moreover, the ways in which non-expert groups receive, utilize, and explicate texts—and the patterns of reception, utilization, and explication—themselves provide useful information, particularly when that information supplements rather than replaces existing critical and academic exegesis.

Keen also disparages online communities for their equivalence to gated communities, in which everyone shares the same opinions and narcissistically mistakes them for truth.[17] Of course, the same allegations of intellectual homogeneity could be made about any community, and the same defenses mounted in response. The allegation seems particularly unwarranted in the context of LibraryThing, however, because its online nature theoretically offers a greater pool (and thus a wider variety) of opinions than a geographically or institutionally fixed community. Moreover, the site's high degree of integration with other institutional and non-institutional sources suggests that if it is a gated community, then the gate is unlocked. It is of course true that LibraryThing will appeal only to particular kinds of people, and, as in any community, its members self-select along a number of tacit social and normative lines, but nonetheless its lack of institutional or geographical barriers to participation is not an insignificant feature, as the wide range of political opinions, tastes, occupations, and backgrounds professed on the site attests.

Finally, convergence does not necessarily mean that existing institutions will be subsumed into—or their traditional roles eclipsed or usurped by—participatory culture. Rather, LibraryThing suggests the potential for new and productive connections to be forged between them, or at the very least for the arts to settle into a bi-stable configuration between existing institutions and participatory culture.[18] Indeed, LibraryThing emphatically does not stand alone, but presents itself as a hub in a diverse matrix that includes traditional institutions and repositories of knowledge which complement its own knowledge work. Nor can it be said that LibraryThing aims to replicate or usurp the role of other institutions. Rather, it aims to do what communities both on- and offline do, which is share opinions and information, and explicate and appropriate ideas and creative works produced by social and cultural institutions.

Clay Shirky makes this point a slightly different way when he suggests that the proliferation of blogs and other vehicles for "amateur" comment and criticism reflect not the death of expert guidance per se but rather a shift from a "filter then publish" model (with the filtering done by professionals such as editors and publishers) toward a "publish then filter" one (under which anyone can publish his or her creative work or opinions, and it is up to readers to utilize ways of filtering that content). In Shirky's words: "The media landscape is transformed, because personal communication and publishing, previously separate functions, now shade into one another. One result is to break the older pattern of professional filtering of the good from the mediocre before publication; now such filtering is increasingly social, and happens after the fact."[19]

Anderson draws the same distinction between pre-filters and post-filters in his account of the long tail. He notes that online recommendations and algorithms are post-filters: they rank and order what is already out there, and thereby channel and amplify consumer behavior rather than trying to predict it (or even to preempt it). In contrast, other sources of recommendation—such as editors, advertisers, managers of physical bookstores, and even academics setting reading lists—act as pre-filters, predicting and delineating what the market will be. Anderson therefore suggests that we are currently undergoing a shift in the underlying structure of the market from one shaped by the emblematic figure of the gatekeeper (who predicts taste) to that of the adviser (who measures it).[20]

Obviously, LibraryThing's methods of recommendation harmonize well with this post-filter model, as they do with the related concept of the "wisdom of crowds": the idea that asking many (non-expert) people and synthesizing or tallying their collective response can be just as accurate as—and often more accurate than—asking one expert.[21] This ethos finds its clearest expression in the wiki phenomenon (which LibraryThing itself embraces), but it is equally if less obviously present in LibraryThing's method of sourcing recommendations from a wide audience (that is, its entire user base) of varying competencies and situations, and allowing patterns of choice and criticism to emerge from across the set of all recommendations.

How Users Connect

Perhaps the first connective element that new users to LibraryThing will encounter is the way in which the site's algorithms can generate recommendations for other books associated with any given book, and can cross-reference a user's entire library with other users' libraries to generate recommendations based on patterns of common ownership (figure 3.2).[22]

A user, from his or her own profile, can also view a ranking of other users with the same books, either weighted by percentage commonality or by raw number of shared books. The idea is to link readers with similar tastes and interests, and then to base recommendations on those common tastes, on the principle that if you like many of the same books as another user, you may appreciate other books in that person's collection. The driving ethos and organizational structure of LibraryThing, then, is affinity: patterns of closeness between members.

ONLINE LITERARY COMMUNITIES [77]

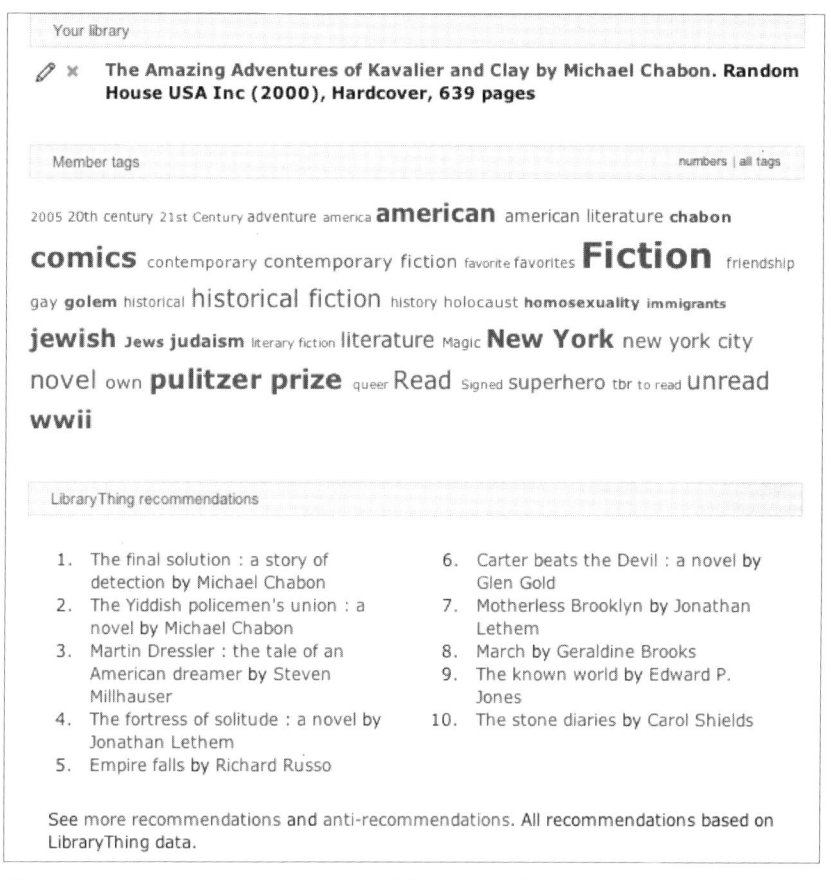

> **Your library**
>
> ✎ ✕ The Amazing Adventures of Kavalier and Clay by Michael Chabon. **Random House USA Inc (2000), Hardcover, 639 pages**
>
> Member tags   numbers | all tags
>
> 2005 20th century 21st Century adventure america **american** american literature chabon **comics** contemporary contemporary fiction favorite favorites **Fiction** friendship gay **golem** historical historical fiction history holocaust **homosexuality immigrants** **jewish** Jews **judaism** literary fiction literature Magic **New York** new york city novel own **pulitzer prize** queer Read Signed superhero tbr to read unread **wwii**
>
> LibraryThing recommendations
>
> 1. The final solution : a story of detection by Michael Chabon
> 2. The Yiddish policemen's union : a novel by Michael Chabon
> 3. Martin Dressler : the tale of an American dreamer by Steven Millhauser
> 4. The fortress of solitude : a novel by Jonathan Lethem
> 5. Empire falls by Richard Russo
> 6. Carter beats the Devil : a novel by Glen Gold
> 7. Motherless Brooklyn by Jonathan Lethem
> 8. March by Geraldine Brooks
> 9. The known world by Edward P. Jones
> 10. The stone diaries by Carol Shields
>
> See more recommendations and anti-recommendations. All recommendations based on LibraryThing data.

Figure 3.2. Recommendations generated by LibraryThing for Michael Chabon, *The Amazing Adventures of Kavalier and Clay*

Arguably the most patently connective aspect of LibraryThing lies in its Groups and Talk sections. Groups are devoted to particular genres, themes, or authors, and they work in some respects like miniature book clubs. By joining groups based on common interests (whether authors, genres, or caffeinated beverages), personal characteristics (such as politics or relationship status), affiliation (for example, students or librarians), or geography, readers can participate in a number of overlapping communities centered on these shared affinities. Users can join or create a group that links them to other members of the group, and each group has its own communal member library (a ranked collection of each member's library) and message forum. The Talk section links all the groups' message forums into a meta-forum, but users can choose to view only threads associated with their groups or that refer to the books in their libraries, or they can view all threads from all groups.

The threads work much like any other Internet discussion forum, but for two features. The first is that each thread displays a list of touchstone works with links to bibliographic and retail data, and the second is that each post shows what it terms the user's "affinity" with the LibraryThing member who made the post. The affinity feature is displayed as a percentage based on how similar the user's library is to the poster's and is meant to indicate the user's mental affinity with the poster, on the assumption that if you share the same taste in books, you probably think the same way. During the writing of this chapter, this feature was suspended, apparently because of technical system resource problems, and it was not clear whether and when it would be reinstated. Nevertheless, another feature that has been initiated allows users to nominate "friends" and to monitor others' "interesting libraries" for the purpose of establishing a more sustained engagement with like-minded users, whether for strictly on-topic purposes or for more general socializing.

Of course, the desire to discuss books with like-minded people is not new; it is, after all, the basis for the advent of book clubs, which predate the Internet. But what is distinct and notable about LibraryThing is that the ability to identify with and participate in a number of groups simultaneously (and to track other readers across those groups) provides a very different model from traditional participatory reading environments, the memberships of which tend to be bounded by institutional, geographical, and/or social factors.

This feature poses complications to existing theorizations of how communities disseminate and interpret texts. One could, for example, categorize LibraryThing's groups as interpretive communities (as first defined by Stanley Fish) and map how those interpretive communities interrelate and how individuals traverse them. Doing so would then expose certain tensions, particularly about community constitution and normativity, within the interpretive community model. Specifically, are the groups really discrete interpretive communities with their own norms and schemes of valuation and meaning production? Or is LibraryThing one single interpretive community? If the former, what of the fact that users so readily traverse (or simultaneously exist within) several communities? If the latter, what of the fact that LibraryThing's members exhibit diversity along a number of axes and profess in their group affiliations different aesthetic preferences, political views, and institutional backgrounds (among other things)?

A number of critics have already raised concerns about the interpretive community model and its abstractness. Fish's model suggests that communities exert a relatively stable normative force and produce consistent meanings, but it does not answer certain important questions about how that normativity arises or is enforced, or how those meanings are produced, other than to suggest that they derive from the interpretive community as opposed to the text or the reader.[23] For example, John Guillory suggests that "the notion of community in the ... discourse of value is always modeled unwittingly on the paradigm of the 'primitive' community, geographically separate, autonomous, and long since nonexistent."[24]

For this reason, Guillory professes a preference for an alternative model proposed by Barbara Herrnstein Smith. To Smith, literary value and meaning are contingent, that is, a changing function of multiple variables.[25] Thus value and meaning do not arise out of a coherent and homogenous community but develop as the result of specific contexts and purposes. Acts of literary evaluation can have multiple forms and functions because those functions are variable, dynamic, and mutable.[26] Smith suggests that even within a community, tastes and preferences may be "conspicuously *divergent*," because individuals will evaluate works according to multiple needs, interests, and resources that other members may privilege differently.[27] In terms of community, Smith notes the "mobility, multiple forms of contact, and numerous levels and modes of interconnectedness of contemporary life ... [such that] contemporary communities are not only internally complex and highly differentiated but also continuously and rapidly reconfigured." She goes on to state that "at any given time ... each of us is a member of many, shifting communities, each of which establishes, for each of its members, multiple social identities, multiple principles of identification with other people, and, accordingly, a collage or grab-bag of allegiances, beliefs, and sets of motives."[28]

Guillory ultimately objects to Smith's theory too, however, on the basis that her claim that each of us belongs to multiple, shifting communities "qualifies out of existence the concept of a community as the basis even of values which are 'local, temporary, and conjectural'—or rather reveals in the very insistence on 'locality' that these notions of community have a surreptitiously geographical basis."[29] Guillory then suggests his own modifications to Smith's model:

> The insistence on the coincidence of contingencies is crucial to Smith's argument, in that it neatly displaces all of the problems dismissed with the rejection of consensus. For example: Because Smith's formulation describes community as a *likeness* of individual subjects, a disagreement as to the value of an object will have to count as prima facie evidence that subjects who disagree belong in effect to different communities. . . . Conversely, there

is no way within this schema to explain agreement between parties whose total economies manifestly diverge. Since no community can be conceived as anything other than a limited population of similar individual subjects, it would seem that we need no analysis of the relation between subjects other than a demarcation of whether they are *like* or *unlike*.[30]

In effect, Guillory endorses a view that seeks to replace the concept of community with affinity as the means by which readers connect. Unlike the strict notion of community, the concept of affinity is not tied to geography nor limited purely to self-identification or subjective perception. Furthermore, affinity can be multidimensional, and can subsist according to multiple criteria and along multiple discursive, political, and economic lines. Perhaps most important, it is not subject to a binary opposition between included and excluded but exists as a continuum; that is, it is a case not of member/nonmember but only of more or less alike. Readers can therefore be situated in multiple different communities (each held together by different forms or clusters of affinity) and to greater or lesser degrees of intensity.

Certainly this conception reflects the LibraryThing experience, whereby users can participate in and range over multiple different, cross-referenced "Groups" (according to various interests and characteristics), which need not have an enduring geographic or temporal nature. Consequently, while these Groups on LibraryThing may demarcate themselves as such, they do not have the boundedness and stability on which Fish's interpretive community model is predicated. Rather, these Groups intersect, and people move between them. While these Groups (or other communities) may exert their own normative force, that force is not inescapable, and members of different groups may find themselves negotiating interpretations with those in another Group (or even with themselves) on the basis of their multiple patterns and degrees of affinity.

This heterogeneity of experience is also evident in the competencies that different users—who are from diverse cultural and professional backgrounds—bring to LibraryThing. The various projects available on the site, from discussions, to blogs, to reviews, to wikis, all give users different mechanisms for participation and engagement, according to their different skills and interests. This conception of locating readers and texts within a constellation of competencies and interests seems to embody the characteristics of what Manuel Castells argues is the new social structure to which the Internet era has given rise. For Castells and others, the unifying or mediating logic that links the Internet with literature (among other things) is the model of the *network*. In Castells's account, "for the first time in history, the basic unit of . . . organization is not a subject, be it an individual . . . or collective. . . . *[T]he unit is the network.*"[31]

Castells distills the ethos of the network as "decentralization, diversification, and customization."[32]

The rise of this "network society" is certainly linked with advances in technology: according to Marshall McLuhan's famous dictum, "The medium is the message" (or massage).[33] In a more contemporary context, Albert-László Barabási notes that connections are a *structural* property of the network.[34] But as the hypertext theorist George Landow observes, it may be unduly short-sighted to reduce such changes solely to changes in technology, as they also need to be viewed in terms of changes in the *practices* by which information is transmitted.[35] Similarly, Jenkins argues of convergence culture that it is more than a technological process bringing together multiple media functions, and is better understood as a "cultural shift," as consumers "seek out new information and make new connections among dispersed media content."[36] In LibraryThing we see this in the insistent linking between bibliographic data, conversations, commercial sites, private blogs, public libraries, and so forth, as well as the site's location in a larger matrix of circulating information and media.

In Raymond Williams's earlier study of broadcasting, he developed his idea of "flow": a total flow of broadcasting as opposed to a sequence of discrete, individual programs.[37] This appears to be the logic of the network: one of connectivity rather than individual units.[38] And as Steven Shaviro observes, networks are "self-generating ... system[s]" that work "though multiple feedback loops."[39] According to network theorists, then, networks are multiple, open structures, always integrating new nodes and seeking new connections. They are also marked by great flexibility, and they resist the conservatism of the traditional canonical model, as their logic is one of movement and connection.[40]

Networks, however, are neither formless nor evenly dispersed. As Bernardo A. Huberman notes, networks (and the World Wide Web specifically) tend to display heavily interlinked clusters or hubs, implying "the existence of communities that share some common affinities."[41] The concept of affinities is also consistent with the notion of the strength of weak ties, first advanced by Mark Granovetter, and which Barabási sees as essential for communicating with the outside world, and as responsible for mediating clusters and hubs within a network.[42]

According to Castells, the form of community that is most appropriate to the logics of the network society is what he calls the virtual community (a concept he adapts from Howard Rheingold). Castells notes that the term "virtual community" is "generally understood as a self-defined electronic network of interactive communication organized around a shared interest or purpose....

Such communities may be relatively formalized . . . or [may] be spontaneously formed by social networks which keep logging into the network to send and retrieve messages in a chosen time pattern (either delayed or in real time)."[43]

In LibraryThing we see evidence of virtual communities in the multiplicity of groups in which one can participate (simultaneously and dynamically), and the fact that new groups and affiliations are constantly being formed almost on a daily basis while others tend to fade away. This reflects Jenkins's observation that "merging knowledge cultures" are "defined through voluntary, temporary, and tactical affiliations."[44] LibraryThing is also something of a broad church, in which clusters of affiliation and community are held together by innumerable weak ties across many axes. Additionally, affinities and linkages generated by the system's algorithms are constantly changing as new libraries are added and existing readers update their libraries.

Implications for Reading, Literature, and Literary Study

Alan Liu argues that the appropriate paradigm for the Internet era is that of knowledge work: the study of the "cultural life of information."[45] This view, then, does not seek to deprecate literary and creative works but demands a renegotiation of our relationship with them. Terry Eagleton argues, from a cultural studies perspective, that literary "texts encode within themselves the mode of cultural production."[46] A network model encourages this view, and encourages an understanding that modes of cultural dissemination similarly come to inhere within the text. The network model both recognizes existing elements of textual categorization and also reconfigures them. Ultimately, it highlights, in a categorical way, an insight contemplated by cultural studies: that texts are consumed as part of a process.[47] Where the network model differs is that earlier models such as that of Jenkins's textual poaching deal with specific encounters, cultural usage, and appropriation, whereas the network model suggests a more expansive view, examining how networks of texts and readers interrelate, grow, and change. This model is an inherently active and participatory one, fostering transient virtual communities of meaning and value production. Indeed, the dynamic and complex flow of information on the Internet has been likened by many critics to the functioning of an ecosystem, casting those who study the flow of that information in the role of social scientists, if not ecologists.[48]

Harold Bloom has stated that "real reading is a lonely activity and does not teach anyone to become a better citizen."[49] The network speaks otherwise. As

LibraryThing strongly suggests, the propagation and preservation of knowledge work is increasingly becoming a communitarian concern. It is difficult to overstate the possibilities for change—and also of return—opened up by the network. Richard Lanham even suggests a movement away from the fixity of the codex text, privileged for its authenticity and authority, toward the flexibility of earlier oral cultures.[50] He further observes that we are asked to believe that the teaching of Western culture has been founded on a print-stable collection of Great Ideas enshrined in Great Books, and we now quarrel about which books are, for our present needs, really Great. But Western education has in its essence been rhetorical, has been based, that is, not on a set of great ideas but on a manner of apprehension; it has taught as central not knowledge but *how* knowledge is held.[51] This question of how, in its many forms and manifestations, is one of the important questions opened up by the network model, of which LibraryThing provides a compelling example. Another important question pertains to the implications for identity, agency, and subjectivity in the network model.

In his elegy to the printed text, Sven Birkerts expresses his fear that the digital age will see the waning of the private self in favor of an inevitable process of social collectivization.[52] LibraryThing may give Birkerts further cause for concern. We often tend to believe that our tastes and preferences, particularly when it comes to objects such as books, are something deeply intimate, something fundamentally telling about our innermost selves and most personal experiences. But LibraryThing's algorithmic linking of users and suggestions for books are startling in their accuracy. During the period in which the site's percentage affinity feature was operational, there was something quite *unheimlich* about reading a forum post with which you very much agreed, and then discovering that your affinity score with that poster was 96 or 97 percent and that your libraries revealed a love of the same books.

But this is not to suggest that algorithms are perfect when it comes to human affairs. In *The Social Life of Information,* Brown and Duguid provide a memorable example when they recount how Amazon.com's algorithmic matching software used Brown's purchasing and browsing history to recommended to him the book *The Social Life of Information*—a book he co-authored. "Computationally, it was impressive to deduce that this new book was of interest. Socially, however, it is thoroughly inept to recommend a book to its author."[53] Nonetheless, algorithmic matching, with its generally startling accuracy and its occasional jarring mismatch, opens up intriguing questions about the uniqueness, coherence, and boundedness of our identities as readers and as people, and suggests that the network model challenges the stability and autonomy not only of canons, texts, and institutions but also of readers.

Landow, drawing on the work of poststructuralist theorists such as Roland Barthes, Jacques Derrida, and Michel Foucault, suggests that, at least in our current era, "the self takes the form of a decentered (or centerless) network of codes that, on another level, also serves as a node within another centerless network."[54] Liu also acknowledges concerns that a network model subordinates agency to utilitarian goals, as people risk becoming merely nodes in the network to be traversed or data sets to be mined.[55] But while such concerns are certainly not trivial, it may be tempting to overstate them. As Landow suggests, the concept of the decentered self has a long pedigree in Western thought. The network era can be seen as merely an evolutionary step in that process of human self-understanding.[56] Nor does a network view necessarily limit human agency. Landow proposes one way to overcome concerns that a network conception deemphasizes "autonomy in favor of participation": to locate consciousness and agency in the very process of that engagement or participation.[57] Moreover, the LibraryThing experience suggests that such a decentered conception of the self does not necessarily result in unstable identities or irreconcilable interpersonal divergence. Rather, quite the opposite may in fact be the case: it may well be the foundation of our personal identities and the very mechanism of our human interconnectedness.

Finally, LibraryThing demonstrates a way in which the algorithmic functioning of computer processes and the irreducible nature of human social acts can be productively combined so that the advantages of both are mutually complementary. In contrast to Brown's experience with Amazon.com, LibraryThing allows for richer comparisons, because users can also look behind the algorithmic matchings and explore personal information about other users in the form of user blogs, biographies, reviews, forum discussions, and so forth. Consequently, while LibraryThing certainly raises a number of genuine concerns about the experience of "literariness" in the Internet era, as well as about how communities and individual identities are constructed online, it is fair to say that it also provides a rich source of background information with which to locate suitable literary works,[58] as well as material capable of prompting new, and potentially meaningful, forms of human social encounter.

Even in respect of these two features, however, LibraryThing displays certain tensions. The richness of information offered by the site is tempered by the fact that only a limited amount of detail about users is made visible, something that, if serving the understandable purpose of respecting the privacy of users, also has effects on the kinds of social interaction that can occur among them.

This feature, which LibraryThing shares with other sites on the World Wide Web that provide forums for social interaction but do not tie users to their real-world identities, also affects the extent to which researchers can accurately assess the nature of the encounters on the site. The limited amount of visible user information means that researchers do not have access to three-dimensional portraits of most users and, aside from their own participation, must rely on the partial evidence of third-party social encounters that can be gleaned from the site's discussion forums. While it is therefore possible to assert with a high degree of confidence that LibraryThing offers the potential for meaningful encounters to occur, further ethnographic research is needed in order to be specific about the extent to which such encounters actually occur. Another factor obscuring the extent to which LibraryThing is capable of fostering an inclusive community is the existence of barriers to entry that may not be directly visible or obvious. For example, most LibraryThing members require, among other things, a sufficient level of wealth to have sustained access to the Internet, and the kinds of educational experiences that make discussions about books and book collections seem like a viable leisure activity in the first place. Consequently, without deprecating the encounters that do occur on LibraryThing, one must note that these may be shaped by forces that are not apparent or easily recuperable.

In this sense the Internet era may not be capable of living up to any utopian promises, whether about the democratization of society and communal inclusiveness or the accessibility and unboundedness of texts and textuality. Rather—much as in every era of human technological and social advancement—it has the potential to solve certain problems and improve on certain practices from the preceding era, while giving rise to its own set of challenges and its own configurations of power and influence.

Notes

1. The number of libraries as of April 18, 2011. This figure is continually growing: as of March 1, 2008, the number was just over 250.
2. On March 1, 2008, LibraryThing had just over 313,000 members and listed 20 million books.
3. The site exists in multiple languages and operates internationally. To date, however, U.S. users and libraries (both institutional and private) appear to predominate. Although this chapter cannot address the ways in which national and cultural variety inflects readers' interactions and use of LibraryThing, these are significant questions which merit further consideration.

4. In this chapter, "communitarian" refers to the promotion of a community constituted by a fellowship of interest(s) and is not intended to carry the term's full historical and philosophical weight and connotations.
5. For accounts of other ways in which the contemporary literary industry is engaging with popular media rather than with traditional cultural gatekeepers, see chapter 2 by Jin Feng and chapter 5 by David Wright in this volume.
6. Henry Jenkins, *Convergence Culture: Where Old and New Media Collide* (New York: New York University Press, 2006), 2.
7. Though Anderson did not coin this phrase: he attributes it to Amazon.com's founder, Jeff Bezos. See Chris Anderson, *The Long Tail: Why the Future of Business Is Selling Less of More* (New York: Hyperion, 2006), 13.
8. Ibid., 53.
9. Ibid., 4.
10. Ibid., 57.
11. Ibid., 99.
12. Andrew Keen, *The Cult of the Amateur: How Today's Internet Is Killing Our Culture* (London: Nicholas Brealey, 2007), 16.
13. Ibid., 16, 20, 30, 63.
14. John Seely Brown and Paul Duguid, *The Social Life of Information*, rev. ed. (Boston: Harvard Business School Press, 2002), 80.
15. Keen, *The Cult of the Amateur*, 105.
16. Ibid., 53.
17. Ibid., 55.
18. See Richard A. Lanham, *The Electronic Word: Democracy, Technology, and the Arts* (Chicago: University of Chicago Press, 1994), 14.
19. Clay Shirky, *Here Comes Everybody: How Change Happens When People Come Together* (London: Penguin, 2009), 81.
20. Anderson, *The Long Tail*, 122.
21. See, for example, James Surowiecki, *The Wisdom of Crowds: Why the Many Are Smarter Than the Few* (London: Abacus, 2005).
22. For an expanded account of algorithmic matching and its interrelationship with (online) word-of-mouth matching, see chapter 5 by David Wright in this volume.
23. See, for example, John Guillory, *Cultural Capital: The Problem of Literary Canon Formation* (Chicago: University of Chicago Press, 1994), 27, 277. See also Stanley Fish, *Is There a Text in This Class? The Authority of Interpretive Communities* (Cambridge: Harvard University Press, 1980), 14, 109.
24. Guillory, *Cultural Capital*, 278.
25. Barbara Herrnstein Smith, *Contingencies of Value: Alternative Perspectives for Critical Theory* (Cambridge: Harvard University Press, 1988), 11.
26. See Smith, *Contingencies of Value*, 28, 39.
27. Ibid., 39.
28. Ibid., 168.
29. Guillory, *Cultural Capital*, 278.
30. Ibid., 286.
31. Manuel Castells, *The Rise of the Network Society*, vol. 1 (Malden, Mass.: Blackwell, 2000), 214.
32. Ibid., 368.

33. See Herbert Marshall McLuhan and Quentin Fiore, *The Medium Is the Massage: An Inventory of Effects* (Corte Madera, Calif.: Gingko Press, 2001).
34. Albert-László Barabási, *Linked: How Everything Is Connected to Everything Else and What It Means for Business, Science, and Everyday Life* (New York: Plume, 2003), 12.
35. See George P. Landow, "What's a Critic to Do? Critical Theory in the Age of Hypertext," in *Hyper/Text/Theory* (Baltimore: Johns Hopkins University Press, 1994), 4. Landow is extrapolating from Friedrich A. Kittler's study of "discourse networks" in the nineteenth century, *Discourse Networks, 1800/1900* (Stanford: Stanford University Press, 1990).
36. Jenkins, *Convergence Culture*, 3.
37. Andrew Milner, *Literature, Culture and Society*, 2nd ed. (London: Routledge, 2005), 114.
38. Castells, *The Rise of the Network Society*, 442–43.
39. Steven Shaviro, *Connected, or What It Means to Live in the Network Society* (Minneapolis: University of Minnesota Press, 2003), 10.
40. Castells, *The Rise of the Network Society*, 502, 71.
41. Bernardo A. Huberman, *The Laws of the Web: Patterns in the Ecology of Information* (Cambridge: MIT Press, 2001), 39. See also Barabási, *Linked*, 64, 170; and Castells, *The Rise of the Network Society*, 502.
42. Barabási, *Linked*, 42–43. See also Castells, *The Rise of the Network Society*, 388–89.
43. Castells, *The Rise of the Network Society*, 386.
44. Jenkins, *Convergence Culture*, 57.
45. Alan Liu, *The Laws of Cool: Knowledge Work and the Culture of Information* (Chicago: University of Chicago Press, 2004), 1.
46. Milner, *Literature, Culture and Society*, 92.
47. Lanham, *The Electronic Word*, 49.
48. Huberman, *The Laws of the Web*, 16.
49. Harold Bloom, *The Western Canon: The Books and School of the Ages* (New York: Harcourt Brace, 1994), 485.
50. Lanham, *The Electronic Word*, xi.
51. Ibid., 24.
52. Sven Birkerts, *The Gutenberg Elegies: The Fate of Reading in an Electronic Age* (Boston: Faber and Faber, 1994), 130.
53. Brown and Duguid, *The Social Life of Information*, xii.
54. George Landow, *Hypertext 3.0: Critical Theory and New Media in an Era of Globalization* (Baltimore: Johns Hopkins University Press, 2006), 127.
55. See Liu, *The Laws of Cool*, 172.
56. Landow, *Hypertext 3.0*, 130.
57. Ibid., 127.
58. Brown and Duguid, *The Social Life of Information*, 187.

4

BUILDING A NATIONAL CULTURE OF READING IN THE "NEW" SOUTH AFRICA

Molly Abel Travis

Speaking to South African publishers and booksellers in 2002, Minister of Education Kader Asmal detailed the Department of Education's "vision of a reading nation" and concluded that to achieve this vision, "we must create a culture of reading."[1] Minister Asmal's call for a national culture of reading in post-apartheid South Africa has become a constant refrain. In a keynote lecture at the 2004 Symposium on Cost of a Culture of Reading, Elinor Sisulu, chair of the Book Development Foundation of the Centre for the Book, a unit of the National Library of South Africa, summarized the cost of failure: "The absence of a widespread culture of reading in South Africa acts as an effective barrier to our development, reconstruction, and international competitiveness."[2] Efforts to build this culture of reading have focused on shaping the practice of reading and on constructing both national and individual identities. These efforts have included reforming school and university literature curricula, promoting multilingualism in a nation of eleven official languages, launching literacy programs, and diversifying the publishing industry. Rather than analyzing the reading practices of individual South Africans, this chapter examines the different conditions of reading that apply to various groups in the context of the new South Africa. The effects of initiatives to create a culture of reading need to be understood in the context of a global economy and in a cultural field marked by radical disjunctions among local, national, and global forces. This analysis of the challenges that South Africa faces makes clear the contingency of reading habits and practices in the English-speaking countries of the developed world, practices that derive from a position of privilege.

Contrary to a long-held belief in South African exceptionalism, political economists argue that South Africa's situation is similar to that of other developing countries.[3] The government has committed itself to a neoliberal economic program that ties its development decisions to the requirements of global capital, which means that solutions to problems such as illiteracy, lack of access to free education, and underfunded schools and libraries will be slow to come from the national government. Thus the real promise in the immediate future would seem to lie in a collaboration between local and global actors that would support the production and distribution of multilingual reading materials and other cultural resources, creating a reciprocal relationship among writers, educators, librarians, printers and publishers, social justice activists, and NGOs—with a national culture of reading generated from the productive proximity of the local and the global.

Cultures of Reading, Nationalisms, and Liberation Movements in South Africa

To create a context for understanding current efforts to build a national reading culture, I want to mention briefly initiatives in other phases of South African nation-building. Archie Dick's analysis of South African women's organizations and the politics of reading in the years immediately after the devastating Anglo-Boer War and before World War I offers valuable insights. In this instance, there were two competing perspectives in the conceptualization of nation-building and the creation of a nation of readers: the ethnic solidarity of Dutch-Afrikaans-speaking women and the imperial affiliation of English-speaking women: "Through their education, book or literature committees, they involved themselves especially with the supply and quality of reading fare, and the regulation of reading itself. These organizations were, moreover, concerned with the kind of history books available and with the development of a national identity. In brief, they assigned a nation-building role to reading."[4] Early reading initiatives of English-speaking women were modeled on the National Home Reading Union (NHRU), an organization formed in London in 1889 and patterned after the Chautauqua movement in the United States. These initiatives aimed to create a nation of readers of the "best" books and to enable the new nation of South Africa to assume its place in the "great federation of Empire."[5] In this formula readers were white and English-speaking, and the best books were those reflecting English history and culture.

In 1903 the South African Home Reading Union (SAHRU) was founded, and gradually situated itself in contrast to the NHRU by accommodating Dutch and Afrikaans readers.[6] The SAHRU gave rise to organizations such as the Afrikaans Christian Women's Society, which was closely allied with the Dutch Reformed Church and committed to *Kerk, Volk en Taal* (Church, Nation, and

Language), and the South African Women's Federation, which "after 1910 soon assumed struggle dimensions, with petitions to government and solidarity with campaigners for Afrikaans language rights."[7] The efforts of Dutch-Afrikaans-speaking women to add non-English reading materials to school curricula and libraries and to support language rights mirrored their own political fight for suffrage. These women made modest strides in using reading to build a new nation, which established a foundation for later struggles in nation-building, in particular—and ironically—the mid-century resistance against Afrikaans as the language of instruction in schools and universities.

Although early women's organizations sought to stock libraries in cities and rural areas with the right kind of books to build the new nation, the role of libraries changed in the intense anti-apartheid resistance later in the twentieth century. In his analysis of the political importance of the Cape Flat township libraries in the 1980s anti-apartheid movements, Dick argues that the libraries' influence extended well beyond the book. In these contested spaces, community activists, grassroots intellectuals, and political agitators used live discussion and performance to refine and circulate ideas, and in so doing "affirmed the library as a space in working class areas with low levels of literacy where the books as props supported a lively tradition of oral discourse and public debate."[8] Many of these discussions concerned censorship and freedom of expression. At the Kensington Public Library in Cape Town, librarian Vincent Kolbe used a sports equipment bag stashed under the circulation desk to conceal not only banned political materials but also copies of banned books such as Salman Rushdie's *Satanic Verses*.[9] In recent years, librarian activists working for the Library and Information Association of South Africa (LIASA) and Free Access to Information and Freedom of Expression (FAIFE) have committed themselves to the creation of a digital commons providing access for all South Africans and have played an important role in the fight against HIV/AIDS by coordinating informational workshops and sponsoring publications in African languages. In this historical trajectory from the empire's handmaidens who sought to create a colonial nation in the image of England to the FAIFE activists who wanted to open South Africa to the digital world of information, one encounters successive cultures of reading that have served both conservative and progressive ends, limiting and liberating nationalist agendas.

Contemporary Curricular Reforms

South Africa's curricular reforms have aimed at developing the right kind of readers to sustain the reimagined nation, attempting to build a national culture through reading. Building a national reading culture is difficult enough, but—as John Guillory's cogent analysis of the effects of confusing school culture with national culture shows—constructing a national culture through school reading is impossible.[10] To begin with, the fact that South African curricular decisions are made by autonomous departments of education in the country's nine provinces greatly complicates this centripetal project of nation-building. Critics of these reforms complain that some of the decisions threaten to create an insular, homogeneous, and biased curriculum—a mirror inversion of apartheid's Christian National Education. A furor arose in April 2001 when the Gauteng Department of Education announced the selection of the set works in the literary curriculum of Gauteng Province, which includes Johannesburg. Among those writers whose books were to be removed from the prescribed list for matriculating students was the Nobel laureate Nadine Gordimer. The advisory panel of teachers rejected Gordimer's novel *July's People* as "deeply racist, superior and patronizing." The evaluators also recommended the removal of a number of Shakespeare's plays from the school list, including *Hamlet,* which several members criticized as "Eurocentric, not optimistic or uplifting."[11] Not all of the "de-selected" works were by white authors: the panel gave the thumbs down to works by black writers, including the short story "Fools" by Njabulo Ndebele, a celebrated South African writer and former vice chancellor of the University of Cape Town, because the story's treatment of introspection was found to be too complex for twelfth graders.

Many of those who criticized these curricular decisions assumed immediately that the evaluators were black. In fact, three of the four evaluators were white and, indeed, were holdovers from the apartheid government.[12] Within a week there was such an international outcry against this process that the Gauteng Department of Education gave way under the pressure. In a fascinating face-off involving international, national, and provincial players, it discontinued its set work evaluation and reversed its decisions. The director of the department, Ignatius Jacobs, attributed the mistake to the fact that the teacher-evaluators were experts in the field of teaching methodology but not literary criticism.[13]

Margriet van der Waal argues that the teachers involved in this process were simply doing their job, adhering to the prescriptions supplied to them by the Gauteng Department of Education. Some of the criteria stressed in the department's guideline document were formulated as follows:

- Does the story have a satisfactory ending?
- Is the language of an acceptable quality?

- Is the tone of the story essentially optimistic, with emphasis on the positive?
- Does the content promote democratic values?[14]

For anyone who values complexity, variety, and creativity in literature, these criteria are troubling, and they are unsuited to a newly democratic country faced with the challenges of recovering and promoting diversity.

We can begin to understand the negative effects of these criteria on the creation of national narratives by considering the implications of two of the prescriptions: "Does the story have a satisfactory ending?" and "Is the tone of the story essentially optimistic, with emphasis on the positive?" These are conservative criteria, which run the risk of transforming history into the stuff of a heritage industry that traffics in essences and avoids the heterogeneous and the dynamic. Targeting tourists as well as those South African citizens who might feel that their traditional culture is in jeopardy, the heritage industry is big business in a nation-building or nation-affirming phase. Additional evaluator comments about *July's People* demonstrate this proclivity to dispense with history: "The message is based on political happenings of the past. This would not be helpful towards efforts at nation building," and "The racial conflict topic would prove to be destructive in a classroom situation."[15]

Multilingualism

South Africa's problems with curricular reforms have resulted from the confusing of school culture with national culture. In his analysis of the unintended negative effects of curricular multiculturalism, Guillory points out that "school culture does not unify the nation culturally so much as it projects out of a curriculum of artifact-based knowledge an imaginary cultural unity never actually coincident with the culture of the nation-state."[16] An example of this effect can be discerned in South Africa's efforts to freeze the many dialects of the nine African languages into what Sinfree Makoni describes as "invented mother tongues." Makoni observes that teachers and students in urban schools in which the language focus is on isiZulu complain that the standardized Zulu of instruction is such a foreign language that the instruction risks alienating students from what is supposed to be their linguistic heritage.[17] In addition, these school texts are freighted with a moralistic value system meant to represent a traditional Zulu lifestyle, which does not resonate with young people who are dealing with such issues as HIV/

AIDS, rape, violence, and poverty.[18] In her research on the literacy practices produced through South African matriculation curricula from 1970 to 2000, Jeanne Prinsloo concludes that not only were students "educated to different purposes according to race and language" during apartheid, but also such practices persist: "English learners have been educated as globally elite subjects with expectations of a global mobility, Afrikaans learners have been constituted as Afrikaner nationalist subjects with expectations of social and economic mobility certainly within their own land, while Zulu learners have been constituted in terms of their Zulu ethnicity and as subaltern subjects."[19]

Roughly 30 percent of the adult population in South Africa is functionally illiterate.[20] While many literacy campaigns have emerged in recent years, schools and libraries—which should be central in these efforts—remain critically underfunded. The new South Africa inherited a library system shaped by an apartheid policy that had manipulated library standards so that the only libraries supported were in small white towns or in the large cities of Johannesburg, Durban, and Cape Town—all of which "service[d] the leisure-time reading habits of the white community."[21] Although rural and small township libraries are under-resourced, they attract patrons who are interested in the libraries' affiliated programs. Many of these libraries are connected to garden projects, life skills classes (for example, money management, beadwork, sewing, brick masonry, Braille), and language instruction.[22]

Librarians across the nine provinces report that indigenous-language speakers seek instruction in English, despite the fact that the constitution recognizes the linguistic rights of all South Africans, and national language policies promote equal access to reading material in the mother tongue(s).[23] To understand this desire to learn English, one should begin by considering the exalted place of English in the liberation struggle. The language wars in South Africa during apartheid culminated in the children's rebellion known as the 1976 Soweto Uprising, in which police opened fire on students who were protesting against the government mandate of Afrikaans as the medium of instruction. Afrikaans was the language associated with the apartheid regime. By contrast, English came to be equated with power, unity, and liberation.[24] Add to this legacy the ascendant position of English in the global and South African economies, and it becomes evident why proficiency in English would appear to be very much a life skill.[25] But language educators and researchers such as Neville Alexander from the University of Cape Town have convincingly argued that first-language education is crucial to teaching and learning. For children whose mother tongue is Afrikaans or any of the nine indigenous languages, instruction in English—or another agreed-upon national second language—should occur only if children have a solid foundation in their first language. Alexander points to the considerable economic and social costs of the low matriculation exam results and high dropout rates of African-language speakers resulting from South Africa's failure to support education in the mother tongue.[26]

Even if South Africa makes a concerted effort to close the gap between its language policy and its practices to create a genuinely multilingual democracy, the process will take many years. Alexander observes that "Afrikaans needed between 50 and 75 years to develop from . . . a lowly patois" into a language of importance.[27] But will the time frame(s) of the global market support the pace and rhythm necessary to grow these African languages? One answer to this question emerges from the current situation of radio and newspapers in South Africa, two media sectors in which indigenous languages typically grow. The advertising industry for radio is characterized by an inertia stemming from prejudice, which results in inadequate support for indigenous-language radio.[28] Newspaper advertising, which can be traced back to the apartheid years, has perpetuated a segmented newspaper industry.[29] Although such segmentation means that there continue to be newspapers in the African languages, Allister Sparks claims that "in a country with a low literacy rate . . . there are too many low-circulation newspapers feeding off a relatively small advertising cake," a scenario that produces under-resourced newsrooms and results in all but a few newspapers attempting to outdo one another with ever more sensationalist tabloid journalism.[30] Thus, what yokes together—but in no way unites—readers in the segmented newspaper industry of the new South Africa is a steady dose of crime and corruption.[31]

Literacy Programs

During a research trip to South Africa in June and July 2007, I was invited by Nombulelo Baba, director of the Isiqalo–First Words in Print project, to accompany her on a three-day site visit to nurseries and preschools in a desolate rural area in Limpopo Province to study the impact of the Isiqalo project, which is run by the National Library of South Africa's Centre for the Book. This ambitious program distributes culturally relevant storybooks written in the dominant home language to all preschool children in the targeted areas, and also conducts workshops for parents and caregivers to enable them to make effective use of the books. The project includes three phases with a total of eleven books.

Despite facing enormous challenges in terms of distributing books to those children (orphaned and rural) who most need them, and finding volunteers to orient and mentor the children's caregivers, who are generally illiterate, this program has had a positive impact.[32] First of all, these are the only books, other than perhaps a Bible, in the homes of the children. Indeed, 90 percent of young South African children have never even seen a book.[33] The nursery directors and caregivers report that the children enjoy the books, ask frequently to have them read, and use the stories as a basis for creating their own narratives. These nurseries, called crèches, and the reading corners in them are among the few bright spots in this landscape with no running water, no gardens, and only a rare chicken or goat. The dedicated women who work at these crèches are not paid. The little money that a few of the children's caregivers can afford to contribute goes toward the children's lunch; the government matches only what the parents and caregivers manage to pay. And, like almost all South African projects to promote African-language publication and cultivate literacy, the Isiqalo–First Words in Print project relies on donors, which means that it is underfunded and in need of government support. The Centre for the Book cannot afford a staff large enough to oversee such a vast distribution of books throughout the country and so must rely on unpaid volunteers, which makes planning and execution uncertain.

To leverage its resources, the Centre for the Book needs to work even more closely with early childhood development (ECD) centers. According to UNESCO's findings, "ECD pays massive dividends in the health and wellbeing of the children—and in national economic terms," with an especially positive impact on children from poor families; unfortunately, a UNESCO global monitoring report showed that as of 2007, the South African government allocated only 1 percent of its education budget for ECD.[34] ECD and literacy programs had to compete in the national budget with such "big ticket" ventures as the Great Limpopo Transfrontier Conservation Park and the FIFA 2010 World Cup, which required massive investments to gain South Africa a place in the global tourist market.

Book Publishing

Elinor Sisilu argues that it is the perpetuation of neoliberal economic policies that has created the most serious problems for those in the book industry in Africa: "Despite advances in some areas the publishing environment in Africa is perhaps even more unfavorable than it was 25 years ago. The World

Bank-inspired structural adjustment policies of the 1980s not only deepened the poverty of the poor and vulnerable communities across the continent through market liberalization and elimination of social programmes, they also dramatically reduced access to books, not least through forcing sharp cutbacks to library expenditure."[35] Annari van der Merwe, a celebrated publisher at Kwela Books in South Africa who has sought out and supported black writers, describes the importance of libraries in creating a reading culture in terms of generations of new readers: the first generation reads newspapers; the second generation reads magazines; the third generation reads books, which are accessed through libraries; and the fourth generation begins to buy books.[36] In addition to their crucial function in this succession of generations of readers, libraries allow readers access to books that they could never afford to buy.[37] Books are very expensive in South Africa: in 2005 a book that cost $10 in the United States and the equivalent of $11 in India and $12 in the UK cost $21 in South Africa, and prices have continued to rise.[38] This price difference results in large part from economies of scale. In the UK, the number of titles published in 2005 was 161,000, compared with 8,177 in South Africa.[39]

The largest segment of adult non-readers lives in the rural areas of South Africa. Ironically, although rural adults rarely read, they are often active writers—writers without publishers. To solve the problem of bringing out the work of the hundreds of writers who came to them for help, staff from the Women in Writing project decided to publish anthologies. As of 2004 they had published six anthologies, which quickly sold out and are now out of print. Because the editors of the anthologies strategically placed pieces from writers across the country in each volume and required each anthologized writer to buy a copy, they extended the market. This project also enabled the writers, most of whom were unemployed, to get a percentage of the earnings from all the copies they sold.[40]

The Community Publishing Project, based in Cape Town at the National Library of South Africa's Centre for the Book, advises, funds, and offers technical support to small publishers and writers' collectives to help them publish and market works produced in their communities. But both self-publishers and small, independent publishing collectives face daunting challenges in their attempts to create a new market for an expanded audience in contemporary South Africa—challenges related not only to the complexities of the language issue but also to the effects of globalization. Without a library market, the only large market for African-language books is the lucrative schoolbook trade— really the only game in town—but this market has been cornered already by the South African affiliates of large European publishers such as Heinemann,

Oxford, and Macmillan. A few independent bookshops stock self-published or small press African-language books, but only grudgingly. These books are nearly impossible to find, hidden under piles of books in English. One bookshop owner in Cape Town complained to me about the poor quality of these books and the fact that no one ever buys them. She accepts them because she feels that she must. It is, after all, the "new" South Africa.

Despite economic challenges, the South African book publishing industry is expanding and diversifying. Not only are established publishers taking risks, but also new publishers and imprints are bringing out unusual voices and genres. Both novice and veteran writers say they are relieved to be able to write about topics other than political oppression.[41] The industry is beginning to venture into publishing in the African languages. The Writings in Nine Tongues catalogue, produced in 2007 by the Publishers' Association of South Africa (PASA) and supplemented in 2010, is a project designed to help publishers recognize the potential of this market. Endorsed and supported by the Department of Arts and Culture and the National Library of South Africa, this catalogue includes nearly five thousand works across genres—novels, short fiction, poetry, essays, and prose. Nhlanhla Ngubane, the chair of PASA, asserts: "Our aim of promoting existing titles in African languages has been largely met . . . and we also believe that the catalogue has acted as a catalyst for the development of new titles. Bringing the literature available in the previously marginalized languages together in one publication, has given publishers an opportunity to identify gaps and niches in the market. Many have revised their publishing plans and we are seeing more and more titles being published in these languages all the time."[42] Although Ngubane claims that the catalogue has promoted the development of new titles, Jessica Hadley Grave, editor of *Bookmark*, the newsmagazine of the South African Booksellers' Association, says that this publishing venture in African languages is limited by a dearth of material. To compensate for this lack and maintain the momentum, the National Library plans to reprint literary classics in the indigenous languages; as of June 2011, forty-six such classics had been reprinted and distributed to public and school libraries across the country.[43] Although the reprinting of "classics" (the inevitable debate that occurs over the definition of this term will likely slow down the process of selection) will help to preserve African languages, this initiative will not solve the problems of access to books for indigenous-language readers and the lack of a market for local literature.

The South African book market is composed primarily of imports, with 75 percent of titles from English-speaking countries and the remaining 25 percent from domestic publishers. Inaugurated in 2006, the Book Fair has been very successful in marketing English-language titles but has also become a trade center in the Black African book market. Stephen Johnson, managing director of Random House South Africa, observes: "In many respects the South African market is still an extension of Charing Cross Road, but the Cape Town Book Fair's focus on local writers and their work will inevitably begin to soften that very British dominance of our market. Having said that, though, the international bestsellers will remain bestsellers here, too, and there's no way that the popularity of a John Grisham is going to pass South African book lovers by."[44]

The Publishers' Association of South Africa and the large Frankfurt Book Fair founded the Cape Town Book Fair. Every press release and piece of information about the Book Fair acknowledges the partnership with the Frankfurter Buchmesse, and the Frankfurt website explains the market appeal of the Cape Town Book Fair not only by making a case for the stability of the South African book market and stating that there are nearly "one million people of German origin" in South Africa, but also by claiming that the fair would be "even more professional and more international in 2010."[45] The 2010 fair began with an exclusive trade day to allow uninterrupted exchange among industry players. But for most of its forty to fifty thousand visitors, the Cape Town Book Fair is an exhilarating experience because so many of the country's writers show up, not only to sign books but also to engage in lively discussions about the cultural, political, social, and economic context of writing and reading. When I visited in 2007, I was fortunate to see not just André Brink and Antjie Krog, who are internationally renowned, but the brilliant novelists Marlene van Niekerk (*Triomf* and *Agaat*) and Shaun Johnson (*The Native Commissioner*) as well, both of whom have won numerous South African and African literary prizes but have barely made a ripple in the international market.

South Africa was the Market Focus project at the 2010 London Book Fair, the British Council's cultural program titled "South Africa: One Nation, Many Voices." Launched in 2004, the Market Focus program was added to the London Book Fair to highlight the publishing industry and international business potential of certain countries with which the UK has a strong trade link. In the first year the program featured Hungary, Poland, Slovenia, and Slovakia, and in subsequent years Australia, New Zealand, Mexico, Spain, the Arab world, and India. In addition to the events that spotlighted South Africa at the fair itself, such companies as Apples & Snakes and Sustained Theatre, supported by the British Council, Arts Council England, and the South African government, coordinated tours of the UK by South African writers. One such tour was the Beyond Words UK series, in which the poets Keorapetse Kgositsile Donato Mattera, Phillippa Yaa de Villiers, and Lebo Mashile participated in seminars, master classes, and workshops designed to promote cultural collaboration and international understanding as well as provide the opportunity for an exchange of skills.[46] The Market Focus was intended to make South Africa more visible in the global market, a carefully orchestrated move in a year when the Rainbow Nation was to be the object of sustained international attention with the wide release of Clint Eastwood's celebrated (and criticized) film *Invictus* and its hosting of the FIFA World Cup games.

Johannesburg now has its own book fair, the Jozi Book Fair, and although it shares some of the concerns of the Cape Town Book Fair (to draw attention to South African literature and promote new writers in a wider market), its orientation is markedly different. The Jozi Book Fair was launched in 2009 by the nongovernmental organization Khanya College, which was established in 1986 "to assist various constituencies within working class and poor communities to respond to the challenges posed by the forces of economic and political globalization." Khanya College's mission involves supporting community organizations, labor unions, and nongovernmental organizations to enhance democracy and effect social change and development.[47] Rather than feature pages devoted to a list of book industry data in the context of a global market, which is the strategy of the Cape Town Book Fair website, the Jozi Book Fair website begins with the central problem of a weak culture of reading in South Africa, which results from a high rate of illiteracy and a lack of libraries, especially in the townships and rural areas. These are the conditions that have prompted its Culture of Reading campaign. The Jozi Book Fair is "a response to the need to rebuild a progressive publishing movement on the continent due to the recent decline of progressive and alternative publishers observed in South Africa and internationally," and it welcomes especially those "publishing houses that are committed to a social justice agenda."[48] But the Jozi Book Fair was not too alternative to participate in the 2010 London Book Fair, which its organizers viewed as an opportunity to learn how to stage a successful fair by drawing on the considerable experience of the London staff. The international venue of the London Book Fair also enhanced the visibility of the Jozi Book Fair and provided a large arena to exhibit and promote the titles of small South African publishers.[49]

South Africa in the Global Mediascape

It is significant that in 2003, in the midst of efforts by South Africans to create a new literature as well as to build communities of new readers, the largest seller in the global market of South African books was Alan Paton's 1948 novel *Cry, the Beloved Country*. This quaint liberal novel was transformed into a multimedia extravaganza as a featured selection of the Oprah Winfrey Book Club, with the context for reading now a website that included many pedagogical components, messages of spiritual uplift from Winfrey, advertising for her television feature on South Africa, and the travel journals of three readers whose letters about the novel won them trips to South Africa for a tour of the book's locales. As Rita Barnard astutely observes, this site "not only fosters the idea of collective reading and shared experience . . . but [Oprah's] reading of the novel is . . . hugely revealing of the ways in which South Africa as mediascape is constructed and consumed at the present time."[50] Derived from "an ethic of emotional similitude," Oprah's "megatext" suggests that "nations will come to signify in a new way, as mediascapes, occasions for certain kinds of stories, and (to be sure) certain kinds of touristic experiences."[51] Oprah's mediascape is occupied by a global collection of readers, including a devoted audience of South Africans—"mostly a white, stay-at-home female audience" in a country with a very small book market.[52]

Ten of Oprah's Book Club choices appear on the list of "101 Books to Read Before You Die" that was unveiled at the 2007 Cape Town Book Fair. The list emerged from a poll conducted by the bookseller Exclusive Books among its customers across South Africa to select "the 101 best novels of all time."[53] Heavily American and British, the titles on this list are mostly from the twentieth century, including many contemporary texts. A large number have been adapted to film, and the popularity of fantasy and romance is evident. This list—with J. R. R. Tolkien's *Lord of the Rings* at number one, J. K. Rowling's *Harry Potter* series at number five, and Dan Brown's *Da Vinci Code* at number nine—is similar to many such lists produced in other countries in the global market (see chapter 5 by David Wright in this volume). The similarity of national lists illustrates the power of large-scale publishers and retailers in the global market to shape national book markets and thus popular taste through the processes of production and distribution so that profitability plays a major role in determining literary value. In the case of the Oprah's Book Club choices, the books that Oprah values are produced in large numbers and distributed globally, with old best-sellers such as *Cry, the Beloved Country* revived and new ones created, even from among older books that were not best-sellers when they first appeared (for example, Toni Morrison's novel *The Bluest Eye*).

In the context of national culture, it is also worth considering what the Exclusive Books list does not contain. There are none of Gordimer's novels and only one by J. M. Coetzee, confirming the belief that these Nobel laureates have always had a much larger international audience than a South African audience. No books appear by the celebrated novelist Zakes Mda, who claims to sell more books in South Africa than Gordimer and Coetzee. There are a mere ten novels by South African writers, and only one from the rest of Africa, Chinua Achebe's *Things Fall Apart,* which barely made the list at number one hundred, sandwiched between Enid Blyton's *Magic Faraway Tree* and A. A. Milne's *Winnie the Pooh.*

South African readers have long been influenced by British and U.S. cultural arbiters. In his analysis of the history of "transnational appropriations" of the textual Atlantic, Andrew van der Vlies argues that the early success of *Cry, the Beloved Country* in the United States, where it was first published, "lent it the aura of an 'international' success before its arrival in the author's native country, playing very well to local, (white) South African English-speaking audiences who then so often looked elsewhere for validation of cultural capital."[54] Of course, transnational appropriations are not unidirectional. Van der Vlies argues that Paton's novel, through its "socio-religious and actively anti-Communist suggestions," allowed U.S. readers during the early years of the cold war to displace "anxieties about ideological conflicts closer to home."[55] More important here than the displacements involved in transnational textual appropriations are the disjunctions among South African readers, for example, the difference between the Exclusive Books readership (mostly stay-at-home white women) and the readers of the matriculation curriculum in which Paton's novel occupies only a tenuous place. Differences multiply when one considers the reading communities of those writers who self-publish African-language books (generally poetry) and distribute them at church gatherings and council meetings. But as different as these cultures are, they are all communities of readers—at a far remove from the millions of South Africans who cannot read at all.

This analysis has considered some of the challenges involved in South Africa's efforts to build a culture of reading in one of the most heterogeneous countries in the world, with one of the world's widest wealth gaps: a nation caught between the pull of the past and the push of the future while bound to neoliberal economic policies. Although these challenges are enormous, they must be met in order to create a foundation for civil society and political engagement in the new South Africa. It will be up to South Africa, acting in its own best interests, to make the right moves in what many observers consider a test case for a new dispensation in global democracy.[56] But how does a developing nation that is so closely tied to and marginalized within global capital go about acting in its own best interests? I would argue that part of the solution can be found in the success of grassroots resistance movements in recent years, movements that have linked local and global justice activists in "campaigns and initiatives intended to protect and represent the dwindling rights and resources of the growing number of people rendered surplus to requirements by the cold globalist wind blowing through the New South Africa."[57] Such campaigns include the Anti-Privatization Forum, Soweto Electricity Crisis Committee, Treatment Action Committee, Western Cape Anti-Eviction Campaign, and Landless People's Movement as well as numerous Jubilee movements fighting for debt repudiation.[58] Libraries are one place in which this kind of grassroots action can be fostered.

A culture of reading in South Africa will develop out of a heterogeneous and dynamic collection of reading cultures, and the task of growing and sustaining these cultures cannot wait on national government reforms that will require lengthy processes of decentralization, de-commodification, and de-globalization. Instead, this challenge might best be met in the short term by creative collaboration between local and global groups in affiliations based on reciprocal exchanges that support production and distribution in the local market. The connection between Khanya College, the Jozi Book Fair, and the London Book Fair is one example. Literacy is always a question of access to resources. Some observers feel that digitization will be the solution to production and distribution, and indeed the publishing group Naspers has been scanning books published in South Africa for its digital archive, which includes books in indigenous languages.[59] But digitization simply reconstitutes the problem of access as one of connectivity in terms of individuals, schools, and libraries. A report by World Wide Worx announced that the number of Internet users in South Africa in 2010 had exceeded 5 million, including a 15 percent increase in 2009.[60] The growth resulted mostly from small businesses upgrading from dial-up to broadband connection. Also, the new Seacom undersea fiber-optic cable that links South Africa to Europe should increase capacity and make connections much faster. But despite the progress, at this writing only 14 percent of South Africans have access to the Internet; township and rural dwellers rely on cybercafés, which are few and far between. On the African continent, South Africa trails behind Egypt, Nigeria, and Morocco in the total number of connections.

Although Africa experienced well over 1,000 percent growth in connectivity in the first decade of the twenty-first century, its total connectivity was still only 6.8 percent as compared with North America at 74.2 percent, Australia at 60.4 percent, Europe at 52 percent, Latin America at 30.5 percent, the Middle East at 28.3 percent, and Asia at 19.4 percent.[61] Predicting the effect of digital technology on the book industry in South Africa, Jessica Hadley Grave points out that South Africans, like Indians, are likely to leapfrog over computers and move directly to cell phones for accessing digital information. In 2007 a new company called CellBook introduced a technology for publishing on mobile phones.[62] Ten million South Africans (one in five) owned cell phones and the number was steadily growing, which would seem to indicate a large target market for this innovative technology. But in the move toward ever briefer communication content—texting and tweeting—it seems unlikely that mobile technology will solve the distribution problems of the book industry anytime soon. The real promise of mobile technology lies in its ability to provide access to information, with Web content adapted for cell phones.

Building a national culture of reading requires South Africans to deal with pressing current problems rather than seeking solace in future solutions. In 2009 the respected education policy analyst Graeme Bloch published a sobering book titled *The Toxic Mix: What's Wrong with South Africa's Schools and How to Fix It*. He calls education in South Africa a national disaster and blames government for failing to transform the inherited tragedy of apartheid schooling and for allowing South Africa's schools to become among the worst in the world. He reports, for example, that 17 percent of schools have no electricity and 79 percent have no library facilities.[63] To solve this problem, he writes, "every person and every institution is going to have to put [their] shoulder to the wheel. The weight of the past and the mistakes of the present are too heavy to be shifted without a general effort by all."[64]

In this context, creating communities of readers across South Africa will require the distribution of print materials in a network that involves indigenous-language writers, publishers, schools, libraries, churches, and community centers in a well-coordinated effort with activist groups, NGOs, and international foundations. Instead of thousands of copies of *The Little Engine That Could*, provided by U.S. foundations committed to fostering literacy in developing countries, one could imagine, for example, those same foundations supporting literacy programs by helping to distribute the children's book *Magopo Wa Rakgadi*, written in the Sepedi language by Mphuhle Annah Mehlape, who lives in the Polokwane region of Limpopo Province—a world away from the Cape Town Book Fair.[65] This distribution would provide a market and a larger audience for the work of a local writer; supply texts in the mother tongue to under-resourced ECDs, schools, and libraries; and make more effective use of the contributions by foundations, NGOs, and a myriad of volunteers from around the world. Initiatives such as the Isiqalo–First Words in Print project could flourish in this expanded network. Building a national culture of reading, then, would become an integral part of the work done in the larger field of South African social movements by those who are already thinking globally and acting locally.

Notes

1. Kader Asmal, speech at the SABA Annual General Meeting, Centre for the Book, Cape Town, August 20, 2002, www.info.gov.za/speech/2002/02120616111001.htm.
2. Elinor Sisulu, "The Culture of Reading and the Book Chain: How Do We Achieve a Quantum Leap?," keynote address at the Symposium on Cost of a Culture of Reading, Cape Town, 2004.
3. See Neil Lazarus, "The South African Ideology: The Myth of Exceptionalism, the Idea of Renaissance," *South Atlantic Quarterly* 103.4 (Fall 2004): 607–28.
4. Archie Dick, "Building a Nation of Readers? Women's Organizations and the Politics of Reading in South Africa, 1900–1914," *Historia* 49.2 (November 2004): 23–25.
5. Ibid., 27–28.
6. Ibid., 35–37.
7. Ibid., 41.
8. Archie L. Dick, "Struggle Libraries under Cover," *Cape Librarian* 50.3 (May–June 2006): 14.
9. Vincent Kolbe, personal interview, Cape Town, July 21, 2007.
10. See John Guillory, *Cultural Capital: The Problem of Literary Canon Formation* (Chicago: University of Chicago Press, 1993).
11. Alex Duval Smith, "Gordimer Insulted at Book Being Called Racist," *Independent Online*, April 17, 2001, www.int.iol.co.za/index.php?set_id=1&click_id=13&art_id=ct20 010417201006208G6356457.
12. Ronald Suresh Roberts, *No Cold Kitchen: A Biography of Nadine Gordimer* (Johannesburg: STE Publishers, 2005), 486–87.
13. Maureen Isaacson, "Gordimer Welcomes U-Turn on Set Book Row," *Independent Online*, April 21, 2001, www.int.iol.co.za/index.php?set_id=1&click_id=13&art_id=ct200104211 8550751C624360.
14. Margriet van der Waal, "'Deeply Racist, Superior and Patronising': The Story of the Stories Children Were Supposed to Read at School," in *Experience and Identity in Recent South African Literature*, ed. Margriet van der Waal and Helen Wilcox (Groningen: University of Groningen, 2003), 42.
15. Roberts, *No Cold Kitchen*, 487.
16. Guillory, *Cultural Capital*, 38.
17. Sinfree Makoni, "African Languages as European Scripts: The Shaping of Communal Memory," in *Negotiating the Past: The Making of Memory in South Africa*, ed. Sarah Nuttall and Carli Coetzee (Cape Town: Oxford University Press, 1998), 245.
18. Van der Waal, "Deeply Racist, Superior and Patronising," 43. See also Rob Noble, "South Africa HIV & AIDS Statistics," www.avert.org/safricastats.htm. South Africa has one of the highest rates of HIV/AIDS in the world. According to the 2010 UNAIDS Report on the Global AIDS Epidemic, which can be accessed at www.unaids.org/globalreport/20101123_GlobalReport_full_en.pdf, 11 percent of the total population is living with HIV, which translates into 17.8 percent of those aged fifteen to forty-nine. South Africa also has the highest incidence of rape in the world.
19. Jeanne Prinsloo, "Learning (Dis)Advantage in Matriculation Language Classrooms," in

Marking Matric: Colloquium Proceedings, ed. Vijay Reddy (Cape Town: HSRC Publishers, 2006), 197.
20. Bev May and Mary Nassimbeni, "Adult Education and Literacy in South African Public Libraries: A National Survey," report for the Print Industries Cluster Council Working Group on Libraries, Cape Town, 2005, 12.
21. Z. Pallo Jordan, address at a fund-raising event for the Mdantsane Library Project, Mdantsane, South Africa, November 22, 2005, www.dac.gov.za/speeches/minister/Speech22 Nov 05.htm.
22. May and Nassimbeni, "Adult Education and Literacy," 58.
23. Ibid., 78.
24. Neville Alexander, "English Unassailable but Unattainable: The Dilemma of Language Policy in South African Education," PRAESA Occasional Papers nos. 3, 17, www.praesa.org.za/images/stories/Occasional_Paper_1/OccPap3.pdf.
25. In a country where, in 2006, the most conservative estimate of adult unemployment was 26 percent (World Factbook) and the more likely figure was closer to 40 percent, all manner of activity must be commodified in an informal economy. Beadwork, for example, is sold to tourists, and English is the language of the tourist markets.
26. Neville Alexander, "Language Policy, Symbolic Power and the Democratic Responsibility of the Post-Apartheid University," *Pretexts: Literary and Cultural Studies* 12.2 (November 2003): 184.
27. Ibid., 188.
28. Ibid., 187.
29. Allister Haddon Sparks, *Beyond the Miracle: Inside the New South Africa* (Chicago: University of Chicago Press, 2003), 192.
30. Ibid., 52–53.
31. The South African Book Development Council's 2007 national survey shows that South African adults are much more likely to read newspapers than books. Two thirds of this population reads for leisure, with 84 percent reading newspapers, 38 percent reading fiction or nonfiction books, and 5 percent reading material on the Internet. South Africa Department of Arts and Culture through the South African Book Development Council, "National Survey into the Reading and Book Reading Behavior of Adult South Africans," June 2007, 11.
32. I derive this conclusion from the research results published by Angela Schaffer and Kathy Watters in summaries of the first two phases of the Isiqalo-FWIP program (Centre for the Book Research Reports, 2003 and 2007), from conversations with Nombulelo Baba, director of the program, and from my observations during the site visits.
33. Elisabeth Anderson, "Inspiring Literacy," National Library of South Africa website, www.nlsa.ac.za/NLSA/News/publications/inspiring-literacy.
34. David Macfarlane, "SA Needs to Plant the Seed to Make It Grow," *Mail and Guardian*, July 20, 2007.
35. Sisulu, "The Culture of Reading and the Book Chain."
36. Annari van der Merwe, interview with Ken Davis, May 2, 2009, audio clip at www.box.net/shared/nob39c2esk.
37. According to book production data, only 1 percent of the South African population regularly buys books, and 51 percent of households report that they have no books in their homes. See "A Short Overview of the South African Book Market," www.capetownbookfair.com/pdf/industry-statistics/bookmarket-south-africa.pdf.

38. Kim Baker, "The Economies of Access to Literature and Information," in *Bibliophilia Africana 8: The Book in Africa*, ed. Cora Ovens (Cape Town: National Library of South Africa, 2005), 148.
39. Jessica Hadley Grave, "A Closer Look at the Book Sector's Future in South Africa," www.buchmesse.de/imperia/celum/documents/SA_Bookmarket_future_full_version_e_12439.pdf.
40. Tembeka Mbobo, Jane Katjavivi, and Yousa Madolo, "Alternative Initiatives in Publishing/Literature and Publishing in Africa," in Ovens, *Bibliophilia Africana 8*, 193.
41. Colleen Higgs, "A New Wave in South African Publishing?" *Cape Librarian* 48.5 (2004): 16–17.
42. Nhlanhla Ngubane, quoted in Grave, "A Closer Look at the Book Sector's Future."
43. Newsletter of the International Federation of Library Associations and Institutions (IFLA), June 2011, www.ifla.org/files/national-libraries/Newsletters/June_2011_0.pdf.
44. Stephen Johnson, quoted in "South Africa: A Book Market on Course for Growth," www.frankfurt-book-fair.com/en/company/press_pr/newsletter/00452/index.html.
45. "Cape Town Book Fair 2010," www.frankfurt-book-fair.com/en/german_book_trade/gcs/cape_town/.
46. Publishers' Association of South Africa website, www.publishsa.co.za/docs/south-africa_market_press_release_2.pdf.
47. Khanya College website, www.khanyacollege.org.za.
48. 2009 Jozi Book Fair Brochure, 2, 3, www.scribd.com/doc/16951413/Jozi-Book-Fair-2009-Brochure.
49. Jozi Book Fair website, www.jozibookfair.org.za/booklaunch3.htm.
50. Rita Barnard, "Oprah's Paton, or South Africa and the Globalization of Suffering," *Safundi: The Journal of South African and American Studies* 7.3 (July 2006): 7.
51. Ibid., 15.
52. Wilma Jean Emanuel Randle, "Let the Young Lions ROAR: Literature and Publishing in South Africa," *Black Issues Book Review* 3.5 (September 2001): 22–27.
53. Exclusive Books website, www.exclusivebooks.com/features/101books.php.
54. Andrew van der Vlies, "Transnational Print Cultures: Books, -Scapes, and the Textual Atlantic," *Safundi: The Journal of South African and American Studies* 8.1 (2007): 46.
55. Ibid. I would add that the novel's universal message of liberal hope, with a focus on individual suffering and redemption in the context of systemic racism, has allowed American readers to displace the issue of race to South Africa—to displace in the negative sense of avoidance through redirection, but also to displace in the constructive sense of sublimation, signifying aesthetic relocation at a necessary distance to allow one to work through trauma and grapple with ethical issues.
56. See, for example, Sparks, *Beyond the Miracle*, x–xii.
57. Lazarus, "The South African Ideology," 615. See also Patrick Bond, *Talk Left, Walk Right: South Africa's Frustrated Global Reforms* (Scottsville, South Africa: University of KwaZulu Natal Press, 2004), 211–38; and Gillian Patricia Hart, *Disabling Globalization: Places of Power in Post-apartheid South Africa* (Berkeley: University of California Press, 2002).
58. Lazarus, "The South African Ideology," 615; Bond, *Talk Left, Walk Right*, 222.
59. Tumi Makgetla, "SA Books Go Online," *Mail and Guardian Online*, June 1, 2007, www.chico.mweb.co.za/art/2007/2007june/070601-online.html.
60. "SA Internet Growth Accelerates," www.worldwideworx.com/archives/234.

61. Dave Smith, "Five Million Now Online as Web Access Grows in South Africa," *Guardian*, January 14, 2010, www.guardian.co.uk/world/2010/jan/14/internet-five-million-south-africa.
62. Grave, "A Closer Look at the Book Sector's Future in South Africa."
63. Graeme Bloch, *The Toxic Mix: What's Wrong with South Africa's Schools and How to Fix It* (Cape Town: Tafelberg, 2009), 82.
64. Ibid., 173.
65. Mphuhle Annah Mehlape, *Mogopo Wa Rakgadi* (Polokwane, South Africa: Community Publishing Project, 2006).

5

LITERARY TASTE AND LIST CULTURE IN A TIME OF "ENDLESS CHOICE"

David Wright

The ways in which we come to know, like, and choose books at the start of the twenty-first century suggest that a reconsideration of some established theoretical narratives about literary taste is merited. This chapter introduces and develops the concept of "list culture" as a means of investigating these issues. The starting point for this analysis is a gap, identified by Elizabeth Long, in the research surrounding the "literary." Researchers have studied numerous elements of literary activity, from the biographies of particular authors to semiotic and psychological accounts of textual interpretation, and from popular literary participation to patterns of literacy. Despite this, Long observes that "how actual readers choose from the vast universe of possible books to read—how they sort through it, make it manageable, and finally settle on a title that they have some reason to believe will provide them with whatever reading experience they are seeking—has remained mysterious."[1]

In the contemporary context there is arguably more at stake than ever before in the resolution of this "mystery," as the "vast possible universe" of books continues to expand. The size, scope, and reach of the book industry has never been greater, despite perennial laments over its inevitable death at the hands of—and here the villain can be chosen from a historical range that extends throughout the twentieth century—film, TV, video, video games, e-mail, and the Internet. The extent of this ongoing growth has led the Mexican critic Gabriel Zaid to speculate mischievously that "in the near future there will be more people writing books than reading them." According to UNESCO estimates, at the dawn of the twenty-first century, 1 million titles were published annually around the world—a figure four times the number of titles published in the decades preceding the invention of television.[2] Stories of abundance of various kinds are persistent in the development of the cultural industries. We can identify them in discourses that emerge from the turn of the twentieth century, from political-economic critiques of the emergence of mass culture in the mid-twentieth century, and more recently in the context of the digital age. The changing strategies of managing this abundance can be revealed through a consideration of the cultural list as a mediating structure.

The Long Tail, a book by the business analyst Chris Anderson, is one of the more recent stories of abundance, and its imagined recasting of the cultural industries is an important stepping-off point for the consideration of list culture in its current incarnation. For Anderson, "many of our assumptions about popular taste are actually artifacts of poor supply-and-demand matching—a market response to inefficient distribution."[3] Based on the remarkable revelation that 98 percent of Amazon.com's top 100,000 books sell at least one copy once a quarter, his thesis is that, in the contemporary cultural industry, producers are following, rather than shaping, the tastes of their consumers. In the context of questions around literary taste and its relation to choices of reading material, literary institutions and expertise are being sidestepped. Readers are able to exchange forms of literary value among themselves through various online fora, including but not limited to those directly connected to retailers, such as the general customer recommendations and the Listmania feature through which users volunteer and share their enthusiasms on Amazon.com. At the same time, these processes allow producers to gather data about preferences through sophisticated data mining and collaborative filtering techniques and subsequently feed this information back to consumers as guides.

Accounts such as Anderson's suggest a logical undermining of traditional forms of cultural authority in place of a relatively "flat" community of engaged readers from which shared ideas of value can emerge. This chapter looks at the literary list in a variety of forms as one persistent technology of circulation that ascribes literary value in quite specific ways in the light of some stories of abundance, which precede Anderson's thesis. The next section addresses one element of this change through a reflection on the changing processes of book recommendation. It connects developments within the book industry with theories of cultural production and more general explanations of the nature of contemporary capitalism to suggest that such accounts might provide interesting answers to the "mystery" of contemporary literary taste.

Recommendation: From (Dis)Interested Critic to Automated Software

Janice Radway has pointed out that understanding the processes by which a book gets into a reader's hands involves unpicking the "socially organized technology of production and distribution."[4] Changes in technologies of production and distribution are themselves likely to imply changes in the nature of relationships between books, their producers, and their readers. Sociological accounts of literary production have emphasized the extent to which the writer is but one of a range of productive actors in the institutional processes that connect books with readers.[5] Accounts of the formation and practice of literary taste have also revealed the ways in which the restricted nature of literary production depends on forms of expert knowledge to manage notions of the "literary."

The most prominent theoretical model in this category is provided by the French sociologist Pierre Bourdieu.[6] For Bourdieu, cultural production is conceptualized as part of the broader characterization of social life as overlapping "fields" of activity, with relative positions of dominance or subordination of actors in fields being determined by the outcome of struggles over economic, social, or cultural capital. The field of cultural production, for example, is divided between producers with a concern for short-term financial profits (large-scale publishers, retailers, best-selling authors) and those disinterested, autonomous producers concerned with art for its own sake, rather than with the economic value of works. Those actors in the field who orient themselves toward the autonomous pole of the field struggle over the value of cultural capital, measurable by critical and academic appreciation, while those actors oriented toward the heteronomous pole compete over economic capital, measured by such indicators of value as sales or the length of a print run. In the Bourdieusian vision of the autonomous literary field, literary value is generated and protected by the actions of protagonists within the literary field and their use of literary expertise. The establishment of this kind of less easily quantifiable value is part of the more general processes within the field of art concerning what Bourdieu terms "illusio," the belief in the distinctive qualities of works of art and their specific separation from the social conditions of their production. Although Bourdieu's model of the literary field largely reflects the social context of the end of the nineteenth century in France, a period when new forms of literary production were required to satisfy the demand from the emerging literate populations of western Europe, we can identify at least four institutions through which the contemporary reading public is informed of what counts as good or bad and worth reading or not.

First, academics and critics continue to "police" the consecrated canons of good literature.[7] These might be the actors who are richest in cultural capital, and whose orientation, rhetorically at least, is to the autonomous literary field: their interest lies in the qualities of literature in and of itself, rather than with the financial rewards of increasing sales. Although they appear "disinterested" in processes of recommendation, for Bourdieu their "interestedness" lies in an intensive commitment to "illusio." They are the most ardent believers in the game of culture because upon it their status rests entirely.

Second, literary reviewers in newspapers, magazines, and other media play a crucial role in the book trade, as they do in a range of spheres of cultural production. Grant Blank's study of the place of reviews in settings as diverse as the restaurant trade and the software industry suggests a key mediating role for the reviewer in providing an authoritative and persuasive reason to make particular choices.[8] In some settings, including book reviews in certain newspapers or magazines, this mediating role is taken up through rhetorical claims to objectivity—a difficult claim to make in the context of the personal interpretation of literary works but one that is aided, or dramatized, by ratings systems that offer, for example, scores out of ten, the award of a number of stars, or the nomenclature of "book of the week." Apparently disinterested, such reviews can be seen as firmly embedded in the institutions of production and promotion—the appearance of a review itself representing a culmination of a series of editorial processes of selection and industry processes of distribution and persuasion rather than a simple beginning of the conversation between reviewer and interested reader. These kinds of expert reviews become key mediators for the visibility of particular titles, which, as James Curran and Susanne Janssen point out, has significant consequences.[9] A book that lends itself to illustration and easy classification within the already known is more likely to be reviewed than one that is more difficult to make media "sense" of. At the very least, there is a symbiotic relationship between autonomous producers and interested promoters of books in the reviewing industry.

Linked to this is the third institution: the growing number of literary prizes, which tread the perilous line between identifying objective criteria of excellence and operating as a promotional tool for the publishing industry.[10] Dismissed by critics of both radical and conservative bents as, to use Bourdieu's terms, evidence of the heteronomization of pure and disinterested notions of literary value, prizes provide key information to consumers, again filtered through the professional judgment of a panel of experts, in navigating their way through the myriad of new and available titles. Finally, publishers and booksellers of various kinds act to shape reading tastes, be it through selecting books to promote or deciding on ways to promote them. Radway describes the processes of book selection in a mail order book club and the practical logic underpinning the club's recommendations to its readers.[11] In the bookshop, the handwritten review or the "staff recommendation" display is used in a similar way to connect buyers and sellers as people with shared interests in reading.[12] In all these processes a relationship is set up between producers and consumers through what Bourdieu would term "cultural intermediaries" (academics, reviewers, prize committees, booksellers) who either claim or are granted the right to act on behalf of readers in guiding them, through various expressions of professional judgment, to the books they might like or should read.

In the "digital age" we need to add a fifth or even a sixth level of mediation, provided by readers as consumers and the technologies that connect them with one another. The story of *The Long Tail* begins with an anecdote about book sales which suggests the significance of these connections. *Touching the Void* is the account of a dramatic Andes climbing accident by Joe Simpson. First published in 1988, it is illustrative for Anderson of the changing strategies for the circulation and measurement of value in the contemporary cultural industries. With the title on its way out of print in the late nineties, sales were revived when another climbing memoir, *Into Thin Air,* was released. Fans of the first book posted online reviews of the second on Amazon.com, which highlighted the apparent superiority of the Simpson story. Anderson explains the building momentum of online word-of-mouth recommendations: "Other shoppers read those reviews, checked out the older book, and added it to their carts. Pretty soon the online bookseller's software noted the patterns in buying behavior—'Readers who bought *Into Thin Air* also bought *Touching the Void*'—and started recommending the two as a pair. People took the suggestion, agreed wholeheartedly, wrote more rhapsodic reviews. More sales, more algorithm-fuelled recommendations—and a powerful, positive feedback loop kicked in."[13] There are two important points underlying this narrative. What Anderson describes is, in one sense, a process of the *democratization* of book recommendation. One could argue that left to the book industry and its promotional tools alone, *Touching the Void* would have disappeared, along with the hundreds of thousands of titles that simply and inevitably fall by the wayside in a context of cultural abundance. Instead it was rescued by enthusiastic readers, who through their own efforts generated additional readers, which led to the older book ultimately outselling the newer one. These readers acted not alone but in concert with the producers of the technical infrastructure through which their ephemeral "word-of-mouth" recommendations could be captured, stored, and analyzed, and the "buzz" around a title, beloved of literary marketeers, could be identified and mapped through the quantification of Web traffic. Alongside this process of democratization, then, this example illustrates another story about the *rationalization* of processes of recommendation through the technical ability to integrate directly the kinds of informal feedback that might otherwise be lost back into the processes of production, selection, and consumption.

The key moment Anderson identifies is the shift from word-of-mouth recommendations to algorithms recognized by software, in which criteria of similarity and difference—the forms of "value" identified and exchanged by reviewers—are coded and automated. These are not infallible and might generate some jarring commonalities, as suggested by the artist Angie Waller in her piece "Data Mining the Amazon."[14] Waller identifies some intriguing patterns of consumption revealed by Amazon.com's collaborative filtering: customers who bought *Mein Kampf,* for example, also bought the soundtrack to *Ally McBeal.* Amazon.com's processes are, however, largely efficient and fiscally productive, arguably more so than traditional forms of recommendation for matching up consumers with the products they want to buy—and increasingly accurate as the transactional data of more online consumers becomes part of the processes of selection.[15] In this regard the ideas of value that emerge from the *Long Tail* thesis reflect what Nigel Thrift has termed the development of "knowing capitalism," in which logistical practices, organized through apparatuses of delivery and control, shape new forms of consuming practice.[16]

Not for the first time the book industry, so often characterized as somehow slow or backward looking, is here at the heart of innovations that alter consuming practices. Rachel Bowlby, for example, has described the emergence of the bookshop with its displays of individually "branded" produce as exemplifying all forms of contemporary self-service shopping.[17] In a similar way, we can see in the processes of collaborative filtering and data mining embedded in the online recommendation process new forms of practice which have quickly become second nature to consumers. For Thrift, these forms of "soft-computing" have become part of how we "decide to decide."[18]

In more general terms, the Amazon.com reviewer as liberated exchanger of literary value fits neatly with what Marek Korczynski and Ursula Ott, following George Ritzer, have termed the "enchanting myths of individual autonomy" that characterize contemporary capitalism.[19] They argue that the idea that people come to products in a liberated way—despite rather than because of the opinions of accredited experts—fails to account for the structures that mediate processes of production and consumption. In the context of debates about literary taste, it is compelling to consider consumers as having freed themselves from "experts" who seek to shore up their own positions by means of restrictive conceptions of literary value. The next section addresses this critique by examining one "mediating structure" that, while enacted and assembled in different ways, has remained remarkably persistent throughout this narrative of change: the list.

"List Culture"

The marketing of cultural products is something that happens to other people. A sophisticated cultural audience, those rich in what Bourdieu terms cultural capital, are perhaps less likely to recognize—or more likely to resist—the idea that their cultural choices are determined by the technical skills of advertisers and marketers. They prefer to see their preferences emerging from more apparently authentic sources, for example, from a knowledgeable reading of critics, or from the narratives of self-discovery that infuse representations of the bookshop browser. This is a position that, in a sense, denies the "industry" aspect of the cultural industries and specifically misrecognizes the complex and subtle means of cross-media promotion so central to the contemporary book industry, which, as Stephen Brown describes, "guarantees in-store promotional support and gets the nation's bibliomanes in a must-read lather."[20]

The list in various forms has played and continues to play a crucial part in this process, as both market information guide and mediating structure of value. This is most obviously manifest in the chart or best-seller lists, which themselves serve this dual purpose. Talking about the musical hit parade, the political economist Jacques Attali describes the necessity for the capitalist production of culture in a time of abundance (this time the 1970s) to find a means of seizing the consumer's attention and providing a way of assessing the value of similar, and similarly priced, products. For Attali, the hit parade "channels, selects and gives value to things that would otherwise have none, that would float undifferentiated."[21] Commodities are brought together in a chart and rendered meaningful not only in relation to one another but also, significantly, in relation to the people who create them. Rhetorically, the role of arbiter is assigned to consumers themselves, but in the context of the hit parade, this perspective conceals the work behind the scenes, where an army of song pluggers and radio playlist managers contrive to make particular songs heard and available to be bought. In the context of the book trade, the purity of the list as a recognition of consumer preference is similarly clouded by arcane and hidden processes of selection. Laura Miller, for example, describes the changing and proprietary methodologies of the calculation of the *New York Times* best-seller list to demonstrate the ways in which such lists do not necessarily reflect those books that have sold the most copies. As well as providing market information for consumers, she argues, they also provide important information for producers, and offer a means of organizing and prioritizing resources in the book industry such that they are "actively participating in the doings of the book world rather than just passively recording it."[22]

In the context of the present-day UK, cultural lists have joined best-seller lists as a staple of Sunday supplements and cultural journalism. Periodic lists of what is being read, listened to, or watched coexist alongside regular polls on the "greatest" books, pop albums, or films, according to critics, reviewers, and, more recently, viewers, listeners, or readers themselves. In this kind of list, the intrinsic "value" or qualities of specific books, films, or music in themselves is replaced with an assessment of their value purely in relation to one another—notwithstanding the differences in genre, tradition, or content that might make them incomparable in any meaningful way. Anderson outlines another element of the superiority of the digital context for the sharing of information when he critiques lists that lump genres together as trying to measure apples against oranges. Filters and recommendations allow more fine-grained list making so that aficionados of more specialized genres of music or literature are able to gauge more accurately what is popular in relation to a specific preferred niche, and so take advantage of the collective tastes of fellow consumers.[23] Even these processes obscure the complex and subtle interactions between producers and consumers through which people come to choose cultural products and, like the star ratings of reviewers, place a patina of rational objectivity on processes of selection. In terms of Bourdieu's model of the field of cultural production, these kinds of evaluations also represent a kind of heteronomy in their recasting of cultural engagement as a form of competition, and the lack of recognition of these processes is evidence of the triumph of the market.

Dismissing lists as either marketing tools or cultural trivia, though, ignores the insights they provide into taste itself and the changing processes through which it is constituted. As John Frow describes, accounts of cultural participation from sociology and, latterly, cultural studies have repeatedly shied away from questions of judgment and evaluation, preferring to concentrate instead on either processes of production or the variously ideological, distinguishing, or resistant processes of consumption.[24] The expression of preferences and the kinds of ranking enabled by participation in list making, though, is an optional extra to the pleasures of cultural consumption in the early twenty-first century. Julian Pinder (in chapter 3 of this volume), for example, describes the potential social connections that emerge from posting and sharing one's tastes for the literary in online forums. What such lists might also represent, particularly in the contemporary context of "endless choice," is a way of rationalizing or mediating processes of production and consumption. The following sections explore this phenomenon by examining the historical antecedents of contemporary list culture and the list as "democratic expression" exemplified by the BBC's Big Read initiative.

One Hundred Books to Read Before You Die: The List as "Canon" and Guide

The concept of the canon is central to all forms of literary value (again, see chapter 3 by Pinder in this volume). Depending on one's ideological position, the canon may represent an immovable core of eternally good literature, knowledge of which is central to being a cultured person, or an elitist/European/patriarchal vision of a coherent and closed social world which denies difference and restricts access. Guillory's account of the contested concept of the canon in the contemporary academy reveals, crucially, that it exists less as a coherent, codified list of works and more as a rather loose assemblage located in the curricula of academic courses and in the minds of literary scholars. Attempts to *formalize* the canon by providing definitive lists of "good books" to read can be seen as "guides" from those who are in the cultural know to those who are not. "No-one," suggests the book historian Jonathan Rose, "who has ever handed students a syllabus of required readings can in good faith object to the principle of a best books list. Though canons can be changed, canonization is inevitable, given we must choose between the millions of books available to us."[25]

Such lists have a long history, and their persistence can be seen today particularly within the pages of lifestyle and cultural magazines. Lists that emerged in the late nineteenth and early twentieth centuries include Sir John Lubbock's *100 Best Books* (which puts forward, among others, the Koran, *Pickwick Papers*, and *Pride and Prejudice*), Arnold Bennett's 1909 guide *Literary Taste: How to Form It* (which also includes the works of Jane Austen and Dickens), and John Cowper Powys's *One Hundred Best Books*.[26] These represent readers as lacking the necessary education to come to these books "naturally," and needing a helping hand to guide them through the choice of possibilities—already bewildering well before *The Long Tail*—as to the "correct" books to read. They can be interpreted as an attempt to manage the emergent mass literate population of the late nineteenth century, and to mark the territory of the already literate cultural elite. While Powys is particularly dismissive of the notion of an instrumental interpretation of reading as a means to "cultivation," his self-consciously subjective guide (which again contains Jane Austen as well as Emily Brontë) signals other implicit aims: "The compiler feels that any one who succeeds in reading, with reasonable receptivity, the books in this list, must become, at the end, a person with whom it would be a delight to share that most classic of all pleasurable arts—the art of intelligent conversation."[27]

Such lists could also be benevolently inspired. Lubbock, for example, was an MP and a president of the Working Men's College who campaigned for early closing legislation so that workers could receive education and enjoy culture. Rose records how Lubbock's list was both gratefully received by aspirant working-class readers as a cultural "roadmap" and simultaneously dismissed by critics such as Matthew Arnold and Henry James.[28] Bennett's guide includes an almost scornful chapter, titled "Your Particular Case," envisioning this aspirant reader. In it Bennett identifies the symptoms of someone who lacks culture but wants to achieve it, without the necessary changes to his whole worldview: "You occasionally buy classical works, and do not read them at all; you practically decide that it is enough to possess them, and that the mere possession of them gives you a 'cachet.' The truth is, you are a sham."[29] Despite this disparagement, both Powys's and Bennett's lists helpfully include the prices of the proposed titles in pounds, shillings, and pence, suggesting that their volumes are a practical guide for aspirant readers to what to buy as well as what to read. As Philip Waller points out, these lists were gleefully received by publishers of the period as means to guide the emerging mass consumer market for books toward specific titles.[30] From the perspective of a cultural elite somewhat fearful of the development of literacy among the masses, as described by John Carey and Patrick Brantlinger, these lists were also a means of guiding them *away* from salacious penny dreadfuls or the corrosive effects of morbid introspection that the unlearned readership of popular novels might generate.[31]

Such benevolently inspired forms of cultural guidance are an accompanying feature to the emergence of mass culture in the early to mid-twentieth century. Joan Shelley Rubin, for example, describes the role of critics in the creation of a middlebrow culture organized around prescribed lists of great books in the United States of the 1930s, 1940s, and 1950s.[32] More recent proponents include E. D. Hirsch's *Cultural Literacy* and Harold Bloom's *The Western Canon: The Books and School of the Ages*.[33] Of as much interest to the argument here, though, is the reemergence of this list as guide, in newspapers, magazines, and in new varieties, in the context of the apparently "endless choices" of the digital age. These kinds of lists, then, might represent an extension of a protective nostalgia, as well as practical instruction for entry into the community of the literate—a response to both abundant choices and abundant readers. Moreover, with their explicit exhortation both to read and to buy particular books, lists can be seen in past and present incarnations alike to bring producers and consumers together in guided ways.

"As Chosen By You": The List as Democracy

In contrast to the concept of the list as canon or guide, more recent innovations in the realm of list culture can be interpreted as rhetorically representing a democratization of literary value: a means of taking away decisions about what counts as worth reading from ennobled literary experts and putting them into the hands of active and engaged communities of readers. The circulation of value among different varieties of fan community, most notably with respect to forms of popular literature, has been a staple of cultural criticism for a number of years, with readers identified as resisting and subverting notions of the literary in pursuit of their particular predilections for romance fiction, science fiction, horror fiction, and other forms of genre fiction. Indeed the sophisticated interpretation of novels by fan readers of various kinds has been central to the emergence of critiques of the canon as elitist, paternalist, and ethnocentric. As critics such as Radway (including in this volume) and Elizabeth Long have observed, though, these forms of celebratory participation are always situated in specific contexts of production, circulation, and distribution, and the popular list might be interpreted as one such context. Frow argues for the centrality of evaluation to the pleasures of popular cultural participation and the "circulating energies" of culture.[34] The lament that *studying* a book stops a reader from *enjoying* it points to the dilemma that analysis is not always an encouragement to action in the same way as a personal or affective response is. Asserting that one book is better than another, regardless of how meaningful that comparison might be according to the parameters laid down by cultural authorities, and having that opinion validated by peers via "list culture" rather than imposed or dismissed by traditional experts, is a significant, if partial, opening up and fragmentation of value and authority.[35]

It can also be argued that, at least in some of their more visible incarnations, "democratic lists" offer a similar form of mediating structure to the list as chart or the list as canon. This can be seen in the example of the BBC's The Big Read, a search for the UK's favorite book carried out by the national broadcaster in 2003.[36] This initiative began with a call for nominations of the favorite novels of BBC TV viewers, BBC radio listeners, and users of the BBC website. After two weeks of open nominations, some 140,000 initial votes were collected and some 6,400 novels nominated. The one hundred books with the most votes were then selected and presented on television in a launch program. This was followed by a series of seven programs over the following seven weeks in which the top twenty-one books were showcased during a series of half-hour films presented by a celebrity proponent of the novel. As with the canonical lists of Bennett, Lubbock, and Powys, these lists included such writers as Dickens and Austen. During each of these programs viewers were encouraged to register further votes by telephone, SMS text message, or the Internet. A running countdown of the relative standings of the final twenty-one was presented throughout the program. Following all these processes a "top five" list was identified. During a live grand finale, further voting was encouraged as the books' champions, accompanied by various celebrity proponents and with a panel of literary experts of various kinds, continued to make the case for and against these five. Finally, *The Lord of the Rings* by J. R. R. Tolkien was named the nation's favorite book.

Using a list as its organizing principle, The Big Read demonstrated an emerging trend for the contemporary literary industry to engage with the mass media, rather than keeping the assumed "high culture" of the former well away from the "popular culture" of the latter.[37] The mass-mediated publicity generated for books by such broadcasting initiatives as Oprah's Book Club in the United States and Richard & Judy's Book Club in the UK is celebrated within the book industry for spreading the word about books. The concentrated attention on the media wrought by such book clubs alters the shape and direction of the struggles within the field, between actors oriented toward the autonomous pole of literary production, in Bourdieu's schema, and those oriented toward the kinds of commercial successes now associated with these initiatives. The mass media, and television in particular, are recognized within the book industry as an important arbiter of contemporary literary taste, which, because of their accessibility, sidestep and indeed actively marginalize traditional forms of scholarly expertise. Moreover, the proliferation of list-centered programs on UK television from the late nineties onwards also suggests that the list is an ideal structure for the organization of taste, owing to the narrative drama inherent in its "countdown." In a sense, The Big Read can be interpreted as a triumph of popular taste over the stuffy, closed world of literary expertise, although some dissenting voices within the "literati" have been dismissive about it. Alluding to the pop singer and footballer celebrity couple David and Victoria Beckham, the novelist Jeanette Winterson described the program as the "Posh and Becks approach to culture."[38]

Despite such objections—indicative perhaps of a firm commitment to autonomous literary value—The Big Read was generally celebrated for promoting reading as a social good and for validating forms of popular taste over exclusionary forms of canon making. Given the collusion between the BBC and the publishing industry in feeding off the publicity that the project generated (seen in branded promotions for titles in the top one hundred list in several major high street retail chains), the list also functions as a site on which agents within the literary field can be brought together, and through which consumers and producers can be provided with the means of directing their actions. Although "literary expertise" is not absent here, its presence is managed in ways that recognize its role in the kind of exclusionary processes of canon formation that the project sought to discourage. As with the technological capture of word of mouth provided by Amazon.com's transactional data and algorithms, other forms of expertise are equally or perhaps even more important. These include access to the technical knowledge with which to manage forms of interactive participation and the forms of marketing and branding expertise which enable the kinds of multiplatform presentation that events such as The Big Read require.

The career of lists is illustrative of the processes of heteronomization of the literary field. This is not simply a rehearsal of tired debates about the ways in which bad old industry corrupts good old culture. Rather it is a way of seeing the list in the light of persistent narratives about the abundant choices available to consumers: as part of processes of rationalization, translation, and mediation, and as a structure embedded in the production of literary taste. In this context, literary lists provide a means of negotiating the "endless" literary choice of the digital age, as much as they can be seen to mediate value in the context of an emerging literate mass in the nineteenth century, or in the context of an emerging commodified "mass culture" in the mid- to late twentieth century.

The evidence of each of these examples, however, suggests that lists are enabling *and* constraining, allowing for the opening up and management of choices. When examined through the lens of theories concerned with "investigating the forms of mediation in contemporary Western societies that allow the co-existence of structures of power with individuals' heightened *sense* of agency and autonomy,"[39] the literary list, even in its contemporary and apparently democratic guise of The Big Read or the Amazon.com recommendation, can be seen as a mediating structure between literary producers and consumers. In this context, agents in the literary field are not simply liberated from conventional perceptions of literary value. Instead they are subject to new forms of governance and require innovative forms of discipline which reflect new forms of choosing available in the digital context. Although academics and literary critics held sway in the management of literary tastes in the Bourdieusian model, the relative decline in the influence of these intermediaries does not mean that readers are entirely free to choose. Instead, new forms of authority and expertise around marketing, media presentation, branding, and the technological organization of abundant choices are coming to characterize the management of the reading public in the contemporary literary field.

Notes

1. Elizabeth Long, *Book Clubs: Women and the Uses of Reading in Everyday Life* (Chicago: University of Chicago Press, 2003), 115.
2. Gabriel Zaid, *So Many Books,* trans. Natasha Wimmer (London: Sort Of Books, 2004), 9.
3. Chris Anderson, *The Long Tail: How Endless Choice Is Creating Unlimited Demand* (London: Random House Business, 2006), 16.
4. Janice Radway, *Reading the Romance: Women, Patriarchy, and Popular Literature* (Chapel Hill: University of North Carolina Press, 1984), 20.
5. See Lewis A. Coser, Charles Kadushin, and Walter W. Powell, *Books: The Culture and Commerce of Publishing* (New York: Basic Books, 1982).
6. See Pierre Bourdieu, *The Field of Cultural Production: Essays on Art and Literature,* ed. and intro. Randal Johnson (Cambridge: Polity, 1993), and *The Rules of Art: Genesis and Structure of the Literary Field,* trans. Susan Emanuel (Cambridge: Polity, 1996).
7. See John Guillory, *Cultural Capital: The Problem of Literary Canon Formation* (Chicago: University of Chicago Press, 1993).
8. See Grant Blank, *Critics, Ratings and Society: The Sociology of Reviews* (Plymouth, UK: Rowman and Littlefield, 2007).
9. See James Curran, "Literary Editors, Social Networks and Cultural Tradition," in *Media Organizations in Society,* ed. James Curran (London: Arnold, 2000), 215–40; and Susanne Janssen, "Reviewing as Social Practice: Institutional Constraints on Critics' Attention for Contemporary Fiction," *Poetics* 24 (1997): 275–97.
10. James F. English, *The Economy of Prestige: Prizes, Awards, and the Circulation of Cultural Value* (Cambridge: Harvard University Press, 2005); John Street, "'Showbusiness of a Serious Kind': A Cultural Politics of the Arts Prize," *Media, Culture and Society* 27 (2005): 818–40.
11. Janice Radway, *A Feeling for Books: The Book-of-the-Month Club, Literary Taste, and Middle-Class Desire* (Chapel Hill: University of North Carolina Press, 1997).
12. David Wright, "'You're Part of the Package': Rationalization and the Status of Expert Knowledge in the Retail Book Trade," *Savoir, Travail et Société* 2 (2004): 17–37.
13. Anderson, *Long Tail,* 15.
14. Angie Waller, "Data Mining the Amazon" (2003), http://couchprojects.com/amazonweb/.

15. J. Ben Schafer, Joseph Konstan, and John Riedle, "E-Commerce Recommendation Applications," *Data Mining and Knowledge Recovery* 5 (2001): 115–53; Sylvain Senecal and Jacques Nantel, "The Influence of Online Product Recommendations on Consumers' Online Choices," *Journal of Retailing* 80 (2004): 159–69.
16. Nigel Thrift, *Knowing Capitalism* (London: Sage, 2005).
17. Rachel Bowlby, *Carried Away: The Invention of Modern Shopping* (London: Faber, 2000).
18. Thrift, *Knowing Capitalism*, 184.
19. Marek Korczynski and Ursula Ott, "The Menu in Society: Mediating Structures of Power and Enchanting Myths of Individual Sovereignty," *Sociology* 40 (2005): 911–28; George Ritzer, *Enchanting a Disenchanted World: Revolutionizing the Means of Consumption* (Thousand Oaks, Calif.: Pine Forge Press, 1999).
20. Stephen Brown, "Rattles from the Swill Bucket," in *Consuming Books: The Marketing and Consumption of Literature*, ed. Stephen Brown (London: Routledge, 2006), 4.
21. Jacques Attali, *Noise: The Political Economy of Music* (Manchester: Manchester University Press, 1985).
22. Laura J. Miller, "The Best-Seller List as Marketing Tool and Historical Fiction," *Book History* 3 (2000): 286–304. See also Alan T. Sorensen, "Bestseller Lists and Product Variety," *Journal of Industrial Economics* 55.4 (2007): 715–38, for a discussion of the impact of bestseller lists on sales.
23. Anderson, *Long Tail*, 112–15.
24. John Frow, *Cultural Studies and Cultural Value* (Oxford: Clarendon Press, 1995).
25. Jonathan Rose, *The Intellectual Life of the British Working Classes* (New Haven: Yale University Press, 2001), 128.
26. Lubbock's list was originally published in the *Pall Mall Gazette* in 1896. It was reprinted in John Lubbock, *The Choice of Books* (Philadelphia: Henry Altemus, 1896). Arnold Bennett, *Literary Taste: How to Form It, with Detailed Instructions for Collecting a Complete Library of English Literature* (1909), Project Gutenberg e-book no. 3640 (2005); John Cowper Powys, *One Hundred Best Books: With Commentary and an Essay on Books and Reading* (1916), Project Gutenberg e-book no. 12914 (2004).
27. Powys, *One Hundred Best Books*, 1
28. Rose, *Intellectual Life of the British Working Classes*, 129.
29. Bennett, *Literary Taste*, 3.
30. P. J. Waller, *Writers, Readers, and Reputations: Literary Life in Britain, 1870–1918* (Oxford: Oxford University Press, 2005).
31. John Carey, *The Intellectuals and the Masses: Pride and Prejudice among the Literary Intelligentsia, 1800–1939* (London: Faber, 1992); Patrick Brantlinger, *The Reading Lesson: The Threat of Mass Literacy in Nineteenth-Century British Fiction* (Bloomington: Indiana University Press, 1998).
32. Joan Shelley Rubin, *The Making of Middlebrow Culture* (Chapel Hill: University of North Carolina Press, 1992).
33. E. D. Hirsch, *Cultural Literacy: What Every American Needs to Know* (New York: Houghton Mifflin, 1987); Harold Bloom, *The Western Canon: The Books and School of the Ages* (New York: Harcourt Brace, 1994).
34. Frow, *Cultural Studies*, 2.
35. The characters in Nick Hornby's *High Fidelity* (London: Indigo, 1996) might also suggest list making as a peculiarly masculine and fetishized version of cultural participation.
36. See David Wright, "The Big Read: Assembling the Popular Canon," *International Journal*

of the Book 4 (2007): 19–26, and "Watching The Big Read with Pierre Bourdieu: Forms of Heteronomy in the Contemporary Literary Field," Centre for Research on Socio-Cultural Change Working Paper Series no. 47 (2007), www.cresc.ac.uk/sites/default/files/wp45.pdf.

37. See Jim Collins, ed., *High-Pop: Making Culture into Popular Entertainment* (Oxford: Blackwell, 2002).
38. Jeannette Winterson, "Book Me Out of This Charade, I Actually *Like* Reading," *The Times*, April 5, 2003.
39. Korczynski and Ott, "The Menu in Society," 914.

6

"KEEPIN' IT REAL"
Incarcerated Women's Readings of African American Urban Fiction

Megan Sweeney

Urban fiction—also known as gangsta lit, street lit, ghetto fiction, and hip-hop fiction—has taken the U.S. publishing world by storm. Bearing titles such as *Thugs and the Women Who Love Them* and *Forever a Hustler's Wife*, urban books feature African Americans who are involved in urban street crime, including drug dealing, hustling, prostitution, and murder. The genre has gained immense popularity, particularly among young black women, since the 1999 publication of Sister Souljah's best-selling novel *The Coldest Winter Ever*. Its roots extend further back, however, to African American novels about ghetto life such as Iceberg Slim's *Pimp: The Story of My Life* (1969) and Donald Goines's *Whoreson: The Story of a Ghetto Pimp* (1972). Although urban fiction writers struggled to find publishers for their work in the late 1990s, some authors now sign six-figure contracts with major publishing houses, and urban books dominate the African American collections in large chain bookstores.[1]

In conducting research with seventy-four women incarcerated in Ohio and Pennsylvania, I learned that urban fiction is equally prominent in women's prisons. The genre is particularly popular among young, lower-class black women, but it has also gained popularity among middle-class black women and white women. According to Darlene,[2] a thirty-five-year-old African American woman, urban books typically feature "a pimp or killer or drug dealer," or "just a everyday life situation: prison, baby mama drama, having a guy being a player." Urban books often start with the protagonists' childhood, "how they used to see their mother get beat up, or how they went to different groups and foster homes and prison," and they sometimes involve courtroom scenes and characters' efforts to "flee the police." The genre has opened up a world of reading for many women who were not readers before coming to prison. As a young black woman named Ronnie explains, she "didn't read hardly at all" but "was hooked" after discovering urban fiction. Now, says Ronnie, "I keep reaching out and reaching out until I find more and more. They all just been good books. They talk about real life."

Some critics argue that urban fiction glorifies crime, reinforces stereotypical images of African Americans, and crowds out far better literature by African American writers. For instance, in "Their Eyes Were Reading Smut," a frequently cited op-ed published in the *New York Times* in 2006, Nick Chiles describes the proliferation of urban fiction as "these nasty books . . . pairing off back in the stockrooms like little paperback rabbits and churning out even more graphic offspring that make Ralph Ellison books cringe into a dusty corner." From Chiles's perspective, "serious" African American writers such as Toni Morrison, Edward P. Jones, and himself are being "surrounded and swallowed whole on the shelves" by "pornography for black women" and "books that glamorize black criminals."[3]

Critics' anxieties about urban fiction are matched by penal officials' anxieties about the genre. Despite women's daily requests for urban books, prison librarians in both Ohio and Pennsylvania exclude the genre because of its depictions of crime and violence. Prisoners who can afford to do so therefore ask family members and friends to order urban books for them through online catalogues such as BlackExpressions.com. If these books make it past the mailroom censor, their recipients share them with other imprisoned readers through what one woman calls the "Underground Book Railroad." I realized the extent of prison officials' anxieties about urban fiction while conducting group discussions with women incarcerated in Ohio. Although we had received permission to discuss a few urban books, a prison official burst in to stop one of our discussions after learning that the books were published by Triple Crown Publications, a firm founded by a former prisoner.[4] The official told me to collect the books and immediately remove them from prison grounds, as if, one prisoner noted, they were "a bomb that no one can touch." Since we were not permitted to read any additional urban books, I asked if we might have a group discussion about two particularly popular books that most of the participants had already read. A penal official insisted, however, that "there can be no discussion of the work."

Although some prisoners echo the concerns of various scholars, librarians, and penal officials in voicing disdain for urban fiction, other prisoners draw attention to the inconsistency of penal officials' attempts to guard the literary gates. Several women foreground the racialized dimensions of the urban fiction ban, noting that violent crime thrillers by the white author James Patterson are the most abundantly stocked books in their prison library. Nena, a twenty-nine-year-old Latina woman, and Boo, a forty-six-year-old African American woman, argue that their warden restricts urban fiction because she is out of touch with the realities that the genre depicts. "We're not all rich people," Nena insists. "We came from the streets. We've been raped doing tricks and left for dead in alleys with dead animals on us." Echoing this sentiment, Boo says of the warden: "She needs to get out of herself and her fantasy world. Life is not a bowl of cherries. Put your feet in someone else's shoes." A young black woman named Lakesha suggests that the prohibition of urban fiction contests incarcerated women's status as readers. Noting that more prisoners watch TV than read books, she argues: "Everything they take away in books we can just watch with our eyes, so it doesn't make sense. I can watch *Prison Break* and I'm sitting in prison!" In Lakesha's view, I should rename my study *Fear of Books*.

Lakesha's comment stayed with me over the course of my research, serving as a crucial reminder of what is at stake in exploring prisoners' reading practices. I must acknowledge that I have felt reservations about the ideological underpinnings of many urban books. Although the books often make reference to the racial oppression that African Americans face, their plots typically focus on black characters' efforts to destroy one another in order to gain class ascendancy and economic power. The books frequently romanticize the role of drug dealer and define success in terms of vast material wealth. Furthermore, they tend to portray female characters as viciously vying for the financial patronage of male drug dealers; many books suggest that supportive relationships among women are well-nigh impossible, and that women can achieve well-being only by establishing a heterosexual, reproductive family unit with a wealthy man. Indeed, the genre may perpetuate the fantasy that African American women can game and romance their way to the top of a system that routinely excludes them from equal opportunity. Finally, urban books often espouse a notion of justice based on individual enactments of revenge, thereby leaving little room for imagining mutuality, cooperation, or shared struggle for collective benefit.

Despite my ideological criticisms of urban fiction, my interactions with women prisoners have pushed me to abdicate the role of literary prison guard and try, instead, to understand how readers use available narrative forms to negotiate their place in the world. Since the prisoners' rights movement of the 1960s and 1970s gave way to the retributive justice framework of the 1980s, prisoners' opportunities for reading and education have sharply declined. During the prison-building campaigns of the 1980s, prisons radically reduced their library budgets, converted library space into cells, and sometimes installed television as a pacification tool. In the prisons where I conducted research, the libraries are funded entirely by revenue from the prisons' vending machines, which means that very limited funds are available for libraries. The decline of prison libraries has also been matched by a drastic reduction in opportunities for higher education in prisons. In 1994, Congress eliminated Pell Grants for prisoners, effectively defunding college programs in U.S. prisons and sparking broader cuts in all levels of educational programming.

Women prisoners' limited access to reading materials has been exacerbated, throughout U.S. penal history, by cultural anxieties about the corruption of women through reading, racialized assumptions about prisoners' incapacity for reflection, and fears that criminals will increase their criminality by reading inappropriate books.[5] The lists of books recently banned in Ohio and Pennsylvania prisons illustrate how race continues to inform penal officials' fears that particular books will jeopardize prison security. In addition to several volumes of contemporary African American urban fiction, the banned books include earlier urban fiction by Iceberg Slim and Donald Goines as well as African American autobiographies such as Maya Angelou's *I Know Why the Caged Bird Sings*,[6] journalist Nathan McCall's *Makes Me Wanna Holler*, former gang member Sanyika Shakur's *Monster: The Autobiography of an L.A. Gang Member*, and lawyer Cupcake Brown's best-seller *A Piece of Cake*. Also banned are books and pamphlets related to racial and class struggles, including "Philosophy of Class Struggle," "Interviews with Assata Shakur," "Debunking the Panther Mythology," and an *Essence* magazine best-seller, *The Willie Lynch Letter and the Making of a Slave*, a 1712 publication that instructs whites about how to maintain blacks in slavery. Books and periodicals that focus on prison issues and include prisoner-authored essays are banned as well, such as *Prison Legal News*, *The Celling of America: An Inside Look at the U.S. Prison Industry*, *Prison Nation: The Warehousing of America's Poor*, and *Journal of Prisoners on Prisons*. Given the disproportionate rate of incarceration for African American women,[7] these restrictions on prisoners' reading and educational opportunities seem to continue historical patterns of treating literacy as the property of white males.[8]

At a time when prisoners are rarely regarded as readers, let alone as human beings capable of deep thought, growth, and change, it seems particularly important to honor prisoners' agency as readers. I attempt to do so in the remainder of this essay by analyzing some of the many roles that urban fiction plays in the lives of incarcerated women.[9] Each of the seventy-four women involved in my research participated in one life narrative interview, one to two interviews about her reading practices, and four to seven group discussions of books.[10] In facilitating the group discussions, I usually asked for readers' initial thoughts about the book and then allowed them to guide the course of the conversation. I posed questions when readers did not have questions that they wanted to pursue, and I sometimes encouraged them to grapple with contradictions that emerged during discussion. I am aware, as Ien Ang argues, that ethnography is "a form of storytelling" and that every cultural description "is not only constructive (or, as some might say, 'fictive'), but also of a provisional nature, creating the discursive objectification and sedimentation of 'culture' through the . . . highlighting of a series of discontinuous occurrences from an ongoing, never-ending flux." In analyzing women's engagement with books, I have tried to account for the ways in which my position as a white, middle-class literature professor shaped my "particular ways of seeing and organizing an ever elusive reality,"[11] and I have learned to recognize how my own investments conditioned my receptivity to the women's thoughts and experiences. At the same time, I realize that women's descriptions of their reading practices cannot be understood as transparent truths about what actually happens when they read. As Bethan Benwell and David Allington argue in chapter 11 of this volume, "statements describing a reader's experiences in reading a particular book may appear to be literal *reports* of events taking place in a preexisting reality, but . . . these must be seen as *accounts* constructing reality."

Although no study can provide an exhaustive picture of the definitive meaning of particular reading practices, some clear patterns emerged across my interviewees' discussions of urban fiction. I highlight some of these patterns in the pages that follow, drawing on individual interviews as well as our group discussions of five urban books that we were permitted to read: Shannon Holmes's *Bad Girlz* (2003), Sister Souljah's *The Coldest Winter Ever*, Danielle Santiago's *Grindin'*, and Tu-Shonda Whitaker's two-part series *Flip Side of the Game* (2004) and *Game Over* (2005). I briefly explore some of the myriad ways in which differently situated women evaluate urban fiction, grapple with the genre's suggestion that crime is a necessary steppingstone to achieve the American dream, and use urban books as templates for reflecting on their own experiences. While it remains crucial to address how the proliferation of urban fiction restricts the range of representations of African Americans, I believe that it is equally crucial—lest we create a prison house of language—to understand how women prisoners use the narratives at hand as tools for shaping their experiences.

Keepin' It Real with Urban Fiction

Like literary critics and penal officials, prisoners sometimes debate the merits of reading urban fiction. Those who criticize the genre express particular concern that it leads women between the ages of eighteen and thirty down the wrong path. According to Starr, a forty-one-year-old African American woman, urban books function "like an old song that filters through your brain and gives you a memory of why that song was good," leading women to keep "plotting to make that stuff come true. Those books glorify their addictions to drugs and money." Other women, including some fans of the genre, contend that urban books discuss drug use in ways that can reactivate readers' addictions. In fact, Miekal, a forty-year-old African American woman who owns an extensive collection of urban books, asked the prison librarian to ban Lisa Lennox's *Crack Head* and Y. Blak Moore's *Slipping* because she believes that their realistic descriptions of crack use will make addicts "slip when they could have wanted to be clean."

Women who enjoy reading urban fiction also evoke its realism in expressing their appreciation for the genre. Urban books "keep it real," these women suggest, by depicting familiar characters, scenes, fashion trends, and speech patterns; in so doing, the books enable women to maintain a sense of connection to their communities, and they conjure a realistic world that exists outside the control of penal officials. According to Darlene, the characters featured in urban books are "so real you can actually feel what they're going through or been through. I can find bits and pieces of me or somebody that's close to me in the urban books." This "realness," Darlene adds, "can take me out of here and away somewhere else other than in my room on my bunk." Miekal describes urban books as a means "to keep it together" by staying connected to life outside the prison. "Urban books is basically just keeping you in touch with what's going on in the streets," she observes, "the latest words they're saying out there, the latest things they're wearing, the latest things they're doing. I like to hear what the lady's got on, you know, she's wearing her miniskirts, and she got on stilettos, and she's looking good, her skin glistening like mocha chocolates." Miekal also likes to read books in which men "take care of their women" by buying them designer jewelry and clothing, but she remains fully aware of the consequences that such a lifestyle invites: "That's drug money, and if you read the book, it tells you eventually he goes down, you know. He's looking at ten to fifteen years or he gets killed." From Miekal's perspective, it makes no sense that women are permitted to read about serial killers but not about what she finds most captivating in urban books: "black men sporting Timberland boots and women wearing Prada."

The fact that urban books employ the vocabulary and speech patterns of African American urban culture is particularly attractive to some readers. An African American woman named Soso specifies that she likes how characters in urban books "use slang, like 'da' instead of 'the,' and 'what fo?' I like how they say 'dat' and not 'that' . . . and things like, 'yo,' 'hey ho,' and 'wassup.' That's how it is in the streets. People use those terms." Readers find it especially inspiring that urban fiction writers have withstood pressures to use standardized English. As Darlene says of the author Zane: "They wanted to change her words around. They say our language is Ebonics or whatever. But she didn't change nothing what she wrote. She stuck with it and now she's like a *major* writer." The mass-produced feel of the genre also adds to readers' sense of its authenticity and accessibility. Nena appreciates Shannon Holmes's *Bad Girlz*, for instance, because "it's not elegantly produced. It doesn't have no extra cover, no picture of the Taj Mahal or magnificent trimming. . . . It's simple. And he explains his whole story in three sentences."

The verisimilitude of urban books enables some readers to participate vicariously in the stories while remaining aware of their fictionality. As a young African American woman, Kaye relishes the fact that urban books feature familiar people and situations. "A lot have to do with growing up in the projects, selling, and using. I did all that," she remarks. "They're about people like you know." Kaye nonetheless emphasizes that urban fiction is not "real." "If it was real," she says, "it would give me more sadness of how their lives turn out." In her view, "the momentum" of urban books "comes from fights, action, and drama," and if the characters had "a nice life . . . it would be like going from the New York City streets to the country roads of Alabama." In fact, Kaye suggests that characters in urban books serve as surrogates, allowing her to experience things that she does not want to experience in real life: "In everything I read, I like stuff that I don't like in my life." Bobbie similarly describes urban books as a means to get her "thuggish feeling out of the way. I put myself where the characters are," she explains, "so it's like okay, you're dealing drugs, I'm dealing drugs. You're killing people, I'm killing people. But I wouldn't really be doing it, you know what I'm saying? I'm just standing back there watching what you're doing."

For women with middle-class backgrounds, urban fiction can provide a vicarious experience of—or association with—a world that seems more "real," gritty, or authentic than the world represented by the suburbs. Bobbie, who grew up in a black, middle-class suburban household, acknowledges that urban books depict "a life that I've never personally lived," yet she values them because they portray a "real" side of life that gets overlooked in "fairy tales like the Huxtable family" from *The Cosby Show*. "I don't feel like I'm in a fantasy world reading [urban books]," says Bobbie. "I don't feel like I'm a six-year-old." For Cassandra, a black woman who was raised in what she calls a "stuffy, sheltered" environment, urban books seem to serve as a means to buttress her sense of racial authenticity or affiliation with street culture. She draws a sharp distinction, for instance, between her own fluency in the language and culture of the street—gleaned from reading urban fiction—and the cultural illiteracy of her "clueless" parents.

Other readers emphasize their distance from the lifestyle depicted in urban fiction and suggest that the books foster their understanding of, and identification with, women whose experiences seem to be reflected in the texts. Wendy, a twenty-eight-year-old African American woman, says of her fellow prisoners, "There's no way on God's green earth I would have ever been around any of these people outside of prison." Because urban books—like the people around her—have a "hustler, ghetto-type feel," Wendy uses them to understand why her fellow prisoners behave as they do. "In some way," she claims, "I'm doing research." Valhalla, a white woman who grew up in upper-middle-class suburbs, likewise explains that she reads urban books to gain "empathy" and "understanding" for people whose lives are "so far from anything I've ever known." When she cannot understand the books' vernacular speech, Valhalla asks her roommate to "translate" it for her. "I don't know nothing about pimps and the crack dealers on the corner and placing all your happiness on how nice your boobs and fur coat is," she acknowledges, "but it's interesting."

Rescripting the American Dream

During one of our group discussions, Kaye characterized urban fiction in these terms: "Hustling is always gonna be on your mind. It's the American dream to live comfortably and to take care of your own. These books are about another way of getting the American dream than the honest way." Kaye's insightful comment highlights the capitalist ideology that undergirds urban fiction. The books insistently focus on the moneymaking prowess of characters and their right to a bigger slice of the economic pie. The desire for class ascendancy is racialized, with African Americans trying to wrest from whites the wealth and privilege that whites have unfairly hoarded. Yet this desire is also the primary motivation for the intraracial conflicts in the novels, and it serves as a point of cross-racial identification for many white readers. As a young white woman named Angel observes: "Some [people] say white people can get a job, get all the breaks, and go to rehab, but if you're mixed or black or Spanish, you don't get that. But [those people] don't understand that people of all races have different lifestyles. . . . I'm not from a rich family. The street is what I know."

In plotting stories of lower-class African American women rising to prosperity, urban fiction may tap into readers' "racial and gender aspirations to live in a world where such stories [a]re possible."[12] Indeed, women prisoners who have struggled for economic survival often appreciate the genre's over-the-top portrayals of characters' moneymaking abilities and lavish lifestyles. For some readers, urban books fuel the fantasy that one might actually achieve the kind of easy wealth that protagonists enjoy. Commenting on Shannon Holmes's *Bad Girlz,* which features two formerly homeless women who become wealthy strippers and prostitutes, Soso acknowledges: "When I'm reading, I can't wait to see the dollar signs! They made money just like that! I wish I had options like that for fast money, with no strings attached." Danielle Santiago's *Grindin',* in which female hustlers seduce, drug, and rob extremely wealthy white men, prompts a similar response from Soso: "If I was their age, I'd get money like they were getting and sit back and relax! You give men drinks and get them high and get their money! I wouldn't have to worry about hustling."

While inhabiting the alluring worlds that urban fiction conjures, other women draw a clear distinction between the books' fantastic and realistic elements. "You have to know where to draw the line from fantasy to reality," Cassandra asserts. Urban books serve as her "get-away books"; she is fully aware that authors "stretch" the truth and try to keep readers "glued to the pages" in depicting drug dealers who make enormous profits. Dismissing the concern that reading such books will make women "want to go out and commit crimes," Cassandra describes urban fiction as "just like a fantasy type thing. . . . It's not like watching *Thelma and Louise* and then you go out robbing."

For other readers, urban books provide opportunities for reflecting on—and trying to resist—their desire to engage in criminal activity. In *Bad Girlz,* an older stripper advises the young protagonist: "Use da game as a stepping-stone. Or it'll use you. . . . Make it out da game fo' it's too late."[13] During one group's discussion of the novel, some women agreed with this philosophy, arguing that you can obtain nice things for your children "in days" rather than struggling for years, and then get out of the game and start your own business. A young black woman named Lefty sharply criticized the older stripper, however, vehemently arguing: "It shows you how people feel like there's no other way to start a life. But there are so many other routes to get started in a beauty parlor. She shouldn't say use the game as a steppingstone! She should say you should do something else to get started with your life. . . . Work at McDonald's! Get financial aid!" Lefty's comments seem particularly significant because she is incarcerated for several robbery charges and has only recently begun to reassess her own efforts to achieve wealth. Earlier in the conversation, Lefty acknowledged that hustling was "a fun life," but she now realizes that "in a lot of black families, money rules. People are materialistic. They feel that's happiness. But when you meet the Man, none of it matters. . . . A lot of people don't realize that the best things in life cost nothing." This discussion of *Bad Girlz* concluded with the following poignant and good-humored exchange, in which Lefty challenged the novel's framework by offering an alternative vision of what matters:

> LEFTY: When you're in jail—I've got robbery cases and bank cases—you think about all the money you got, but it don't be shit now that you're in jail. My Pop-pop said you appreciate all you've got when you work hard for it. He worked and had benefits. It sounds corny but when you experience all this [time in prison], you wish you would have listened. It took years to get what they get in a day, but you probably had something to show for it. And all these people who have SUVs with movie screens and everything else, who wants to watch TV when you're going down the street?
>
> CANDI: She did have big speakers. [general laughter]
>
> NENA: When people have a fifteen-inch TV screen in their car, *that's* corny.
>
> BOO: Yeah, you should save that for the house.
>
> LEFTY: You could invest in college, not a TV or a pair of Jordans. I didn't appreciate that before.

Over the course of our group discussions, I began to recognize that some urban books present more opportunities than others for contextualizing characters' actions in relation to broader social and political issues. For instance, Sister Souljah's *The Coldest Winter Ever* and Danielle Santiago's *Grindin'* generate divergent interpretive possibilities through their depictions of the drug trade. Although *The Coldest Winter Ever* is often deemed the progenitor of contemporary urban fiction, it differs from most of its literary offspring in explicitly critiquing the drug trade for spawning destruction and ruthless competition within the African American community. *Grindin'* seems more typical of the genre in its legitimization of the drug trade as a means of "stackin' for the future."[14] In comparing these two novels, I do not mean to champion *The Coldest Winter Ever* as the ideal to which urban fiction should aspire. In fact, I find problematic the novel's homophobic vision of the monogamous, heterosexual, male-governed family as the salvation of the African American community. The comparison nonetheless seems instructive because it draws attention to the kinds of interpretive possibilities that urban books do and do not open up for readers.

The Coldest Winter Ever features Winter Santiaga, a selfish young woman whose father is an extremely wealthy drug kingpin. When Winter's father gets arrested, her mother becomes addicted to crack, her younger sisters end up in foster care, and Winter herself engages in ruthless criminal activity that lands her in prison. Winter nonetheless valorizes her father's criminal activity in these terms: "He got at least *twenty years of good high living* out of the business" while a "regular nigga worked all week for change to get to work plus a beer to forget about how hard he worked." Winter also contends that drug dealers help America "to be rich" and employ "half the men in the ghetto," who otherwise could not get jobs. Sister Souljah—who appears as a character in the novel—counters this logic, however, by arguing that "drugs is a government game. A way to rob us of our best black men, our army. Everyone who plays the game loses. Then they get you right back where we started, in slavery! Then they get to say 'This time you did it to yourself.'"[15] *The Coldest Winter Ever* reinforces this perspective in an appendix—which has no parallel among other urban books—that includes detailed analyses of the novel's main characters, as well as Sister Souljah's responses to ten interview questions.

As women debated the merits of Winter's logic during our group discussions, some argued that "the good living, the cars, the clothes, the jewels" were not worth going to prison, while others maintained that it would be worth spending time in prison if you made a million dollars, "as opposed to struggling until you're seventy-five and you never get a million dollars." All of the women felt persuaded, however, by Sister Souljah's argument that the drug trade is a form of modern-day slavery. Her argument prompted Monique, a twenty-nine-year-old African American woman, to reflect on her own role in enslaving others through selling drugs: "You're putting boundaries and holds on a whole 'nother being because when you do sell the drugs . . . you limit other people's ability to do certain things, whether it's provide for their family, take care of theirself, or get an education because they're just gonna continue to chase that high, you know. Instead of just having them straight put shackles on us and take us to another country and put us to work, we're shackling ourself." Valhalla reflected that drug dealers themselves become slaves because "they don't prepare for anything else" and then "they can't get out of it; they're trapped." *The Coldest Winter Ever* thus opened up possibilities for women to reflect critically on commonsense justifications of the drug trade.

By contrast, Danielle Santiago's *Grindin'* implicitly justifies participation in the drug trade as necessary for achieving economic success. Although Chaz, the protagonist's boyfriend, has suffered because of his mother's drug addiction, *Grindin'* does not critique his role as a drug seller. In fact, when Chaz asks if the protagonist, Kennedy, can live with the fact that he's going to stay in the game, Kennedy says, "I guess I don't have a choice if I want to be with you."[16] For some readers, the novel's endorsement of a ruthless capitalist ideology accords with their sense of what is required for success in a fiercely competitive world. During a group discussion, Kaye argued that Chaz "won't make someone else's mother stop using if he stops selling. The dealers are not the ones making the problem." Drawing on media representations of the high cost of being a star, several women also asserted that despite Chaz's huge success as a rap star, he must continue selling drugs in order to have enough money. "After they pay for the videos and all that, stars don't have any money," Nez argued. "That lifestyle's expensive. So Chaz had to hustle." Readers in the group agreed, moreover, that Kennedy had no choice but to allow Chaz to continue selling drugs because she "gets a lot of money from him," and "once you see how much money you can make, it's hard to let go." For women who look to urban fiction as a reflection of the real world, *Grindin'* thus generates few possibilities for imagining employment options that do not revolve around "the game." In fact, Nez—who wants to "go legit" upon her release from prison—has learned from *Grindin'* that strip clubs have become popular, so she plans to open a business that can supply strip clubs with sex toys and exotic costumes.

The constructions of the drug trade in *The Coldest Winter Ever* and *Grindin'* are yoked to their constructions of education. *The Coldest Winter Ever* depicts Sister Souljah, the character, as an avid reader who is always surrounded by books, and it emphasizes that a former drug dealer named Midnight is able to leave the game because he has educated himself. In their readings of *The Coldest Winter Ever*, women in my study tend to follow the novel's lead in emphasizing that Midnight's education enables his escape from a criminal lifestyle, while Winter's lack of education keeps her wedded to the game. Such a perspective resonates with women who prioritize education in their own efforts to leave crime behind. At the other end of the spectrum, Santiago's *Grindin'* suggests that higher education leads to a false sense of superiority and a distance from the realities that most black people face. Kennedy refers to her aunt who has a master's degree as a "snooty rich know-it-all," and she harshly criticizes Brooke, a "black yuppie" marketing executive who graduated from Yale University and assumes "that she [i]s better than most black women." Kennedy says to Brooke, "Your skin may be black, but you don't know shit about being black."[17] During the group discussion of *Grindin'*, women indicated that Kennedy's comments resonate with their own suspicion that education can distance people from their communities and the realities of everyday life. My status as a middle-class university professor and the fact that most of the women had dropped out of high school seemed to inflect this conversation in significant ways. Nez and Soso discussed the characters' education levels in ways that enabled them to feel empowered. "Kennedy could survive in Brooke's world but Brooke couldn't survive in Kennedy's world," Nez insisted, suggesting that "street smarts" are more versatile than formal education. She and Soso then argued that whereas "people from the projects just do what they know how to do," well-educated people "have breakdowns," "turn to drugs," "have complicated problems in their lives," and "wear masks" in an effort to conceal who they really are.

Kaye responded to Kennedy's comments by announcing, "I still want education," and by emphasizing her own ability to be "a chameleon" and function in "two different worlds." While asserting that she "can talk business but . . . can also swear with the best sailor," Kaye nonetheless drew attention to the gulf between Brooke's experiences and her own. "I'm from the projects," she emphasized, adding that Brooke "probably never had to endure life or steal something to survive. Students from Yale think they're the best and they get the top jobs." This sense that those who "never had to endure life . . . get the top jobs" undergirds the suggestion, in many urban books, that people from the projects must participate in crime in order to succeed. On one level, then, *Grindin'* highlights the disparities that differing levels of privilege and education can produce. On another level, however, the novel provides few possibilities for readers to gain new information about alternative worlds and subject positions that they might inhabit. As they invoke the American dream, urban books thus prompt some readers to grapple with issues of power and privilege, yet they often reinforce ideologies that help to maintain current structures of inequality.

Writerly Reading Practices

While urban books reflect settings and situations that seem familiar to many readers, their social realism is not matched by psychological realism; many of the books are plot-driven rather than character-driven, and their thin character portrayals offer few insights into the psychology, motivations, or internal struggles of the protagonists. Nonetheless, many women respond to urban books as if they offered deeper character portraits than they do. These readers seem to assume such a close proximity between their own and the characters' experiences that they use urban books as templates, as paint-by-numbers canvases that allow them to fill in characters' portraits with their own psychological interiority. In this sense, the women engage in what José

Esteban Muñoz calls a practice of "disidentification," which entails "tactically and simultaneously work[ing] on, with, and against a cultural form" in order to "invest it with new life."[18]

For instance, Tu-Shonda Whitaker's *Flip Side of the Game* and its sequel, *Game Over,* prompted many readers to reflect deeply on their own actions and relationships. Whitaker's novels focus on Vera Wright-Turner, a young woman who is struggling to develop a healthy relationship with her mother. Vera's mother, Rowanda, tried to abandon her when she was born by placing her in a trash can; Rowanda was fifteen years old and addicted to crack, and she did not believe that she could provide a good home for her daughter. Vera was rescued and raised by her aunt, and during the present time of the novels, she is learning to forgive her mother—who is recovering from her addiction—and to accept responsibility for her own actions. During our group discussions of Whitaker's novels, several women expressed their sense of identification with Vera as a neglected daughter and/or with Rowanda as a neglectful mother. Nena, who engages intensely with every urban book she reads, identified so strongly with Vera's feelings of neglect *and* with Rowanda's neglect of her daughter that she said of Whitaker's novels, "On a scale of one to ten, I'd rate these books a twenty!" Although she deeply sympathizes with Vera, Nena said of her during our discussion: "I could have just kicked her ass sometimes. I wouldn't have such a strong opinion if I hadn't experienced it. But when I've experienced 98 percent of the book—all the consequences, wanting to kill myself, all her thoughts and feelings—I could really relate to her. It helps me keep my own head on straight." Noting Vera's tendency to blame Rowanda for her problems, Nena added: 'The number one thing is how [the books] make you think about choice. . . . It's up to us. We can't blame others for our consequences." Just as Vera had to learn that "she's not eight years old," Nena acknowledged that she is learning to view herself as "a twenty-nine-year-old woman and not a three-year-old. I'm learning to get comfortable in my own skin." Later in the conversation, Nena also drew parallels between the guilt and shame that Vera feels for being Rowanda's daughter and the feelings that her own son may have toward her, particularly since he was born addicted to heroin. Furthermore, referring to Vera's decision to monitor her mother through a hidden camera while she is babysitting for Vera's child, Nena acknowledged: "I was thinking about how I would feel as an addict, like they're never gonna trust me. I would be upset and hurt. But then I flipped the script and realized I was only clean eight out of twenty-nine years of my life. I've been in mental hospitals, rehab, and every time I said, 'I'm gonna be mature, etc., etc.' and every time I got high." Nena's concluding comment—"My family abandoned me, but I can't change anyone but me"—underscores how discussing urban books offers some women an opportunity to reaffirm their insights and emerging self-conceptions.

Monique performed a particularly striking disidentificatory reading—working on, with, and against the books in order to suit her own needs—during her group's discussion of materialism in Whitaker's *Flip Side of the Game* and *Game Over*. Tyra initiated the conversation by drawing attention to the books' quasi-obsessive emphases on brand-name clothing, cars, and furniture. Vera is "too materialistic," she argued, and the novels focus excessively on the fact that she is "wearing Prada" or sitting "on a Coach red leather sofa." In responding to Tyra's critique, some other readers insisted that the novels offer a realistic representation of life in the ghetto. According to Mocha: "A lot of people are materialistic that's from the ghetto. . . . That's what everybody looks up to, the Donna Karan, the JLo, the Sean John." Monique, who was deeply invested in urban fiction at the time of the conversation, insisted instead that Whitaker's inclusion of brand names merely represents effective description. Drawing comparisons with writers outside the urban fiction genre, Monique argued: "The writer was just very detailed in all of her descriptions . . . so you could just visualize for yourself and take a walk with [Vera]. . . . It's not necessarily being materialistic, but they just describe it to a 'T' so you can get a feel for what they want you to feel. . . . I've read books where I never attached to the book because they didn't put me in that walk with them."

Monique's efforts to deflect Tyra's critique, and thereby defend urban fiction as a whole, reflect her appreciation for the genre, which has played a key role in her efforts to "get [her]self together." She finds Whitaker's novels inspiring, for instance, because they "tell you the real deal while also showing you . . . that you can make a better life for yourself." Monique likes that Vera "came from a trash bag, and her mother was strung out, but she also owned her own business and got herself together and wasn't using that as a crutch. She used that as a building tool. Through all her struggles and her strifes and her history and her past, she overcame that, and she built a firm foundation with her husband, who's educated." Even when Vera was trading sexual favors for men's financial support, "she didn't just go and buy cars and go to clubs," Monique notes. "She went to college. . . . She had a business. . . . So I respect her hand and how she played it." Because she is struggling to develop a good relationship with her own mother, Monique also deeply admires Vera's efforts to repair her relationship with her mother. Monique's disidentificatory reading of Whitaker's novels thus enables her to defend a genre that has played a crucial role in her endeavors to make positive changes in her life.

Urban fiction inspires such enthusiasm in some readers that they transition from the role of writerly reader to the role of literal author; one woman involved in my study has already published her first book and has two others under contract. The genre allows readers to consider their experiences and speech patterns as worthy of representation in a book, and it suggests that readers can become authors simply by writing about what they know. Indeed, many writers of urban books promote a democratization of authorship, inviting their readers to correspond with them and to engage in dialogue about reading and writing. "Some of the authors even ask you do you have a story to tell, or how could you relate to this book," Darlene observes, "and they even say you could write me a letter here and I will respond."

Other women's enthusiasm for urban fiction wanes over time, and they sometimes conclude that they must leave urban books behind if they want to embrace a new way of being in the world. Christine, a young white woman who read nothing but urban books when she entered prison, now wants to read other kinds of books because she is "getting out of the street mentality" and feels "like a different person." In fact, Christine has come to believe that urban fiction is not good for incarcerated women because it suggests that "no matter how hard you try to escape" a criminal lifestyle, you will never be able to do so. As Christine illustrates, women usually move beyond urban books because they want to go somewhere else on their personal journeys; they are looking for other ways to script their own realities and other stories to tell about their lives. In the words of Rose: "If I'm reading to take my mind to another place, obviously I don't want to read the Triple Crown books because I don't want to go to that place. . . . I've been down that road."

"Maybe you should write another book called *Fear of Books*." As I reflect on women prisoners' engagements with urban fiction, Lakesha's comment pushes me to reckon with the lingering discomfort that the genre inspires in me. This discomfort does not stem from prisoners reading the books. As this essay illustrates, incarcerated women read urban books in complex and varied ways. Although some of the books script a self-referential universe that provides few avenues for readers to "take [their] mind to another place," women demonstrate resourcefulness and creativity in using urban books as tools for lending meaning to their experiences. As they enter the protagonists' stories, women sometimes reflect on their own experiences as children and parents, drug users and drug sellers, and victims and perpetrators. Some women gain greater self-awareness, learn from the characters' mistakes, increase their sense of agency, and even develop empathy for others. In their group discussions of urban books, readers sometimes push one another to think about important issues such as the ethics of the game, gendered violence, and possibilities for carving out new ways of living. While some women find pleasure and comfort in maintaining a singular focus on urban fiction, others determine that they must leave urban books behind as they seek to rescript their lives. Regardless of the particular outcomes of women's engagements with the genre, I firmly believe that neither penal officials nor literary critics should police these engagements.

Nonetheless, I continue to feel uncomfortable about urban fiction because it reinforces dominant ideologies that fuel conditions of inequality and thereby help to create a pipeline to prisons. Like so many other cultural forms—from true crime books to countless law-and-order television shows such as *CSI: Crime Scene Investigation*—urban fiction offers no "trace of an imagination of a society without crime as we know it" and no sense of "a collective fate" or "shared destiny" necessary for imagining a society without crime.[19] Narratives about murder, Sara Knox argues, say "so much about *what a culture knows* and *what it will not let itself know*."[20] By focusing on drug dealing and involvement in the game as necessary for gaining a foothold in our racist, capitalist economy, urban books divert attention from our need, as a society, to change the structure of the game and make the playing field more fair. Moreover, in celebrating protagonists' mastery of the game, urban fiction often reinforces an ethic of violence, ruthless competition, materialism, and revenge, thereby occluding possibilities for mutuality and collective efforts to achieve social justice. It bears repeating, however, that this ethic is not unique to urban fiction; the genre is but one manifestation of the sacrificial logic that pervades our culture and governs U.S. penal policy. Our current failure to approach communal safety and well-being from the perspective of social equality and social justice—rather than from the perspective of "Fuck with mines and I will annihilate yours"[21]—represents an impoverishment of our social imagination. This limited social imagination, far more than any book that could make its way into prisoners' hands, is what truly warrants fear.

Notes

1. Like their predecessors Slim and Goines, many contemporary urban fiction writers began by publishing their own books and marketing them on street corners, in clubs, and in barbershops and beauty salons. Large publishing houses that now sponsor urban fiction include Atria Books (Simon & Schuster), One World Books (Random House), Hachette Books (Warner Books), Griffin (St. Martin's Press), and Urban Books (Kensington).

2. Each woman chose a pseudonym to protect her privacy.
3. Nick Chiles, "Their Eyes Were Reading Smut," *New York Times,* January 4, 2006.
4. Vickie Stringer founded Triple Crown Publications in 2001. At the time of this writing, seven out of twenty-six authors sponsored by Triple Crown were incarcerated. Stringer explains that she publishes imprisoned authors' works "because being formerly incarcerated myself, I knew that no one else will do it." Angela Bronner, "The Queen behind Triple Crown: BV's '5 Questions' for Author Vickie Stringer," www.triplecrownpublications.com/data/publicity14.doc.
5. For more information about the history of reading and education in U.S. prisons, see Megan Sweeney, *Reading Is My Window: Books and the Art of Reading in Women's Prisons* (Chapel Hill: University of North Carolina Press, 2010).
6. Angelou's autobiography is on the list "because they say it's about child rape," says Ohio's chief librarian, but as she notes, the rape "is a very small part of the autobiography."
7. Although in 2006 African Americans represented only 12.8 percent of the U.S. population, black women accounted for 28 percent of all incarcerated women and were 3.1 times more likely to be incarcerated than white women. Bureau of Justice Statistics, "Prisoners in 2006," www.ojp.usdoj.gov/bjs/abstract/p06.htm. According to a 2007 study from the Pew Center on the States, one in one hundred black women between the ages of thirty-five and thirty-nine was behind bars, as opposed to one in 355 white women in that age group. Adam Liptak, "1 in 100 U.S. Adults behind Bars, New Study Says," *New York Times,* February 28, 2008.
8. Catherine Prendergast, *Literacy and Racial Justice: The Politics of Learning after* Brown v. Board of Education (Carbondale: Southern Illinois University Press, 2003), 37.
9. For further discussion of women prisoners' engagements with urban books, see Sweeney, *Reading Is My Window.*
10. For this portion of my research, I conducted 140 individual interviews and forty group conversations. Each individual interview lasted between forty-five minutes and two hours, and each group discussion lasted between ninety minutes and two hours.
11. Ien Ang, "Ethnography and Radical Contextualism in Audience Studies," in *The Audience and Its Landscape,* ed. James Hay, Lawrence Grossberg, and Ellen Wartella (Boulder: Westview Press, 1996), 255–56.
12. Claudia Tate, *Domestic Allegories of Political Desire: The Black Heroine's Text at the Turn of the Century* (New York: Oxford University Press, 1992), 6.
13. Shannon Holmes, *Bad Girlz* (New York: Atria, 2003), 170.
14. Danielle Santiago, *Grindin'* (New York: Atria, 2006), 161.
15. Sister Souljah, *The Coldest Winter Ever* (New York: Pocket Star Books, 1999), 201, 118, 354.
16. Santiago, *Grindin',* 178.
17. Ibid., 27, 101.
18. José Esteban Muñoz, *Disidentifications: Queers of Color and the Performance of Politics* (Minneapolis: University of Minnesota Press, 1999), 12.
19. Avery F. Gordon, *Keeping Good Time: Reflections on Knowledge, Power, and People* (Boulder: Paradigm Publishers, 2004), 60, 61.
20. Sara L. Knox, *Murder: A Tale of Modern American Life* (Durham: Duke University Press, 1998), 17.
21. Santiago, *Grindin',* 221.

7

PRODUCING MEANING THROUGH INTERACTION
Book Groups and the Social Context of Reading

Joan Bessman Taylor

As the book historian Robert Darnton has observed: "The inner experience of ordinary readers may always elude us. But we should at least be able to reconstruct a good deal of the social context of reading."[1] As established and recognizable reading communities, book discussion groups provide an access point into the social context of reading to which Darnton refers and also offer a means to uncover the often elusive reading practices of real rather than imagine ., implied, or ideal readers.[2] These group discussions provide elaboration of the act of reading, illustrating that the reading process must be conceptualized as a continuum of events beginning before a reader picks up the book and continuing long after one puts it down. Rather than a bounded, discrete activity that can be readily identified, quantified, and evaluated, reading is dynamic and prolonged, without an identifiable start or end. It is "embedded in cultural and political formations: collaborative, negotiated and partially determined by shared social practices and discourses."[3] For book group members, this continuum of reading includes aspects such as anticipation of reading, reflection on what has been read and one's experience of the process, discussion of these elements, and reflection on that discussion.

Whether carried out alone or in the context of a group, reading is inherently social. This premise underlies much of the sociological research on reading, work that formerly focused on literacy but shifted in the 1990s to a conceptualization of reading as a social practice.[4] A newer line of work, rooted in anthropology and sociolinguistics, sees reading as "an external, social act, performed by people in interaction and in a particular context."[5] As Paul Armstrong asserts: "Reading has a social, political dimension because we make sense of texts by forming hypotheses about meaning that emerge from the assumptions and conventions we bring from our other experiences with literature and life.

Those presuppositions, expectations, and habits of understanding are defining aspects of our existence as social beings. Reading is a social experience in which we find our beliefs and conventions engaged and challenged by our other ways of seeing, judging, and behaving."[6] Even prior to any reading event, "reading must be taught, and socialization into reading always takes place within specific social relationships."[7] Whether a person "stumbles" on a title (an act that, though seemingly serendipitous, is actually the product of collection development negotiations made by librarians, booksellers, or other providers), explicitly asks someone for a suggestion, queries a system (designed by someone with data collected from reader statistics, reviews, and so on), or is given a book by someone else, the very selection of a text to read involves interactions of a social nature.

In the case of book groups and their formalized discussions, the social dimensions of reading are more explicit and therefore more observable. In the analysis that follows, I aim to inform our general understanding of reading practices and to avoid dichotomizing reading as either solitary or collective. Recognizing that book groups privilege face-to-face and, increasingly, screen-to-screen discussion, I attend to the interpretive strategies specific to this kind of group book talk in an attempt to understand how discussion affects everything these readers do as part of membership—including but not limited to choosing books, taking notes, researching authors, and deciding whether or not to finish a book.

Context of the Research

My claims about contemporary reading and book discussion groups in this chapter are informed by five years of participant observation in six open-to-the-public adult recreational book groups reading varied works and meeting in public spaces in the midwestern United States. Five of the six groups made my active participation a condition of access, requiring me to read each month's selection and talk about it. Although Cover-to-Cover did not explicitly require me to participate fully, and its members were numerous and sufficiently vocal to permit a lurker comfortably, I did participate whenever possible. The sample was limited to six groups, as this was the maximum number I deemed manageable, given the groups' stipulations for attendance and my own requirement that meetings not conflict with one another. The groups selected included Cover-to-Cover, a group of mostly middle-aged white women focused on popular literary works; Table Talk, a group of black women focused on works by and about African Americans; the Science Fiction Group, a mostly male group reading works of science fiction and fantasy; the Normal Person's Book Discussion Group (NPBDG), a mixed-gender group with a focus on literary fiction; the Mystery Group, a group of middle-aged white women discussing popular mysteries; and the Great Books group, a mixed-gender, multigenerational group who followed the guidelines and Shared Inquiry Model of the Great Books Foundation in their reading of canonical texts. Cover-to-Cover and Table Talk met in public libraries, the Mystery Group in a chain bookstore, the Science Fiction Group in an independent bookstore, the NPBDG in campus meeting rooms of the local university, and Great Books at a local Baha'i center. As with all groups that are open to the public, attendance fluctuated somewhat, but each had a strong core membership of between four (Science Fiction Group) and twelve (Cover-to-Cover and Great Books). Meeting once a month from one to two hours, three of the groups met twelve months out of the year, and three (Great Books and the two library-run groups) met for ten months, breaking for two months in the summer.

Data were collected from October 2001 through August 2006 and derived from field notes spanning my attendance at 225 meetings, transcripts from a year of tape-recorded meetings of each group, group handouts, and e-mail correspondence. Using QSR NVivo software, I performed qualitative analysis using a combined methods approach. This included using the "start list" approach of Matthew Miles and A. Michael Huberman[8] and the constant comparative method of Barney Glaser and Anselm Strauss.[9] Initial coding of data was conducted with a start list of codes based on sensitizing concepts[10] garnered from my review of the related literature (including concepts said to exist, to be absent, and to need further investigation), group participation over time, and preliminary analysis conducted as part of my pilot study. The start list was revised as data were reviewed line by line and other categories were added. Data analysis proceeded through use of the constant comparative method and the processes of open and axial coding as described by Strauss and Juliet Corbin.[11] Ultimately categories were grouped into themes that provide the basis for my findings described here.

Discussibility

The significance of discussion is articulated through the notion of discussibility, a concept that pervades popular guides for reading groups in the

United States and the discourse commonly surrounding them, as well as the published international research on book group practices.[12] Though it is "something intuitively appreciated by certain booksellers,"[13] discussibility has not been explicitly defined beyond being that quality that makes a book well suited for fostering group discussion. Toward a definition, Elizabeth Long suggests: "To be 'discussible' a book must be interesting as well as good; otherwise, reading and talking about it will fall into the category of the onerous and unpleasurable 'shoulds' that reading groups . . . are anxious to avoid because they bury members' own desires under the pressure of an obligation to legitimate culture."[14] I unpack the notion of discussibility in work published elsewhere,[15] but for our purposes here it is useful to note a finding of Jenny Hartley's survey of over 250 book groups in the UK, in which she asked participants to list the books their groups had read together. She found that "quite a few books . . . distinguished themselves as crossovers, going well in some groups and badly in others."[16] Readers relate that they derive the most satisfaction from discussions of books with which they disagreed or were dissatisfied, or about which members disagreed with one another.[17] As one reader told me, if the book is "too succinct and too funny and too clear," then discussion becomes "a bit of a problem." This suggests that, more than just a feature of books, discussibility may be a precipitate of the mixing of particular books with particular readers.

My fieldwork indicates that when a group finds a book to be well written, thorough, and/or unanimously well liked by its members, the discussion about it is dominated by one form of talk, what I call "reading as dissection." When it is disliked by some or is perceived as having gaps or flaws in its structure or content, another type of discussion takes precedence, which I call "reading as creation." Each of these forms of discussion reveals activities and processes that are often elided and thereby obscured when we refer to them singularly and collectively as "the act of reading."

Reading as Dissection or Creation

It was in reading as dissection that the material book was paid the most attention, though this represented only the minority of discussions—or the smaller proportion of the discussion when both types occurred. In the meetings I observed, direct references to the book under discussion could be divided into two types: references to the cover, front matter (title page, frontispiece, copyright page, table of contents, acknowledgments), and back matter (references, information about the author); and references to the narrative content of the book. The first type of references constitutes discussion of what Gérard Genette has termed "paratexts." He describes the paratext as being "a zone between text and off-text, a zone not only of transition but also of *transaction*," and presents these features as elements of "influence on the public, an influence that—whether well or poorly understood and achieved—is at the service of a better reception for the text."[18] This transactional power of paratexts was apparent, for instance, in the NPBDG's discussion of *The Puttermesser Papers* by Cynthia Ozick. Though the main title of the book calls it "Papers," its subtitle and the publisher's data identify the book as "A Novel." When the NPBDG examined the copyright page, this revealed yet another identity for the work: several of the chapters had been previously published as short stories. The readers then turned to the "About the Author" section for clues as to what genre Ozick usually publishes in. Reading that she had won four O. Henry first prizes, the group recognized her as primarily a writer of short stories. Through analysis of the book's paratextual elements, these readers were able to situate the book, a necessary condition for their making sense of it. In so doing, they provide substance to Karin Littau's claims that "it is as impossible to disengage the materiality of a text from its meaning as a work as it is to disengage the understanding of a work from the physical forms in which we receive it."[19] Ultimately the unusual format of the work was cited as part of its appeal.

Readers generally talked about the book from memory, or occasionally from notes, but opened and referred to the physical book itself in only a few circumstances. Most direct quoting occurred when there was confusion about the events or chronology of the story, such as when the members of Table Talk tried to determine if the letters featured in the climax of Walter Mosley's novel *The Man in My Basement* were intended by the main character to be mailed, or whether he knew they would never be sent. Recognizing that a difference of intention would alter the outcome of the plot, the women returned to the book for elucidation.

Other references to the material book occurred when readers agreed on having enjoyed the book and, having little else to say about it other than "Isn't this passage great?" wanted to pick apart the devices used to achieve such a result. This tendency to return to the actual language of the work in instances of evaluation is not exclusive to the groups in this study but is corroborated in more recently conducted work.[20] The material book was also consulted when such discussion was part of a group's standard repertoire of inquiry, for example, the Science Fiction Group's standing question "Is the title appropriate?"

and the Great Books group's monthly use of the Shared Inquiry Model's question "Where in the text did you find support for that?" In each of these cases, direct consultation with the material book assisted the readers in appreciating or trying to comprehend what the author had accomplished, or in helping them evaluate the attempts of cultural authorities such as reviewers and publishers to influence the perspectives or tastes of readers. These meetings became a stringing together of quotes with members taking turns reading their favorite passages or those passages that helped clarify matters such as the book's chronology.

Reading as Creation of the Ideal Text

Although group members spent some time addressing the material aspects of the book they were discussing, and did on occasion quote directly from it, these were not the activities that appeared to be the most significant in the book group discussions I witnessed. The majority of the groups' time in meetings was spent in creative processes: discussing the ways the book could have been different, talking about what members would have preferred to have had included, and identifying gaps in the narrative. Borrowing from Jasper Fforde's novel *Lost in a Good Book*, the Science Fiction Group in my study even gave these gaps a name—"bloopholes"—which, according to the novel, is a "term used to describe a narrative hole [left] by the author that renders his/her work seemingly impossible."[21] Through the process of filling in what the author did not, or making suggestions for features that would make a book better, readers shared ideas about how to bring the work closer to their ideal, usually advocating for fuller character development and more closure on the major issues or conflicts presented. In this manner they embodied and extended Richard Gerrig's description of the act of reading as performative: "The task of the reader is much like the task of the actor. . . . They [readers] must use their own experiences of the world to bridge gaps in texts. They must bring both facts and emotions to bear on the construction of the world of the text."[22] Observing them creating the text they wished they had read— the ideal text—I termed this practice "reading as creation." In an instance of self-reflection, during the discussion of Elizabeth Moon's *Trading in Danger*, one reader described his contribution to this process. "I'm just spewing fan fiction," he observed. "There's nothing in there that says any of this."

The product of these reading interactions is not a tangible, reproducible item. This ideal text is, to borrow Wolfgang Iser's phrasing, "virtual in character" and indeed derives its dynamism from this very virtuality.[23] I draw on Iser here because his conceptualization of reading provides a starting point—albeit a limited one—for thinking about reading as creative and performative. He describes reading as the interaction between the text and the reader, as an interaction between partners in a communication process. Iser's reference to communication is an ostensible acknowledgment that social forces play a role in reading, yet this is constrained by both his assumption that a reader functions individually—somehow outside of what Elizabeth Long calls "the social infrastructure of reading,"[24] necessary for any reading to occur—and his assertion that reading differs from "all forms of social interaction" in that "with reading there is no face-to-face situation."[25]

Discussions between members of a reading community are, often literally, face-to-face situations, but they also make tangible those unformulated deliberations that are the result of any reader's existence as a social being inevitably influenced by the coexistence of others. These deliberations include interpretations based on personal values that are shaped by societal values and also matters of taste that, as Pierre Bourdieu has demonstrated, are socially conditioned. Meanings derived from books are in part learned responses, as vocabulary and strategies for comprehension are taught to us from an early age and perpetuated by participation in interpretive communities; but they are also reactive in that they incorporate rejection or acceptance of the ideas of others. In this way readers, both present and dispersed, direct interpretation. Although Iser attributes to the reader some interpretive power, he grants the text an even greater degree of sway over the creation of meaning. In Iser's estimation, it is solely the gaps or blanks in the text that serve as catalysts for making meaning. During their discussions, book groups recognize the text's role in meaning production but also demonstrate that the illumination, creation, and resolution of gaps in meaning can come about through other readers, both real and imagined.[26] It is from this dynamism that is the ideal text—virtual in that it is not formalized in writing but real in its effect—becomes observable through the interactions of readers. This dynamism was apparent when the participants in my study recognized the possibilities for the content and shape of works, even when this recognition resulted not from what they had read but from what they imagined. This recognition in turn transformed their expectations for reading.[27]

Roland Barthes maintains that we gain access to the ideal text "by several entrances, none of which can be authoritatively declared to be the main one . . . based as it is on the infinity of language."[28] He describes the networks of an ideal text as "many" and "indeterminable." Through analysis of my collected data and participation in meetings over time, I have recognized a range of "entrances" or ways of gaining access to a text's meanings that figure into the realization of the ideal text. These strategies illuminate the ways in which readers make sense of what they read through negotiation with one another. This negotiation goes beyond what Daniel Allington and Bethan Benwell in chapter 11 of this volume describe as the process of creating "consensus"—of readers changing their interpretations relative to the responses of the group's members and ultimately selecting meaning from the already voiced "group acceptable interpretations"—to the initiation of another meaning altogether. My prolonged exposure to group talk suggests that attributing any interpretation to a single book group reader or individual speech act is overly simplistic in that the group and its dynamic deliberations and protocols have influenced the reading before it was even conducted. The cumulative context and the confluence of ideas within group discussions over time produce new, previously unarticulated meanings that unite in unanticipated ways. (Indeed the text referred to in subsequent discussions will not be the one that readers currently hold in hand.) And though, as Barthes states, the "number of systems of meaning . . . is never closed,"[29] I have witnessed three aspects of the kind of discussion that contributes to the creation of the ideal text emerging with particular frequency. These are (1) an assessment of the degree of prior knowledge readers feel they have been expected to bring to a work, (2) an analysis of the material aspects of the book, and (3) the identification and filling in of gaps in the narrative or development of a work.

Prior Knowledge

My observation revealed that a major factor in a group's creation of the ideal text was the perception of the author's expectation of prior knowledge on the part of the reader. Readers were, for example, confronted with concepts or ideas that were not explained but that they felt they were assumed to know in order to engage with a work. This requirement of prior knowledge included facts and social situations, but also knowledge of other written works. Sometimes group members were pleased at being credited with extensive or specialized knowledge in an area; sometimes they felt insulted by the assumption that they were ignorant about a particular topic; and at other times they became frustrated by the expectation that they would have expert knowledge beyond what was provided in the book.

This frustration generated by the requirement of prior knowledge is illustrated by a discussion in which several members of the Science Fiction Group criticized author Larry Niven for not explaining some of the complex scientific concepts on which the plot of his *Ringworld's Children* relies. One member summed this up, saying: "You have to understand gravity, you have to understand centrifugal force, you have to understand magnetics, you have to understand light speed. There's a lot of fundamental scientific principles that if you don't get the fundamentals off the top of your head, Niven isn't going to explain them." This lack of explanation left some members of the group feeling as though they had missed out on much of the work's potential. In addition to the need for knowledge about facts, readers sometimes found that they were better able to understand a plot or a character's motivation if they had read other works by the same author. Similarly, they sometimes recognized that there was an implied expectation in the content—or lack of content—in a work they had read in comparison to works by other authors writing in the genre or dealing with similar themes. With series books this reliance on intertextuality is not surprising, as familiarity with characters over time is a long-recognized factor in the appeal of such works.[30] Much of the discussion surrounding *Ringworld's Children* became a tying together of information gathered from the series as a whole and a comparison of Niven's concepts to those of other science fiction writers. For example, when I asked if Niven's "Known Space" was the largest world we know of in science fiction, the Science Fiction Group reminded me of a book we had read previously by Stephen Baxter describing a Dyson sphere. Combining what they recalled of the dimensions of it with their recollections of the universe in Arthur C. Clarke's novels, they began to estimate how large the Ringworld was in comparison. Determining the size of the universe described by Niven required readers to have knowledge not only of his work but also of works by other authors. In this way, construction of the ideal text can sometimes involve a confluence of multiple works from within a subgenre.

Hans Robert Jauss has articulated this materialization of author expectations and assumptions as the shaping of the "horizon of expectations": "A literary work . . . does not present itself as something absolutely new . . . but predisposes its audience to a very specific kind of reception by announcements, overt and covert signals, familiar characteristics, or implicit allusions. It awakens memories of that which was already read, brings the reader to a specific emotional attitude, and with its beginning arouses expectations for the 'middle and end,' which can then be maintained intact or altered, reoriented, or even fulfilled ironically in the course of the reading according to specific rules of the genre."[31] Readers did, as Jauss describes, invoke their prior reading experiences to help supplement their understanding of the work under discussion. Their familiarity with other works by the same author or by different authors helped them confront a work and provided them with ideas about the boundaries of what was possible for the work at hand. Even with series books, however, the assumption of prior knowledge was sometimes disruptive or disappointing, usually because of a difference between what was revealed in the books when read in the order in which they were written and what the reader felt expected to know. In reference to Valerie Malmont's novel *Death, Snow, and Mistletoe,* one member of the Mystery Group described this phenomenon, saying: "It doesn't stand alone. It suffers from the typical mystery problem in that it assumes you've read the other books."

Just as authorial expectations of readers can sometimes be inferred from texts, readers' expectations of authors are often revealed through discussion. Book group members make these an explicit facet of meaning production, voicing them prior to reading during the book selection process (determining the potential discussibility of a book) and through their inclusion of standard discussion questions asked each month, such as "Was the book what you expected?" This question and others similar to it provide the catalyst for the reading event that follows. For instance, in response to Stephen King's novel *The Eye of the Dragon,* one reader answered the question: "No. I expected Peter to get out of the castle, raise an army, and come back and kick some butt. I wanted Peter to prove he was innocent." In this case, as in many others, thwarted expectations lead to consideration of other directions the book could have taken. Examining what they anticipated would happen over the course of reading allows readers to reflect on reading in a way that makes for dynamic discussion in which other readers who have experienced the same work can compare ideas and generate new ones. The tension between author expectations and reader expectations could be debilitating but instead serves as a medium for creativity. In this way, readers are not predisposed to "a very specific kind of reception" following the leads embedded in the literary work but are instead "resisting readers,"[32] creating a new (if not always an oppositional) reading of the book. Each reading does not remain a "discrete exercise," as has been claimed of book group reading,[33] but rather evidences an accumulation of experience.

The Material Aspects of the Book

The second major characteristic emerging from discussions around the creation of the ideal text involved critiquing material aspects such as the length of a book, and suggesting tools to assist the reader in the process of interpretation. Just as readers discussed material aspects of a book as part of what I have called reading as dissection, they also did so when talking about the version of the book they wished they had read in place of the one they did read. In this case, however, this included expressing a wish for changes to a book's physical dimensions or for features not already present. Sometimes disappointment was expressed over the book's length—that it was either too short or too long—suggesting dissatisfaction with characterization, plot development, or the inclusion of unnecessary details burdening the reader's experience of the work. At other times readers evinced the desire, often related to issues of length, for the inclusion of particular attributes missing from the book.

In every book group discussion I attended, the book's length was a topic of conversation. This attention groups paid to length is particularly interesting, given that it is an aspect rarely mentioned in book reviewing sources, especially in the case of fiction works. On occasion the number of pages is listed as part of a book's citation in the heading of a review, but elaboration on the relationship of length to reading experience is rare. And yet discussion of a book's length—both its actual length and whether or not it felt long to read, expressed through comments such as "It was a quick read" or "It seemed to go on forever"—was often the icebreaker that got the conversation going. Groups were careful when selecting books over three hundred pages, as they recognized that to finish a long book in time for the discussion sometimes required special scheduling, given members' busy lives. Some readers belonged to multiple book groups and so had to budget their reading time accordingly.

As Ellen Moore and Kira Stevens describe in their "demands for a fantastic book group book," a "great book group book is neither too long for what it has to say, nor so short that you get teased but not satisfied."[34] These standards are, of course, relative. As I considered the issue of book length while conducting observations, I was struck by how clearly readers described their personal requirements in this respect. Given the expectation that members must read the book in a limited time, and that some people read faster than others, I expected that some readers would always prefer shorter books over longer ones, but this was not the case. Sometimes the same person who complained about a book's being too long one month commented that the next month's selection would have benefited from being longer.

The reaction of one group, the NPBDG, to two books of approximately equal length offers an interesting case in point. *The Time of Our Singing* by Richard Powers and *The Amazing Adventures of Kavalier and Clay* by Michael Chabon are roughly equal in length. The former runs 631 pages and the latter 656 pages. Despite enjoying Powers's book, some members of the group responded negatively to its length, saying, "This one could've been shorter" and "He has so many ideas in his head and he cannot seem to bring himself to not give us every one of them. . . . This man needs an editor." They liked the book yet were simultaneously annoyed by it, agreeing that some parts could have been omitted without the plot suffering. Though they found Powers's writing to be beautiful, they resented being bombarded with details they considered unimportant while being expected to remember fundamental information that was mentioned only once. Because it was so easy to lose track of key details, one reader even suggested that using CliffsNotes alongside the book would make it more enjoyable, even though this would mean additional reading. Similarly, another reader remarked that she "would have liked an annotated version" of the book that elaborated on the music referred to throughout the novel, especially the operas alluded to in chapter titles. Another reader expressed surprise at the lack of a standard paratextual element, a chapter listing at the beginning of the book, since the chapter titles provided within the book seemed intended to escort the reader through the detailed narrative. The ideal text for these readers would have included reminders or signposts throughout the narrative of what had happened earlier on and further explication of the subject providing the book's setting.

The discussion of Chabon's book had a very different tenor from that of Powers's. One reader stated after reading *Amazing Adventures* that Chabon was "right now at the top of my list as best writers in the world. . . . I think he's a great writer. When you read it there was nothing that went clunk, you know? When you read it, it is all right." This reader nonetheless agreed with the group that the ending of the book was somewhat disappointing. Rather than resenting the fact that the book was long, however, this group determined that for it to be ideal, it could actually have been longer, in fact twice as long. One reader remarked, "It could have gone on another six hundred pages." Another wanted answers: "I guess I am just surprised that Joe is living in the end, you know what I mean? He had such a burden of guilt. It seems like, how is he going to keep going? Is that suddenly all resolved for him?" Here the desire is for resolution of some of the aspects of the book left unaddressed rather than for parts of the book to be excised, as was the case with *The Time of Our Singing*.

During my years as a participant observer of book groups, I often heard readers express the sentiment that if an author includes a character, he or she should be developed fully. For the participants in my study, and for many of the readers described in other researchers' work, it is character development that allows readers to engage with a story and to care about what happens in it. This does not mean that the characters have to be likeable, just that they have to be sufficiently developed for readers to be able to believe that they could exist in the real world. As Sharon from the Cover-to-Cover group put it: "Depending on how long the book is, if I get thirty or forty pages into it and I discover I don't care what happens to these characters, then I don't go any further with it. I have to care. The characters have to be described well enough. I have to care what happens to them."[35]

In addition to commenting on the length of a book—and regardless of whether a work is fiction or nonfiction—readers often propose additional features that would enable them to derive more meaning from the book. During the discussion of Monica Ali's *Brick Lane,* for example, Jerry shared his "cheat sheet of character names and who everyone was" with the group to help stimulate discussion. Similarly, while discussing Octavia Butler's *Parable of the Sower,* Diana remarked that the author would have served the reader better if she had included an appendix of the scriptures referred to throughout the novel. Other tools created or proposed by the readers I observed included timelines of events, family trees, glossaries, maps, and photographs. Part of the creation of the ideal text, then, is the collaborative development of such tools. Whether in real time during discussion, or prior to the monthly meeting in anticipation of discussion and with the group's needs in mind, the conceptualizing of these tools exemplifies the social nature of reading.

Filling in Gaps or "Bloopholes"

The third important aspect contributing to the creation of the ideal text involved readers identifying gaps or "bloopholes" in a work. Iser describes individual reading as a filling in of gaps, and a similar process can be seen to occur when works are brought before a group for discussion. When reading for pleasure, the readers I observed found some of the gaps in a work's plot distracting or disruptive, but these same gaps became seeds for negotiating options, for improvising, and for creative flights of fancy within the group context. During discussion, readers supplemented the work under consideration by filling in these gaps with details from their own life experiences or their interactions with others in order to gain a better understanding of aspects of the narrative such as character motivation.

Many plot gaps were viewed by the readers in my study as the result of insufficiently developed characterization. Readers wanted to know where characters were coming from, so to speak, and when they were not provided with this information in the work, they collectively supplied it themselves. Members of the Mystery Group often filled in information that would explain how or why a character was able to do the heinous things he or she did, such as how a serial killer could lack a conscience and kill repeatedly. They wanted details about a character's history or psychology that were rarely present in the work. The Table Talk group often interpreted negative character actions as the result of breakdowns in the family structure or as the consequence of an individual's being subjected over time to racial prejudice. On one occasion when the NPBDG was trying to make sense of a character's detachment from other people, suggestions were made that he "just wasn't a social person" or that "maybe he's got Alzheimer's, you could almost see that." The group members looked to the text for cues but still needed elaboration of their own in order to find the explanation they sought. For each of the groups, the identification of gaps often resulted in discussions about ethics.

Returning once again to the Science Fiction Group's discussion of *Ringworld's Children* provides evidence of the ethical considerations engaged in by readers. One member asked the group: "Were you appalled by the use of antimatter to blow a big chunk in the Ringworld? You know, you're the admiral of the fleet and we've got three people in there. Let's blow a hole in Ringworld. We know we might kill a billion people but just go ahead and screw 'em. I'll be the greatest single genocidal maniac in history." A second member, trying to understand why the admiral, in an effort to retrieve three crewmen, would consider actions that might destroy countless people and an entire world in the process, proposes: "They'd rather blow it up than let the Kzin or the Trinocs or anybody else get a hold of it. . . . They are in a system fighting each other to make sure nobody else can get to the Ringworld." Building on what was present in the work, this reader extended the known details to arrive at a logical explanation for events.

Table Talk's discussion of *The Known World* by Edward P. Jones evidences another instance in which interpretive strategies led to ethical considerations. As the group commented on the repeated and euphemistic references to masturbation in the book, the members tried to understand its role in the plot and why the main character engages in the taboo act. One reader sparked conversation with her statement "I was wondering if he did that so that he wouldn't sleep with his wife. Because he didn't want to have more children. . . . He didn't want to have more children to be born into the same cycle of slavery." The gap in the story provided an opening for these readers to empathize with a character they otherwise disliked, and to grapple with how African Americans could themselves have become slave owners.

Sometimes "bloopholes" were not filled in but were noted and discussed, leaving each individual member to embrace multiple possibilities. These sometimes extended beyond the timeframe or plot of the book, or took the shape of relating the book's events to real-life situations. For instance, during the discussion of *The Terminal Experiment* by Robert J. Sawyer, one reader asked, "If the soulwave were found to exist, do you think it would affect your behavior or change the behavior of humanity in general?" The group then proceeded to speculate on what it would mean if animals were known to have a soul, why those in the novel thought it was at ten weeks that the fetus gets a "soulwave," and the implications that such an occurrence would have in our culture for political positions on abortion. Ultimately, members observed that the book did not draw conclusions about anything, a situation that permitted those reading it to entertain their own conclusions.

The back-and-forth interaction between what is written on the page and what readers find there is mediated and negotiated by extending the process beyond that of a single reader's experience. With book group reading, multiple meanings and interpretations as well as varied creative adaptations intermingle to become the ideal text. The ideal text cannot be quantified or outlined but is fluid and constantly evolving. It does, however, have substance in that it influences future book group discussions. After its ideation, it becomes a factor in the range of possibilities to which other works are compared. That is, the ideal text influences decisions regarding the discussibility of other works considered for book group focus as well as judgments about the success or quality of any given work. Book groups make tangible the fact that it is not just recorded texts that figure in the horizon of expectations and not just the values of society as a whole within any given historical moment that provide the criteria by which books are judged. The horizon of expectations includes the virtual texts that emerge through interaction—both face-to-face and among members of an imagined community of readers. Through their interactions with the selected book and with one another during discussion, book groups give substance to Barthes's assertion that "the Text is experienced only in an activity of production" and that it is a "social space."[36] This dynamic endeavor—reading as creation—makes tangible the social aspects inherent in all reading and transforms our understanding of where the act of reading begins and ends.

Notes

1. Robert Darnton, "What Is the History of Books?" in *Reading in America: Literature and Social History,* ed. Cathy N. Davidson (Baltimore: Johns Hopkins University Press, 1989), 45.
2. See Robert Darnton, "Key Concepts," in *Readers and Reading,* ed. Andrew Bennett (New York: Longman, 1995), 235–40.
3. Bethan Benwell, "'A Pathetic and Racist and Awful Character': Ethnomethodological Approaches to the Reception of Diasporic Fiction," *Language and Literature* 18 (2009): 309.
4. Wendy Griswold, Terry McDonnell, and Nathan Wright, "Reading and the Reading Class in the Twenty-first Century," *Annual Review of Sociology* 31 (2005): 132.
5. Meredith Rogers Cherland, *Private Practices: Girls Reading Fiction and Constructing Identity* (London: Taylor & Francis, 1994), 5.
6. Paul B. Armstrong, *Play and the Politics of Reading* (Ithaca: Cornell University Press, 2005), ix.
7. Elizabeth Long, *Book Clubs: Women and the Uses of Reading in Everyday Life* (Chicago: University of Chicago Press, 2003), 8–9.
8. Matthew B. Miles and A. Michael Huberman, *Qualitative Data Analysis: An Expanded Sourcebook* (Thousand Oaks, Calif.: Sage, 1994), 50–89.
9. Barney G. Glaser and Anselm L. Strauss, *The Discovery of Grounded Theory: Strategies for Qualitative Research* (Chicago: Aldine Publishing Company, 1967), 45–78, 101–16.
10. Herbert Blumer, "What Is Wrong with Social Theory?" *Symbolic Interactionism: Perspective and Method* (Englewood Cliffs, N.J.: Prentice-Hall, 1969), 140–52.
11. Anselm Strauss and Juliet Corbin, *Basics of Qualitative Research: Techniques and Procedures for Developing Grounded Theory* (Thousand Oaks, Calif.: Sage, 1998), 101–42.
12. Two examples among many guides include Ellen Moore and Kira Stevens, *Good Books Lately: The One-Stop Resource for Book Groups and Other Greedy Readers* (New York: St. Martin's Press, 2004); and Pat Neblett, *Circles of Sisterhood: A Book Discussion Guide for Women of Color* (New York: Harlem River Press, 1997).
13. DeNel Rehberg Sedo, "Badges of Wisdom, Spaces for Being: A Study of Contemporary Women's Book Clubs" (Ph.D. diss., Simon Fraser University, 2009), 233.
14. Long, *Book Clubs,* 123.
15. See Joan Bessman Taylor, "When Adults Talk in Circles: Book Groups and Contemporary Reading Practices" (Ph.D. diss., University of Illinois at Urbana–Champaign, 2007), and "Good for What? Nonappeal, Discussibility and Book Groups (Part 2)," *Reference and User Services Quarterly* 47.1 (2007): 26–31.
16. Jenny Hartley, *Reading Groups* (Oxford: Oxford University Press, 2001), 66.
17. Many personal accounts are included in Ellen Slezak, ed., *The Book Group Book: A Thoughtful Guide to Forming and Enjoying a Stimulating Book Discussion Group* (Chicago: Chicago Review Press, 1995).
18. Gérard Genette, introduction to *Paratexts: Thresholds of Interpretation* (Cambridge: Cambridge University Press, 1997), 2.
19. Karin Littau, *Theories of Reading: Books, Bodies and Bibliomania* (Cambridge: Polity, 2006), 29.
20. Joan Swann and Daniel Allington, "Reading Groups and the Language of Literary Texts: A Case Study in Social Reading," *Language and Literature* 18 (2009), 254.

21. Jasper Fforde, *Lost in a Good Book* (New York: Penguin, 2004), 298.
22. Richard J. Gerrig, *Experiencing Narrative Worlds* (New Haven: Yale University Press, 1993), 17.
23. Wolfgang Iser, "Interaction between Text and Reader," in Bennett, *Readers and Reading*, 21.
24. Long, *Book Clubs*, 8.
25. Iser, "Interaction between Text and Reader," 22.
26. I use "imagined" here in a manner inspired by Benedict Anderson's description of imagined communities in *Imagined Communities: Reflections on the Origin and Spread of Nationalism* (Verso: London, 1983), 6. I mean to imply that readers are consciously and subconsciously aware of and influenced by other readers and reading practices even if they do not personally know them.
27. This change of expectations was most obvious when readers discussed possible choices of books for future group focus, in particular in their deliberations about whether a book would be discussible.
28. Roland Barthes, *S/Z* (New York: Farrar, Straus & Giroux, 1974), 5.
29. Ibid., 6.
30. Joyce G. Saricks, *Readers' Advisory Service in the Public Library* (Chicago: ALA Editions, 2005), 50–55.
31. Hans Robert Jauss, *Toward an Aesthetic of Reception,* trans. Timothy Bahti (Minneapolis: University of Minnesota Press, 1982).
32. Judith Fetterley, *The Resisting Reader: A Feminist Approach to American Fiction* (Bloomington: Indiana University Press, 1988).
33. Jane M. Barstow, "Reading in Groups: Women's Clubs and College Literature Classes," *Publishing Research Quarterly* 18.4 (2003): 7.
34. Moore and Stevens, *Good Books Lately,* 225.
35. Personal interview, November 25, 2001.
36. Roland Barthes, *Image-Music-Text,* trans. Stephen Heath (New York: Farrar, Straus and Giroux, 1977), 164.

8

GENRE IN THE MARKETPLACE
The Scene of Bookselling in Canada

Julie Rak

In a collection about reading, it might seem odd to discuss something that at first glance is not about reading at all: the culture of bookstores and the kinds of information they codify and embody. But before a book can be read, it must be acquired in some fashion. There are many ways to get books into the hands of readers. For example, they can be given as gifts, awarded as prizes, borrowed from libraries, or even stolen. But at some point in the journey to readers, a book must be bought and sold like any other commodity, and unless it is bought directly from a publisher, it must be purchased from a bookstore, online retailer, or other type of retailer. Although most people who understand themselves to be readers do not think of their books as commodities, and many academics who study books—with the notable exception of book historians and publishing historians—do not think very much about the material circumstances of book acquisition, the scene of bookselling is closely linked to the reading cycle. But so far, little research has been conducted into the role of the contemporary bookstore in getting books to readers, and none at all has been carried out about the role that genre, and generic categorization, plays in organizing knowledge for readers in bookstores. Like reading itself, bookstores have cultures, and they aim to encourage the production of certain kinds of reading subjects who want to read (and purchase) books. In this essay I argue that at the heart of this transaction between potential readers and booksellers is an understanding of genre as a form of social production that organizes knowledge in the bookstore and determines how books make their sojourn from writers to publishers to sellers, and finally to readers.

Why Genre Matters

What is genre, and why does it matter? Originally "genre" signified the organization of information into types or kinds. This led to an understanding of any genre as static, or as a closed system, with classification as its method.[1] The classic understanding of genre as taxonomic and a matter of "pure" classification, particularly in literary studies, has been challenged by theorists in the fields of rhetoric and composition.[2] Genre, these theorists claim, is intimately involved in making social life possible. To understand genre better as a social force in its own right, we can treat it as what Pierre Bourdieu would call a method of "position taking" in the cultural field,[3] a way of organizing knowledge which has the effect of producing knowledge in its effort to organize it. This act of generic classification has at its heart an ideology of ordering which tries to make its own subjects as individuals interact with institutions, in what Charles Bazerman calls the expectations of "communicative social space" that are found in any use of genre.[4] This kind of approach requires a return to a study of genre, not as an aesthetic category but as an important part of the production of meaning in culture. As Nick Lacey has pointed out, genre "is of little use critically but of great use in 'common sense' terms, which is how mass audiences use the concept."[5] Scholars who use what Richard Coe and others have called "the new genre theories"[6] have made use of Mikhail Bakhtin's work on speech genres to argue that genre is part of every social process,[7] and that genre structures the terms of engagement for spoken and written utterances. In the field of information sciences, Geoffrey Bowker and Susan Starr characterize "genre systems" (which they understand as the complex interaction of multiple genres) as encompassing many levels of the act of classification, including the making of lists and other types of codification practices.[8]

Following the lead of theorists who see genres governing many types of social interaction while simultaneously functioning as examples of classification, I understand the role of genre in bookstores to be *scene-setting*, because genres within the physical space of bookstores both set limits and create possibilities for knowledge transmission. In the case of reading, bookstores represent one kind of setting where the opening act of reading can take place. Since readers come to bookstores to get certain kinds of knowledge, to experience the physicality of a book in terms of its feel, look, or smell, or even just to talk to or be with other people who like books, genres organize those experiences for readers and show them what kinds of things might be useful for them to know as well as which books to buy. Genre offers, in the words of Janet Giltrow, "background knowledge" about any text or event which forms a type of agreement between the producer or receiver of utterances that is mutual and unspoken.[9] In doing this, genres provide a type of grammar that does far more than merely organize books on shelves. Genres, often without the knowledge of people who use them every day, structure the culture of bookstores and become the first part of the social nature of reading within what is most often a capitalist framework of marketplace transaction.[10] As Amy Devitt says in *Writing Genres:* "Genre pervades human lives. As people go about their business, interacting with others and trying to get along in the world, they use genres to ease their way, to meet expectations, to save time. People recognize genres, though not usually the power of genres."[11]

Genres are also, however, part of practices that form the heart of the Foucauldian power/knowledge nexus within the context of everyday activity: "In a society such as ours . . . there are manifold relations of power that permeate, characterize and constitute the social body, and these relations of power cannot themselves be established, consolidated nor implemented without the production, accumulation, circulation and functioning of a discourse."[12] In other words, genres produce the conditions of power, even as they can be used to access certain types of power. Whereas Michel Foucault most often looked at the limits of epistemic knowledge formations in order to critique the redeployment of power within the status quo,[13] Carolyn Miller and other New Rhetorical theorists of genre have pointed out that genres can also be a type of social action that can form a counter-practice to the status quo, depending on how they are deployed. A genre *acts* in the world because its effects of restriction and allowance are spatial and temporal. As Miller has argued, genres exhibit "exigence," which is a "form of social knowledge—a mutual construing of objects, events, interests and purposes that not only links them but makes them what they are."[14]

Genre as Social (Bookstore) Action

In this study of Canadian bookstores following the entrance of Chapters Indigo—the largest bookstore chain in Canada—into the Canadian book market, I focus on the scene of bookselling as a way to think about genre as social action intimately connected with the ideologies of space and materiality within the context of global and local capitalist systems. For this study, I saw ideas about the "local" operating as strongly within independent bookstores as among independent publishers who see themselves as committed to a region or a constituency,[15] and I wanted to determine whether local conditions affected the role genre played in the organizational life of a particular store and of its staff. I also wanted to see how some independent bookstores handled books produced by large mainstream presses such as Random House and HarperCollins. In their catalogues and on the backs of their books, large presses provide classification rubrics such as "nonfiction" or "history," and I wanted to know whether independent stores followed this way of understanding genre taxonomically, or whether generic classifications were handled in some other manner.

I asked managers or buyers at eleven independent urban bookstores across Canada to talk about how they understood genre, or even nonfiction, as part of their everyday work practices.[16] I compared their responses to those in an interview I did with a manager of a large urban Chapters Indigo store, to see how a multinational bookstore chain treats issues connected to genre, and to investigate how, after the advent of Chapters and its widely decried gutting of the independent bookstore system, independents make use of genre as social action as they sell books.

During the course of these interviews, I found that the reorganization of generic types within the physical environment of independent stores forms part of a loose set of tactics that independent bookstores use in order to continue to do business in the wake of the arrival of big-box bookstores. These tactics include what I call "the web of classification" that independent bookstore managers and owners use to classify books by genre, place them in stores, and sell them to readers. Although large publishers clearly expect sellers to use the rubrics on the back of their books, not one independent bookseller I interviewed acknowledged using these. Instead, booksellers rely on their own readings of publishing catalogues, the opinions of trusted publishing representatives who point out which books will sell to the constituency of a particular bookstore, the opinions of staff members about which books should be shelved where in a store (sometimes determined collectively in meetings), and their own feelings about what kinds of books should be sold in their store and where they should be sold. In the case of difficult-to-categorize books, or books that seem to fit in many genres, staff will "cross-shelve" copies of a book in different sections, or will create new categories—such as "Armchair Travel" or "Graphic Novel"—to handle new kinds of books. I refer to this way of doing classification as a "web" because this strategy consists of numerous interconnected assumptions and considerations, many of which are cultural in the sense that independent stores have a "culture" that affects which books are sold there, and social in the sense that social norms help to create the categories of classification that independent store managers and owners use. This way of classifying and shelving books could be seen as a tactic in Michel de Certeau's sense,[17] an everyday response to the globalized book trade's attempt to standardize generic practices and ignore cultural specificity in the bookselling environment.

The web of classification is quite different from what I go on to demonstrate with the case of Chapters Indigo, which forms much more of a seamless rela-

GENRE IN THE MARKETPLACE

Figure 8.1. Bookmark II interior

tionship between the generic typologies used by large publishers and the generic classification systems that the chain uses in every one of its stores, without variation. In this sense, Chapters Indigo performs the social work of global classification and participates fully in the type of standardization that critics of globalization warn about. But the independent book trade's use of tactics shows that globalization has not eliminated the presence of small independent sellers in the Canadian book trade and, I suggest, will not be able to do so, since genres themselves are dynamic and notoriously difficult to fix for any length of time, despite the fact that fixity is one of their features. To provide a picture of my findings, I present here three case studies of stores in Canada which enact the spatial organization of genre in a variety of ways: Bookmark II in Halifax, Nova Scotia; the Toronto Women's Bookstore in Toronto, Ontario; and Chapters Indigo in Edmonton, Alberta.

Bookmark II, Halifax, Nova Scotia

This independent bookstore is a mainstay of street and intellectual life in the Halifax downtown core. At this writing there is no Chapters Indigo or Coles Books nearby, and the economic depression of the Maritimes means that there are not a lot of big-box stores around anyway. The exterior of the store features the store's name in rounded brown letters on a yellow background. The inside is what I consider a monument to generic classification (figure 8.1).

The entire store is painted bright yellow and is lit with fluorescent lights. There are no comfortable chairs and no area for children. As figure 8.1 shows, the wall supports have generic categories such as "Travel" or "Psychology" printed right on them in large letters, and opaque panels above the shelves repeat the categories. Center-aisle displays, shown in figure 8.2, also have classification markers on them, including what I will discuss as an educational juxtaposition: "Nonfiction" shares shelving with "True Crime."

The spatial organization of Bookmark II tells a story about the importance of genres and the importance of bookstores to genres themselves. This is not immediately obvious: even store manager Michael Hamm admits that he did not see how the spatial organization of the store was deliberate before he began to describe it himself.[18] But the arrangement of nonfiction sections such as "Politics," "Current Affairs," and "History" at the front indicates that Bookmark II sees the selling of nonfiction as central to its mandate. There are several reasons for this. Bookmark II forges very strong community affiliations with its customers in order to make a profit. Many of the customers were described by Hamm as politically left-wing, and so the store specializes in selling left-wing political books. It also sells books about local history and local issues to locals, although tourists from cruise ships also come to the store from the harbor and buy some of these books as well. Hamm made sure to tell me that this store is very different from what he called "a mall store," which he describes as more "family-driven and television-driven," in contrast to a "book review–driven" store like Bookmark II. Hamm made these remarks in discussing whether a book review, a reading event such as Canada Reads, or a television program creates the tie-ins that attract people to a store. Bookmark II's orientation toward book reviews means that its manager and staff see the store as catering to an intellectual clientele who love books and are fiercely devoted to the store's culture (and to the survival of independent bookstores). As Hamm says: "We're a small bookstore, so our success comes from community involvement. . . . [S]o when there's a segment of the population that is underrepresented, we see that as an opportunity for community involvement." This store's culture and its commitment to social justice in the community contribute to the decisions about generic classification that take place within it.

Since Bookmark II sees itself as a store that caters to intellectuals, it sells many kinds of nonfiction, particularly books with a left-wing take on current affairs, and it expects its customers to want these books, and to be able to find

GENRE IN THE MARKETPLACE [165]

Figure 8.2. "True Crime" and "Nonfiction"

them easily. Therefore, although the store's layout would not seem to encourage browsing, Hamm says that the location of sections encourages "flow" through the store from the front to the back, and the labels help customers get quickly to the books they need. Unlike in many stores, current affairs and political science rather than current fiction are shelved up front to signify their importance to the store's culture and customers. Science fiction and detective books, genres with dedicated fan cultures, are located at the back of the store, far away from the front desk, because those customers never need help from staff and will go only to those sections, ignoring all others. They are impervious to sales techniques. But the center aisles of the store tell a different story. Here is where books that are more difficult to classify are placed, near the front desk so that staff can help customers more easily. "Nonfiction," far from being generic in an academic sense, is presented in the store as the left-wing equivalent of "True Crime." That section, for instance, is where readers can find the story of Reena Virk, a teenage girl who was murdered in Vancouver during the 1990s by other teenage girls in a race-motivated crime. The section is also "double-faced," or shelved with "Biography," another catchall section. Although the field of biography studies sees biography as clearly generic and as separate from autobiography, it is significant that in the environment of this bookstore, "Biography" competes with "Political Memoir" and functions as a way to shelve life writing that is not about current events. According to Hamm, the store staff try to resolve dilemmas about where to put a book by cross-shelving, that is, placing multiple copies of biographies in the "Current Events" sections and then helping customers to make connections between events and lives. Here is a clear case of tactics, in which staff resolve a possible classification problem by using a provisional tactic.

The politics of genre also factors into the creation of new genres in the context of the community-based store culture. In an interesting community service move, Bookmark II created a separate section called "Queer Studies" in response to a GLBT (gay, lesbian, bisexual, transgendered) reading group which came in and asked for one. After some debate about whether it was a good idea not to "mainstream" books for this group of readers, Bookmark II created this classification and placed it in the store where these readers would feel, as Hamm says, "comfortable," even though he would rather shelve gay mysteries in the mystery section. In the case of Bookmark II, the staff do not make use of the generic labels on the back of books, and this disregard for how large publishers classify books means that segments of its community participate in generic decision making within the web of classification. In this respect, the store's success in its community does not serve the interests of multinational companies and how they want books to be marketed; the production of genre as a social phenomenon serves, in a small way, to disrupt global flows of information and capital.

The Toronto Women's Bookstore, Toronto, Ontario

Although a number of writers in the media have blamed the arrival of big-box generalist stores in the Canadian book market during the early 1990s for the disappearance of many independent bookstores, the advent of generalist stores is not necessarily seen as a problem by managers and owners whose stores were able to continue to do business in the new climate.[19] For specialty stores like the Toronto Women's Bookstore, specialization provides an opportunity to think differently about everything to do with running a business, including the classification of stock. In the case of this store, its chosen mandate as an outlet designed to encourage and promote the writing of women of color and writing by people dedicated to antiracist work has made it, in the words of its manager Kristen Hogan, "possibly the most successful feminist bookstore in North America."[20]

The Toronto Women's Bookstore sees reading as a political act which is central to social change. The store's sign and the first page on its website display this quotation by the African American feminist writer Alice Walker: "If a book doesn't make us better, then what on earth is it for?"[21] The store's organization reflects its commitment to alternative business practices: it is a nonprofit store governed by a board of directors rather than a small business that must turn a profit. The money made from selling books used for University of Toronto courses allows the staff to stock progressive titles—even when these do not make much money—and to run writing workshops and events for writers who are women of color.

The physical organization of the store also reflects its mandate and principles. Unlike any other store I saw, the Toronto Women's Bookstore does not divide its sections into fiction and nonfiction, a strategy confirmed by Hogan. The exceptions were the children's section, which contains a nonfiction area, and the "Canadian Nonfiction" section, although the latter does not contain solely nonfiction books. This is because, as Hogan said to me, women's experiences have often been treated as if they were fictional, and as a result, the store philosophy is that fiction has just as much power to change lives as nonfiction does. Accordingly, the sections are organized along the lines of identity politics, whereby fiction and nonfiction are shelved together. According to Hogan, this shelving practice also offsets the problem, found in feminism itself, of the whiteness within feminism which places the experiences—and writing—of women of color as a supplement. Classification still produces some problems, as in the dilemma over shelving Cherrie Moraga's writing: Does her work go in the "Chicana/Hispanic" section or into the "Lesbian" section? As at Bookmark II, problems like this are most often solved by cross-shelving books. At this store, shelving works as a tactic not only to get readers for books but also to educate readers about the politics of generic classification by shifting its boundaries. Here we can clearly see genre operating as social action, at the level of the store's organization itself.

Chapters Indigo, Whyte Avenue Store, Edmonton, Alberta

When Coles and Smithbooks merged to form Chapters Indigo, which opened big-box bookstores across Canada in 1995, it was widely believed that such stores caused the closure of independent stores in Canada. The existence of big-box chains has often been cited as a major reason for independent store closures.[22] Indigo Books and Music now owns Chapters, Classic Books, and the World's Biggest Bookstore. It is unsurprising that critics of the store openly voice their dislike of its status as Canada's only big-box bookstore chain, its commercial feel, and its lack of community involvement. One example of this type of criticism is a 2007 post on *The Torontoist* blog, of interest here because it takes Chapters Indigo to task for its lack of "intuitive" generic classification systems. According to the writer of *The Torontoist*, "the simple task of trying to find a book [at Chapters Indigo] is complicated and made more difficult by tables, displays, and towers of 'lifestyle' items that must be overcome before proceeding to an actual book section. Even then, though, the quest can become more tedious . . . [because of] the perpetually perplexing, arbitrary categorization system."[23]

As I have shown, classification systems can appear to be idiosyncratic in a store environment, but the difference here is that a Chapters Indigo store does *not* have a local culture because it is part of a chain. Its generic classifications therefore appear to be arbitrary to this writer, who expects bookstores to have local cultures. As a chain, however, Chapters manages its stores centrally, and so it can be seen as less like other bookstores and more like other kinds of retail stores. This is not necessarily how the staff at the store want to see Chapters Indigo. During my interview with Katherine Connaught, the assistant manager of a Chapters Indigo store on Whyte Avenue in Edmonton, she was careful to point out that there is some difference in the way Chapters stores order books. The Whyte Avenue area, Connaught said, is "artsy," and so there are more art books in the store than in a west end store, which has more tourists and so stocks more travel books. Different Chapters Indigo stores do try to respond to customer requests and do create new sections based on customers' requests. Furthermore, Connaught mentioned that even at a big-box store like Chapters Indigo, staff members work there because of their love for books, and not because books are retail items: "I don't find bookselling to be retail. I'm actually a hairdresser by trade [so I know what retail is]. I think it's different because retail-wide, people say they want to work in retail. But in bookstores, you're there because you want to sell books. . . . I think people get into it because they love reading, they love books." This attitude toward books and bookselling chimes with the views expressed by managers such as Michael Hamm and Kristen Hogan about why they love working in the book industry.

A look at generic classification at store level, however, does show that Chapters functions as a multinational chain which links much more seamlessly to the production of large mainstream publishers such as HarperCollins and Random House. The Chapters Indigo store on Whyte Avenue is large and well lit and features an escalator at its center. The ground floor contains best-sellers, magazines, and gift items, while the second floor hosts the coffee shop, music store, and books. Roughly half the books on the second floor are fiction. The nonfiction books are classified—Connaught used the phrase "broken up"— into dozens of subcategories, each with a "New and Hot" section. Chapters Indigo does not differentiate between mass market paperbacks, trade paperbacks, and hardbacks, with one exception. The section "Fiction and Literature," Connaught explained, was formerly called "Classics," and it included books that were not generically identifiable as science fiction, fantasy, horror, true crime, or mystery. This was the only time I saw evidence of generic decision making that did not simply adopt what large mainstream publishers said about their books.

Unlike any of the independent stores I visited, Chapters Indigo classifies and shelves its books according to the generic markers on the back cover of each book. Classification is managed through the store's sophisticated computer system, and permission from the head office must be sought if an individual store wishes to change its sections. Sections such as "Hot Nonfiction" are always located at the front of a store or on its first floor, and are always stocked with what the Toronto office says should be in the section. "Hot" always means best-selling. The store sells gifts, CDs, cards, and magazines in addition to books, and many stores feature a Starbucks coffee shop. Unlike the independent stores I visited, Chapters did not organize its store for customer flow, in part because each store attempts to follow the same layout. Books are carried unless they do not sell. Lower-volume sellers might be allowed to stay, but if they do not sell quickly or steadily, an argument must be made to the head office for their inclusion. The Chapters Indigo I visited does not generally sell what it calls "specialty" books—by which it means books by smaller presses—because it does not see itself competing with the independent retailers in the area. In fact, Connaught said, they often recommend that customers go to those stores "because they have a different clientele."

The ideology of classification at Chapters Indigo confirms its big-box structure, since it attempts to link its systems seamlessly with those of large publishers. It would be a mistake to say that Chapters caters exclusively to general readers who would never read books published by small Canadian presses— the poetry section does stock books from small presses, for example—and its manager did express some of the same idealized sentiments about books that echo the comments of independent store staff. The layout of the store, however, its centrally controlled management structure, and its treatment of books as retail items no different from other commodities found at big-box stores mean that the store does not participate in community life in the same way that independent stores do, and does not subscribe to the ideals of the book trade that the independent stores espouse in order to stay competitive. Chapters Indigo's treatment of genre as a transparent practice that generally does not require tactical management is clearly successful for many of those who shop at the store, but the hostility that supporters of independent bookstores have toward the chain shows that this form of generic classification actually works at the level of a *techne* that excludes groups of people who expect a different type of knowledge management at a bookstore.

What does the theory of genre as communicative action have to say about the acts of classification in each of these bookstores? First, it is clear that genre *does* matter to the environment of a bookstore. In the case of Bookmark II, the act of classifying nonfiction books and then placing them strategically within the store fits with an understanding of the store's clientele and culture. Here we see that something as "invisible" as the placement of books illustrates the importance of genres as part of everyday communicative life between people: they offer rules for how to live, how to "know" one's place socially, and how to act inside or outside a system. Moreover, often in an unnoticed way, genres set the rules for interaction, including who is allowed to be legitimately in a group, and who is not allowed to belong. The request made by the GLBT reading group for a separate section indicates that the group itself experienced exclusion because of generic choices, and its members decided to intervene at the level of systemic ordering rather than simply asking for more books that they wanted to read.

Kristen Hogan's comments about the Toronto Women's Bookstore indicate that generic choices—for instance, the decision made by the staff *not* to organize their store generically—are political and that classification systems do not work in ideologically neutral ways. Anne Freadman describes genres working in this way as "ceremonials," that is, as "games which situate other games" and determine how any symbolic interaction between different parties is to be carried out.[24] Genres therefore have much to tell us about discursive communities, including "what sorts of communication . . . a genre encourage[s]" and "who can—and who cannot—use this genre."[25] At the Toronto Women's Bookstore, the belief that women's lives have been treated as if they were fictional, and the belief that the politics of more commonly found generic ordering in stores can be racist, directly affect how books are categorized and shelved. Here we can see that genres not only structure what we know and how we know it but also work to exclude certain kinds of knowledge because in the terms of the system, that knowledge cannot even be transmitted or admitted.

Like Louis Althusser's good subjects, genres seem to "work all right by themselves" without our having to think much about them.[26] Nevertheless, the tendency of Devitt and other genre theorists to see genres as powerful but value neutral must be counterbalanced by Foucault's picture of the episteme as the quiet organizing of power/knowledge itself. The examples I provided—out of a total of eleven interviews—demonstrate the difference between the ways independent stores classify books without reference to publishers' categories and Chapters Indigo's close adherence to publisher classification systems. Canadian independent booksellers decide what *kinds* of books to order in keeping with their store culture and other factors unrelated to publishers' wishes, while Chapters Indigo, as a chain retailer, is much more closely aligned with mainstream publishers' generic classification of books. It will come as little surprise that Chapters Indigo was the store that did not make tactical use of classification, because as a big-box retailer it does not have a clear store "identity" that it uses to forge relationships with its customers. What was surprising to me was how the independent stores I visited managed to survive, and even thrive, by using classification as one tactic among many to create a counter-practice to big-box retailing and retain the community-centered feel of books and bookstores, which many readers seem to enjoy. Unlike other culture industries, bookselling attracts customers who often do *not* endorse big-box retailing and who actively wish to oppose the forces of globalization, even as they participate in what I call everyday capitalism. In some localities at least, genre as a social practice is used to bring books to readers, readers to books, and—these entrepreneurs hope—new and useful ideas to the people who need them.

Notes

This project was funded by a Standard Research Grant from the Social Sciences and Humanities Research Council, and by a Killam Operating Grant (University of Alberta). I thank Danielle Fuller, Laurie McNeill, and Daphne Read for their advice and support.

1. Amy Devitt, *Writing Genres* (Carbondale: Southern Illinois University Press, 2004), 6–7.
2. See Heather Dubrow's summary in chapter 4 of *Genre* (London: Methuen, 1982). Also see John Frow's discussion of the development of genre studies in *Genre* (New York: Routledge, 2006), 70–71; and David Duff's introduction to *Modern Genre Theory* (Harlow, UK: Longman, 2000), 8–19.
3. Pierre Bourdieu, "The Field of Cultural Production," in *The Field of Cultural Production: Essays on Art and Literature,* ed. Randal Johnson (Cambridge: Polity, 2000), 33–35.
4. Charles Bazerman, "Genre and Identity: Citizenship in the Age of the Internet and the Age of Global Capitalism," in *The Rhetoric and Ideology of Genre: Strategies for Stability*

and Change, ed. Richard M. Coe, Lorelei Lingard, and Tatiana Teslenko (Cresskill, N.J.: Hampton Press, 2001), 17.
5. Nick Lacey, *Narrative and Genre: Key Concepts in Media Studies* (New York: St Martin's Press, 2000), 212.
6. Richard M. Coe, Lorelei Lingard, and Tatiana Teslenko, "Genre as Action, Strategy, and *Différance*: An Introduction," in *The Rhetoric and Ideology of Genre*, 2–3.
7. Devitt, *Writing Genres*, 33–34; Frow, *Genre*, 12; Aviva Freedman and Peter Medway, "Locating Genre Studies: Antecedents and Prospects," in *Genre and the New Rhetoric*, ed. Freedman and Medway (London: Taylor & Francis, 1994), 1.
8. Geoffrey C. Bowker and Susan Leigh Starr, *Sorting Things Out: Classification and Its Consequences* (Cambridge: MIT Press, 1999), 138.
9. Janet Giltrow, "Genre and the Pragmatic Concept of Background Knowledge," in Freedman and Medway, *Genre and the New Rhetoric*, 155.
10. Libraries also provide another place where these types of transactions about books occur. At the Beyond the Book conference, some papers alluded to the need for adoption by libraries of strategies used by bookstores. See abstracts for Eve and for McKechnie et al. on the Beyond the Book website, www.beyondthebook.bham.ac.uk.
11. Devitt, *Writing Genres*, 1.
12. Michel Foucault, *Power/Knowledge: Selected Interviews and Other Writings, 1972–1977*, ed. Colin Gordon (New York: Pantheon, 1980), 93.
13. Michel Foucault, *The Order of Things: An Archaeology of the Human Sciences* (New York: Vintage Books, 1994), 63–70.
14. Carolyn Miller, "Genre as Social Action," in Freedman and Medway, *Genre and the New Rhetoric*, 30.
15. Frank Davey, *Canadian Literary Power* (Edmonton: NeWest Press, 1994), 98; Danielle Fuller, *Writing the Everyday: Women's Textual Communities in Atlantic Canada* (Montreal: McGill–Queen's University Press, 2004), 42–46.
16. I kept my study within Canada and in English-language bookstores in order to keep my sample manageable, and because the history of the book trade in Canada differs from that in the United States. With the exception of the Toronto Women's Bookstore (which does have a lot of generalist content), I chose self-described "generalist" stores because they most closely resemble the operation of Chapters Indigo. My sample included stores from almost every region of Canada: the western provinces, Atlantic Canada, and central Canada. I interviewed only one store manager for Chapters Indigo because, as she told me, the classification systems for each store are centrally managed: there is no difference between stores. Interviews were conducted with open-ended questions at eleven independent stores and one branch of Chapters Indigo and were taped either at the store location or in a café nearby. They ran from one to two hours.
17. Michel de Certeau, *The Practice of Everyday Life* (Berkeley: University of California Press, 1984), 34.
18. All summaries and quotations in this section are from my interview with Michael Hamm, Bookmark II, Halifax.
19. Anna Miller, "Who's Afraid of the Big Bad Box-Store?," *National Post*, April 5, 2008, Weekend section.
20. All summaries and quotations in this section refer to my interview with Kristen Hogan, the Toronto Women's Bookstore, Toronto.
21. www.womensbookstore.com.

22. In 2008, Susan Delean cited big-box stores as a factor in the closure of her store, Ballenford Books, in Toronto. *T.O.* weblog, "Ballenford Books to Close," www.blogto.com/books_lit/2008/03/ballenford_books_to_close/. See also Ken Jones and Michael Doucet, *The Impact of Big Box Development on Toronto's Retail Structure* (Toronto: Centre for the Study of Commercial Activity, Ryerson Polytechnic University, 1999); Dominic Ali, "Fear and Trembling at Book Expo America," *Vancouver Sun,* June 17, 2000; Robert Fulford, "The Turmoil over Chapters Book Chain," *National Post,* July 21, 2000.
23. "Villain: Chapters, Indigo, Coles, Smithbooks, Etc.," http://torontoist.com/2007/12/villain_chapter.php.
24. Anne Freadman, "Anyone for Tennis?" in Freedman and Medway, *Genre and the New Rhetoric,* 46–47.
25. Coe, Lingard, and Teslenko, "Genre as Action," 6.
26. Louis Althusse, *For Marx,* trans. Ben Brewster (London: Verso, 1990), 135.

2
METHODS

9

NEW LITERARY CULTURES
Mapping the Digital Networks of Toni Morrison

Ed Finn

As the publishing industry scrambles to adapt to the shifting realities of electronic texts and the decline of traditional models of authorship and criticism, reading practices are expanding to include new kinds of social exchange. Although readers have always been involved in literary conversations and forms of distinction that differ profoundly from those of professional critics, millions of cultural consumers are now empowered to participate in previously closed literary conversations among authors, critics, and publishers, and to express forms of mass distinction through their purchases and evaluations of books. The twenty-first century has brought significant changes to the social lives of books, as a text can engage thousands of people in a vast, asynchronous conversation without operating through the mass-mediated forms of professional reviewing publications or indeed print of any kind. Cultural processes of distinction have increasingly moved online, from bookselling itself to reviewing, recommendations, and other expressions of individual literary taste. In this chapter I argue for a new consideration of the reader as an increasingly active contributor and collaborator in literary conversations and the act of literary distinction. Taking the career of Toni Morrison as a case study in contemporary authorial fame, I use methodologies from the digital humanities to describe these collective literary exchanges in aggregate as they have emerged in book reviews and purchase decisions. These tools allow us to extend our conceptions of literary review and reception to include reading communities and processes of elevation and canon-building not usually considered in studies of taste formation.

Throughout this chapter I use the words "distinction" and "prestige" interchangeably as I argue that everyday readers are playing a growing role in defining literary fame. Prestige has moved beyond "specific consecration" within a cultural field, as Pierre Bourdieu defined it, to encompass the more complex and contingent realities that Bourdieu himself later realized have created a literary landscape in which "the boundary has never been as blurred between the experimental work and the *bestseller*."[1] More familiar to literary scholars will be the words "canon" and "canonicity." I take John Guillory's *Cultural Capital* as my starting point here, particularly his contention that canons are deeply rooted in the rhetoric of the syllabus and the "pedagogic imaginary" of the university.[2] But whereas Guillory and many other contributors to the canon debates keep their sights trained on the school, I argue for a definition of canonicity that also incorporates popular culture and commercial success, in which the school is one site of authority among many. This kind of extension is essential for effectively interpreting contemporary American literature, where authorial fame and commercial prominence play significant roles in determining which authors are read both within and beyond the academy. As John K. Young puts it in his work on contemporary black authorship in the marketplace, we are witnessing "postmodernism's merger between canonicity and commercialism," a world in which Morrison's repeated appearances on *Oprah* do not tarnish her canonical status but rather enhance it by introducing her work to new audiences.[3]

This argument does not mean to conflate canonicity and literary consumption, but rather aims to explore empirically some of the sites where the two are most closely connected: the digital shopping cart and the book review. The shifts in reading culture that I have described serve both to make visible the rules by which literary superstructures such as canons operate in shaping large sectors of the literary marketplace, and to change those rules gradually, as a growing proportion of all acts of literary distinction (purchases, reviews, and so forth) take place, and are shared, online. In essence, these data point to evolving processes of cultural elevation in which canonical prestige is both directly and indirectly connected to what James English calls "the economy of prestige"—literary prizes, media coverage, and the considerable importance of lists.[4] As David Wright argues in chapter 5 of this volume, the architectures of selection driving consumption and reviewing practices at websites like Amazon are changing the rules of literary taste-making. Whereas Wright offers a theorization of lists in reception studies and literary taste, in this chapter I investigate how one prominent author has been discussed and categorized by professional critics, readers, and the marketplace itself, as interpreted by automated recommendation systems.

Scholars have considered each of these three sources of data separately in research that I briefly address below, but synthesizing them here will allow us to understand better the public game of literary culture, in which all of these influences play out simultaneously through texts, evaluations, and purchases. This analysis of contemporary literary culture takes the case study as its model, considering an author who is one of America's most prominent living writers. Toni Morrison makes a particularly appropriate subject for this research because of her own efforts to engage directly with her readers, as she has demonstrated through her repeated appearances on Oprah's Book Club, among many other things. Morrison explained her philosophy clearly while discussing *Paradise* on *Oprah*: "Novels are for talking about and quarrelling about and engaging in some powerful way. However that happens, at a reading group, a study group, a classroom or just some friends getting together, it's a delightful, desirable thing to do. And I think it helps. Reading is solitary, but that's not its only life. It should have a talking life, a discourse that follows."[5] The talking life of books is my central concern here: the ways in which readers talk about books and the ways in which books talk to one another.

Books Talking: Morrison Review Networks

My approach in this chapter is to ask how new architectures of connection are changing existing models of cultural exchange—to ask not whether online literary cultures are better or worse than what we had before but rather how they work. To that end I am drawn to a metaphor that shares a long history with Morrison's critical reception: the trope of the talking book. As Henry Louis Gates argues in his seminal text on African American literary criticism *The Signifying Monkey*, "Black people, the evidence suggests, had to represent themselves as 'speaking subjects' before they could even begin to destroy their status as objects, as commodities, within Western culture."[6] The particular attention to "Negro expression," to use Zora Neale Hurston's term, is a hallmark of African American authorship that functions not only as a way of establishing distinct forms of cultural and racial identity but also as a vital first step in breaking the shackles of silencing objectification imposed by slavery. To be a black writer, Gates argues, requires more than mastering classical white forms of literary discourse; it demands innovation not just in content but in form. Morrison's deep ties to this legacy of the talking book, expressed most famously by Hurston and Ishmael Reed, go beyond what Gates calls the way "black texts 'talk' to other black texts"[7] to question, as Morrison did in her Nobel lecture, the stakes of literary conversation itself.[8]

In this light, the interactions traced out in this chapter are merely amplified and indexed versions of cultural exchanges that have gone on as long as people have written and shared books. In the network diagrams displayed here, we can see the efficiency with which Morrison's texts have been woven into many literary conversations, linking together historically and culturally diverse canons. These "talking books" engage readers in various kinds of exchange, the most obvious of which is consumption: the products recommended by Amazon's "Customers Who Bought This Item Also Bought" feature. It is important to distinguish between the act of purchasing a book and the act of reading it; what we are considering here are networks of literary aspiration and desire as they are expressed through the purchase of a material good rather than the intellectual act of "consuming" a book in reading it page by page. These networks fluctuate through marketing campaigns, academic years, summer vacations, and other influences, all of which remain opaque behind the calculations of Amazon's algorithms. In this chapter I consider one synchronic "snapshot" of recommendations, in part because of the technical challenges of visualizing the way these networks shift over time, but diachronic analysis is a fruitful area for future research.

To create the visualizations displayed here, I mapped out the networks of texts linked through these user purchase decisions, starting with Morrison's best-known novel, *Beloved*, and tracing the first ten books that were recommended from each product page.[9] A link from *Beloved* to *Ceremony*, for instance, indicates that shoppers on the *Beloved* page would see an image of *Ceremony* underneath the "Customers Who Bought . . ." banner.[10] Taken in aggregate, the recommendations offer a way to read Amazon's best guesses about literary desire at a given point in time, and as they are also potentially subject to influence from marketing campaigns, movie tie-ins, and the like, they operate in a feedback loop involving publishers and booksellers as well as consumers. The feedback is clearly imperfect and contingent, but we can take Amazon's success as the world's largest bookseller to indicate that its algorithms work, and that they are reasonably efficient at discerning and satisfying readers' consumer desires.

Beloved, arguably Morrison's most famous work, points readers toward three books by authors other than Morrison herself: Ralph Ellison's *Invisible Man*, a CliffsNotes guide to *Beloved*, and Leslie Marmon Silko's *Ceremony* (figure 9.1). In other words, Ellison and Silko are the basic cultural points along which Amazon's shopping carts are triangulating Morrison. Paired with *Beloved*, Ellison's seminal text establishes a clear link between the two authors as pillars of the African American literary canon, and few readers or scholars would be surprised that the literary marketplace has made this connection. Yet if we accept these recommendations as fair evidence of Amazon customer

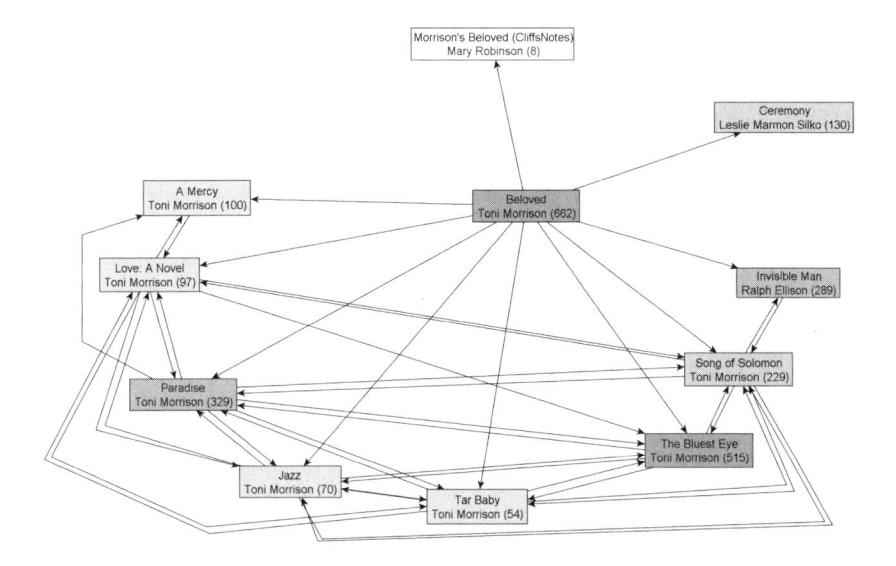

Figure 9.1. Amazon recommendations from *Beloved*

shopping practices, as an inscription of literary consumption, the strong affiliation of Morrison and Silko suggests that other cultural force lines are equally important. Both novelists address some of the darkest moments in U.S. history, exploring victimization and the powers of narrative to rebalance the cultural record and "rememory" events that many would prefer be forgotten.

Tracing these initial links reveals new subnets with their own complex prestige structures. *Ceremony* turns into a portal for Native American fiction that is entirely distinct from the rest of Morrison's literary universe (figure 9.2). At this point we can begin to see patterns that bear out Guillory's argument that "judgments with canonical force are institutionally located" and that the most significant of these are educational institutions.[11] The ghosts of countless syllabi haunt this network, most notably in the way that genre distinctions are overruled when sufficiently prestigious texts "rise above" the local canon to become affiliated with other "masterpieces" in the broad super-canon of literary greatness.[12] Likewise, other grouping influences can overcome authorial boundaries: Roberto Bolaño's *2666* connects to this network via *A Mercy*, which weaves Morrison's work into a collection of other contemporary novels (figure 9.3).

The interconnections between these wide-ranging texts—*Netherland, Unaccustomed Earth,* and *The White Tiger,* in addition to Bolaño—suggest both the

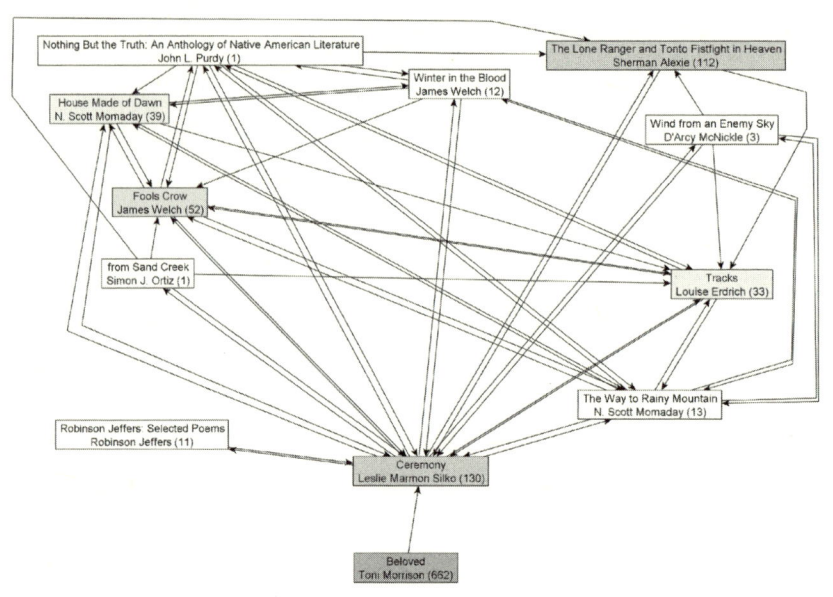

Figure 9.2. Amazon recommendations from *Ceremony*

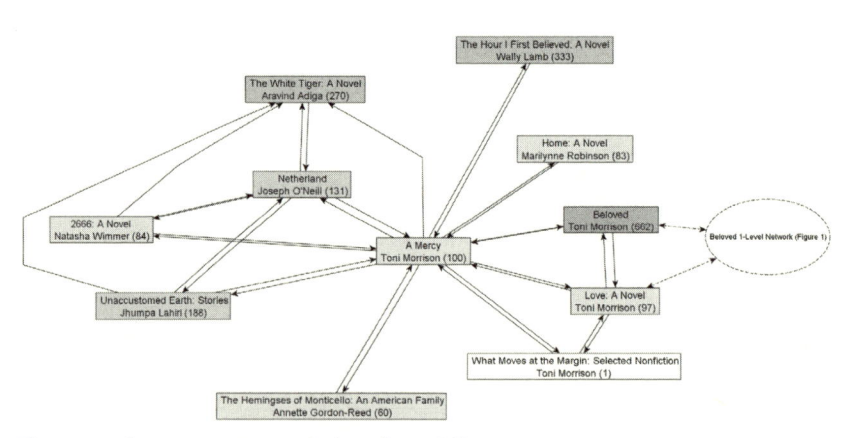

Figure 9.3. Amazon recommendations from *A Mercy*

power of temporality and "newness" as an organizing category, and the shift in *A Mercy* to the subject of coloniality. With *A Mercy*, Morrison builds a new avenue for her work, linking it to the burgeoning field of postcolonial literature and thereby recontextualizing her role as an American writer. Amazon readers have associated *2666* and *A Mercy* in both directions, suggesting that a state of fluid transfer exists between these two cultural zones. This is a dramatic difference from the unidirectional link from *Beloved* to *Ceremony,* marking a distinction between readers who buy both Morrison and Silko (many of them students, no doubt) and those readers who purchase Silko alone, or purely within a Native American literary canon. The difference suggests an imbalance of power: if we imagine these arrows as one-lane roads on which readers can travel, this link might ferry them away from Morrison into many happy years of traveling among Native American fiction.

For all of these surprising leaps, Morrison's work forms a tightly interconnected subgroup in my models of the Amazon network at larger scales.[13] Along with other distinct subgroups, such as Native American fiction, this Morrison cluster exists within a more tangled web of high canonical texts, ranging from American classics by authors such as Mark Twain and Nathaniel Hawthorne to Fyodor Dostoevsky, James Joyce, and William Shakespeare. One intriguing result of this research is the difference in structure between the African American and Native American literary canons as they are reflected in the Amazon marketplace. In the typical genre grouping, one would expect a fairly extensive set of interior connections with limited connections to other canonical networks through only the most prestigious works. Yet the African American writers Morrison is associated with, particularly Ellison, have clearly entered a broader American canon that includes F. Scott Fitzgerald, Ernest Hemingway, and Hawthorne, joining those older writers as part of an "all-star" American list.

We can get a clearer sense of this larger American canon and the forces driving it by ranking texts according to the number of incoming connections they receive in the network, which is a basic definition of "prestige" in social network analysis (figure 9.4).[14] To put these figures in perspective, the average node in the network received only 5.2 links, with genre affiliation playing a major role in governing prestige. *Tracks,* for example, received all of its endorsements from other Native American books, while *The Great Gatsby* was part of a network of American classics including William Faulkner, Ellison, Hawthorne, John Steinbeck, and Hurston.

As one moves further down the rankings, Amazon prestige inflects this mass canonicity in some surprising ways. The established white canon survives in the form of Fitzgerald, Twain, and attendant CliffsNotes, while newer Native American and African American classics round out the list. These chart-toppers reflect the enduring power of canonical tenure in American literature in Guillory's sense, epitomized here by Fitzgerald's and Twain's now ubiquitous novels, as well as the gradual shift in classroom syllabi to expand the Great American Reading List. The prestige on display here mirrors a particular kind

Table 9.4. Prestige rankings in Amazon network (3 levels out from *Beloved*)

RANK	TITLE	AUTHOR	LINKS
1	*Tracks*	Louise Erdrich	29
1	*The Great Gatsby*	F. Scott Fitzgerald	29
3	*Ceremony*	Leslie Marmon Silko	24
4	*Fitzgerald's The Great Gatsby (CliffsNotes)*	CliffsNotes	22
5	*Their Eyes Were Watching God*	Zora Neale Hurston	20
6	*Song of Solomon*	Toni Morrison	19
6	*The Adventures of Huckleberry Finn*	Mark Twain	19
8	*Hawthorne's The Scarlet Letter (CliffsNotes)*	CliffsNotes	18
8	*The Bluest Eye*	Toni Morrison	18
8	*Invisible Man*	Ralph Ellison	18
11	*Beloved*	Toni Morrison	17
11	*Jazz*	Toni Morrison	17
11	*Fools Crow*	James Welch	17
14	*The Adventures of Huckleberry Finn (CliffsNotes)*	CliffsNotes	16
14	*To Kill a Mockingbird (CliffsNotes)*	CliffsNotes	16
14	*Crime and Punishment*	Fyodor Dostoevsky	16
14	*Four Souls: A Novel*	Louise Erdrich	16
14	*The Crucible*	Arthur Miller	16
19	*Paradise (Oprah's Book Club)*	Toni Morrison	15
19	*The Lone Ranger and Tonto Fistfight in Heaven*	Sherman Alexie	15
19	*Crime and Punishment*	Fyodor Dostoyevsky[1]	15
19	*The Scarlet Letter*	Nathaniel Hawthorne	15
19	*Death of a Salesman*	Arthur Miller	15
24	*A Mercy*	Toni Morrison	14

1. Amazon typically combines different editions of a single book and recommends only one, but in this instance a different spelling of the author's last name has created two competing entries for *Crime and Punishment*.

of academic prestige, the widely acknowledged canon of high school reading lists and major anthologies, and figure 9.4 marks the point at which these academic institutions interface with the market.[15] The speed with which Louise Erdrich, Silko, and Morrison have achieved their canonical status is, in literary-historical terms, breathtaking: *Ceremony* and *Song of Solomon* were both published in 1977 and *Tracks* in 1988, meaning that in just a few decades these books have risen to the top at America's largest bookstore, suggesting their centrality in the wider field of popular literature. We know this anecdotally, from high school and college syllabi, from survey classes and exam reading lists, but these data from Amazon confirm their material presence at the heart of the literary marketplace, as icons that are still heavily invested in by readers. A look at the diagram as a whole corroborates the ghostly presence of thousands of school assignments in shaping these networks of purchases, an effect I return to later in discussing reader reviews of Morrison's work. The presence of CliffsNotes texts in these prestige rankings underscores the point that students drive a huge percentage of these purchase decisions, and they are driven in turn by the teachers, school boards, and academic critics who set syllabi.

The strong presence of CliffsNotes in the Amazon network marks one of the many subnets or minor genres present—and at times almost invisible—within the larger space of Morrison's literary network. The degree to which CliffsNotes volumes mutually reinforce ties among themselves through consumer purchases suggests another metric for measuring lines of force and influence in these recommendations: the clique. Adapted once again from social network theory, "clique" is a term used to define a group in which all members are connected to all other members or to a minimum number of other members.[16] Morrison's networks are full of small cliques—clusters of three or four texts that are completely interconnected—but when we look only at the largest cliques present, striking patterns emerge. In figure 9.5 I have charted out the largest cliques to be found within three links of *Beloved*. The largest single clique consists of eight Morrison novels, but by expanding our definition to include groups with at least six members (in technical terms, a clique of $k = 6$), we can see all of the major clustering forces at work. When we privilege groups over individual "all-star texts," we see a very different kind of prestige at work in the contemporary literary marketplace.

The Native American canon I identified earlier unfurling from *Ceremony* exists here as well, but in a cluster of texts written exclusively by Erdrich. Morrison's works also inhabit their own clique, as do Faulkner's and Bolaño's, confirming in all three cases that authorship is a powerful factor governing purchasing decisions. More interesting, however, is the question of why Morrison, Faulkner, Erdrich, and Bolaño are authors whose works clump together by name more consistently than any other writers in this network. I posit an answer in several pieces. First, not many authors have a minimum of seven books in this elite network of recommendations surrounding *Beloved,* and their texts do not link closely enough with any other cluster to create a $k = 6$ clique. Second, and more excitingly, these authors demonstrate something sufficiently distinctive and compelling in their writing that causes their works to be tightly affiliated. Simply put, readers purchase more than one of their books, and all of the texts visible in figure 9.5 lead consistently to the others. This is a sign both of some ineffable authorial uniqueness and of marketable literary

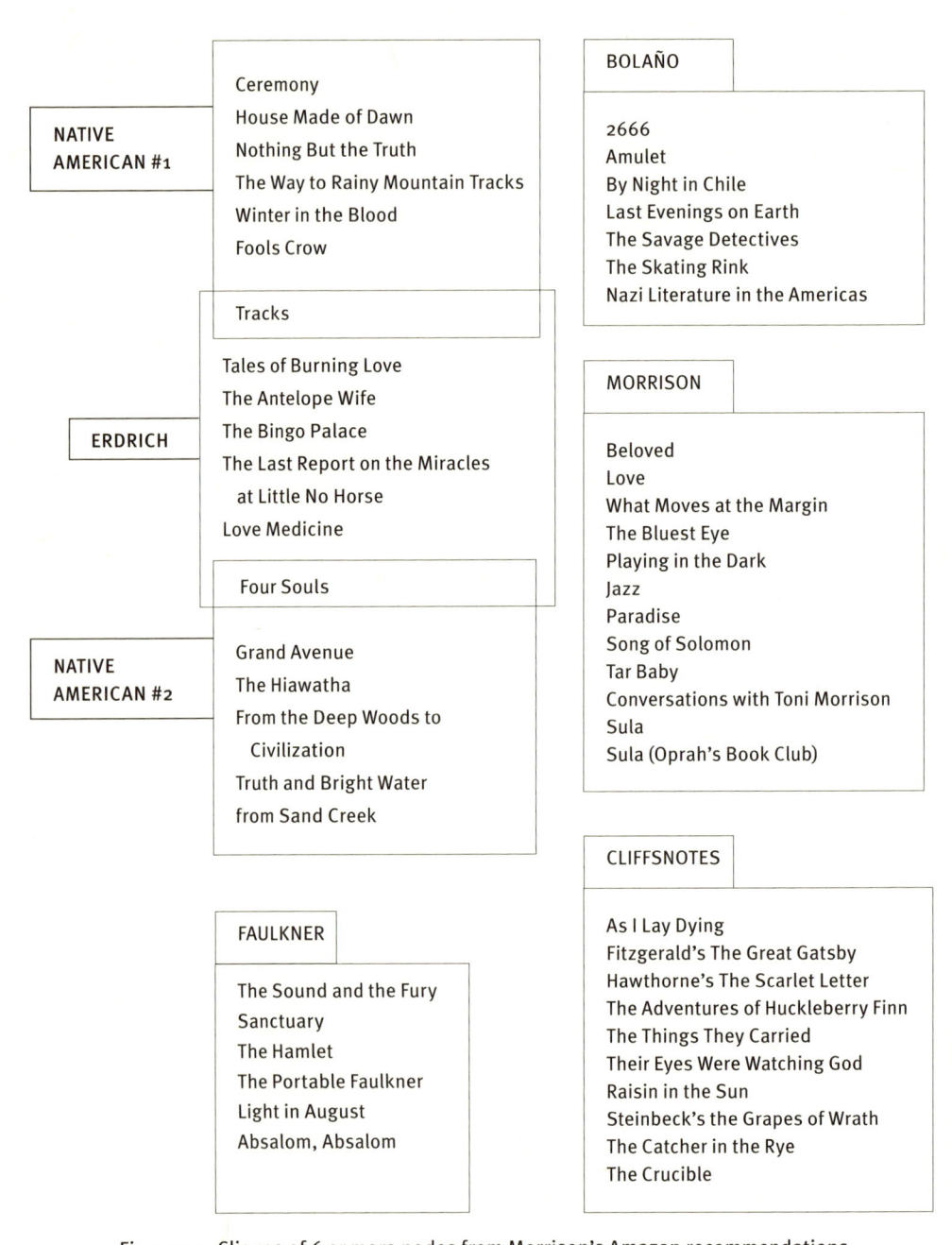

NATIVE AMERICAN #1
- Ceremony
- House Made of Dawn
- Nothing But the Truth
- The Way to Rainy Mountain Tracks
- Winter in the Blood
- Fools Crow

BOLAÑO
- 2666
- Amulet
- By Night in Chile
- Last Evenings on Earth
- The Savage Detectives
- The Skating Rink
- Nazi Literature in the Americas

ERDRICH
- Tracks
- Tales of Burning Love
- The Antelope Wife
- The Bingo Palace
- The Last Report on the Miracles at Little No Horse
- Love Medicine
- Four Souls

MORRISON
- Beloved
- Love
- What Moves at the Margin
- The Bluest Eye
- Playing in the Dark
- Jazz
- Paradise
- Song of Solomon
- Tar Baby
- Conversations with Toni Morrison
- Sula
- Sula (Oprah's Book Club)

NATIVE AMERICAN #2
- Grand Avenue
- The Hiawatha
- From the Deep Woods to Civilization
- Truth and Bright Water
- from Sand Creek

FAULKNER
- The Sound and the Fury
- Sanctuary
- The Hamlet
- The Portable Faulkner
- Light in August
- Absalom, Absalom

CLIFFSNOTES
- As I Lay Dying
- Fitzgerald's The Great Gatsby
- Hawthorne's The Scarlet Letter
- The Adventures of Huckleberry Finn
- The Things They Carried
- Their Eyes Were Watching God
- Raisin in the Sun
- Steinbeck's the Grapes of Wrath
- The Catcher in the Rye
- The Crucible

Figure 9.5. Cliques of 6 or more nodes from Morrison's Amazon recommendations

consistency; it also is the commercial triumph of an authorial brand. As John Cheever once described himself, "I'm a brand name like corn flakes, or shredded wheat."[17] In different ways, Faulkner, Erdrich, and Bolaño also share the role of interlocutor with Morrison, relating narratives from a distinct culture to the larger American mainstream.

I take this as an instance in which the market asserts itself, treating authors more like brands than teaching tools. If the single-author syllabus is a comparative rarity in contemporary American education, particularly in the high school and lower-level university courses most likely to drive large numbers of book sales, then the prestige listings in figure 9.4 seem more likely to derive from more widely taught multi-author, multi-genre courses and summer reading lists, in distinction to the clusters of figure 9.5. What these clusters mark instead, I argue, is the sustained impact of other forces: book clubs, particularly Oprah's, and reading practices that take place outside formal education. Faulkner's situation here is enlightening. Given his status as a writer whose influence on Morrison has long been a topic of critical discussion, some of the most interesting questions here relate to the significance of his work in the network as a whole. In terms of prestige, Faulkner scores surprisingly low, with his most prestigious book, *Absalom, Absalom!* in a three-way tie for twenty-fourth place. The fact that Oprah picked three of his other novels for the Book Club in 2005 seems to have had little long-term impact on prestige but might help explain why so many consumers have been investing repeatedly in the Faulkner clique. In short, Faulkner's work presents a compelling example of divergence between the academic and the commercial marketplace of literary prestige. As one rough measure, consider the inversion between Amazon "prestige" and the number of MLA bibliography citations mentioning either author: 1,928 for Morrison and 3,877 for Faulkner.[18] On Amazon, Faulkner is one of many authors filling in the corners between the big hits, with *As I Lay Dying* pointing toward *Beloved,* perhaps as a Book Club artifact, but receiving no reciprocal link in return. Even when the *Beloved*-centered network is extended out to three levels, the two authors are connected only indirectly, via Ellison and Hurston.

If these texts make up a supporting cast for the literary stars of the marketplace, there is another pervasive clique that fulfills a very similar function. The CliffsNotes clique proves that readers become loyal to the brand, purchasing other editions consistently. The texts explicated by this sub-network of literary guidebooks are in many ways the clearest sighting yet of a difficult-to-define popular American literary canon. *The Grapes of Wrath, The Scarlet Letter, The Catcher in the Rye:* these are books millions of high school students read every year. Ironically, we glimpse this canon of American literature through a doubly normative filter, restricted first to the lucrative center of the study aid market (those racks of CliffsNotes editions at bookstores clearly aiming for the most frequently assigned texts) and second to only the texts most frequently purchased together. This is a commercially and intellectually "safe" canon, the only nonwhite, non-male author present being Lorraine Hansberry, writer of an earlier generation's protest narrative *A Raisin in the Sun*. A work must be sufficiently culturally reputable for something so disreputable as a CliffsNotes edition to be written for it, a fact that works in parallel with James English's observations on the importance of scandal to literary prize systems.[19] In many ways CliffsNotes represents the pinnacle of a certain kind of literary consumption: the need to gain a basic kind of cultural capital as quickly and easily as possible in order to earn some credential such as passing a class, writing a paper, or passing as a knowledgeable reader in conversation.

The only other non-authorial clique structure present in this network is the cluster of three overlapping groups revealed in figure 9.5. Erdrich works as the intermediary between two subgroups of Native American fiction. Her novel *Tracks* links to a set of more "prestigious" works that already appear in the upper rankings of our prestige diagram: widely recognized novels such as *Ceremony, Fools Crow,* and *House Made of Dawn*. The other cluster, linked through *Four Souls,* reveals another intriguing second-order canon at work in Morrison's network. In fact, with the exception of *Four Souls,* all the novels in this cluster achieve their limited prestige only by internal links to one another, creating a small, mutually informed structure with limited connections to the larger network. If Erdrich connects to a larger Native American canon via *Tracks,* here she also links to a more insular literary island made up exclusively of books by male Native American writers published since the mid-1990s.

Like the recommendations graph and the syllabus itself, the clique is a reductionist tactic, an attempt to explore the relationships between texts as they operate in groups. The patterns that emerge from Amazon's networks of recommendations seem to be clearly tied to market signals. They echo the way books are grouped in a bookstore, sorting texts by genre, by author, and by function (CliffsNotes). This abstraction of clustering, with the focal length of our critical instrument set at $k = 6$, reveals recognizable patterns, but changing the settings to $k = 4$ would reveal a much more chaotic range of cultural signals at war in the literary marketplace and the diversity of the reading choices people make. Perhaps the most striking discovery here is not that these landscapes of literary desire and acquisition are chaotic but that they are still governed by easily recognizable rules of attraction and connection which shape the choices that bring us into contact with the books we read. The competing forces of the marketplace end up reproducing familiar rules and categories, a process that plays out in different ways when we change our focus from the patterns of automated systems to the deliberate choices of individual critics and readers.

The Culture Game: Morrison and Professional Reviews

Exploring recommendations networks is a deceptive sort of empirical research, as it involves analyzing the output of other models and algorithms that have already groomed and regularized the data of normal human interaction. However Amazon defines the associations it tracks, it has already eliminated the misspelled and misplaced titles, abandoned shopping carts, and other lost texts that define the material and digital experience with literary commodities. We get a very different perspective on authorial prestige when we consider the book reviews of professional critics. Here we encounter another kind of social algorithm, the system by which, as Bourdieu argues, critics "reproduce . . . the space within which they are themselves classified."[20] Scholars of this arena have tended to focus on the critical independence of the reviewers, particularly in the literary field, where many are authors themselves.[21] Reviewers are acutely conscious of the actions of their peers and geometries of prestige within the spaces of literary criticism, and they often operate according to a loose consensus model in which positive and negative evaluations can quickly multiply.[22] We can see these phenomena borne out in Morrison's case in a number of ways, particularly in the way reviewers situate each new work from this highly prestigious author within the constellation of her previously acknowledged successes. Since the publication of her first novel, *The Bluest Eye,* at the relatively late age of thirty-nine, Morrison's stature has grown rapidly. In the decades since then, reviews of her work have taken on tropes and repeated themes of their own as writers grapple with her fame, her literary legacy, and the complex interweaving of characters and narratives across her novels.

One way to explore this decades-long performance of literary reception is to consider her professional reviews in aggregate by exploring those books, writers, and characters that have appeared in three or more reviews of Morrison's work across the entire span of her authorial career. In figure 9.6 we can see the breadth of reader response to her fiction in references to names that range from Herman Melville and William Faulkner to Hurston, Alice Walker, and James Baldwin. In these figures, connections are defined as nouns that appear together in the same review; the nodes in this figure have been further limited to only those co-occurrences that occurred in four or more reviews (out of a total corpus of seventy-five reviews).[23] I have limited the definition of these nodes to include only capitalized proper nouns, assembling a dictionary based on all such nouns to appear more than once in either corpus, professional reviews and reviews on Amazon.[24] Like the professional corpus, the set of Amazon reviews I analyze next comprises all reviews of Morrison's books written by consumers until the data were collected in September 2009. At 112,920 words, the professional corpus averages out to 1,506 words per review. The larger Amazon corpus, at 374,845 words, has only 174 words in the average review. Figure 9.6 represents the central conceptual canon of these professional reviews: the consistent references that reviewers have made in connection to Morrison's work spanning her career. Centrality is roughly approximated here by placing the more well-connected nodes closer to the center of the diagram. Each node is connected to some percentage of other nodes in the network (represented numerically in gray boxes to the right of each node). Morrison is connected to every node here since her name was mentioned in all seventy-five reviews of her work; therefore, her centrality measure is 1.0. The resulting diagram presents one perspective on the core of Morrison's professional literary self, a portrait of the author painted by her own professional interlocutors, the critics.

The temporal axis makes its presence felt in these reviews through the higher prestige accorded to earlier texts (the date of publication for Morrison's novels is noted parenthetically in the figure). These early works define the Morrisonian frame of reference: the novels *Song of Solomon, Beloved, The Bluest Eye,* and *Sula* all play important roles for reviewers as both critical yardsticks and guideposts for readers contemplating a new publication. *Song of Solomon,* in particular, stands out as the most well connected of all Morrison's novels, and its immediate neighbors include all other Morrison fiction. In another sense, Morrison's earlier temporal foundations are also on display here: about a third of all the authors present in this diagram are titans such as Faulkner, Walt Whitman, and Twain. Her reviewers place her in the same constellation as these American "classics" in part because of comparisons to their fiction and in part because of her own critical response to the American literary tradition in *Playing in the Dark,* in which she argues for the profound impact of the (often silenced, often erased) African figure on the American psyche. In this sense, the network reflects Morrison's position as a particularly polyvalent figure in American letters as an editor, writer, provocateur, academic, critic, and leading proponent of the African American studies movement.

The "Morrison" node at the center of this network pulls together a diverse

NEW LITERARY CULTURES [191]

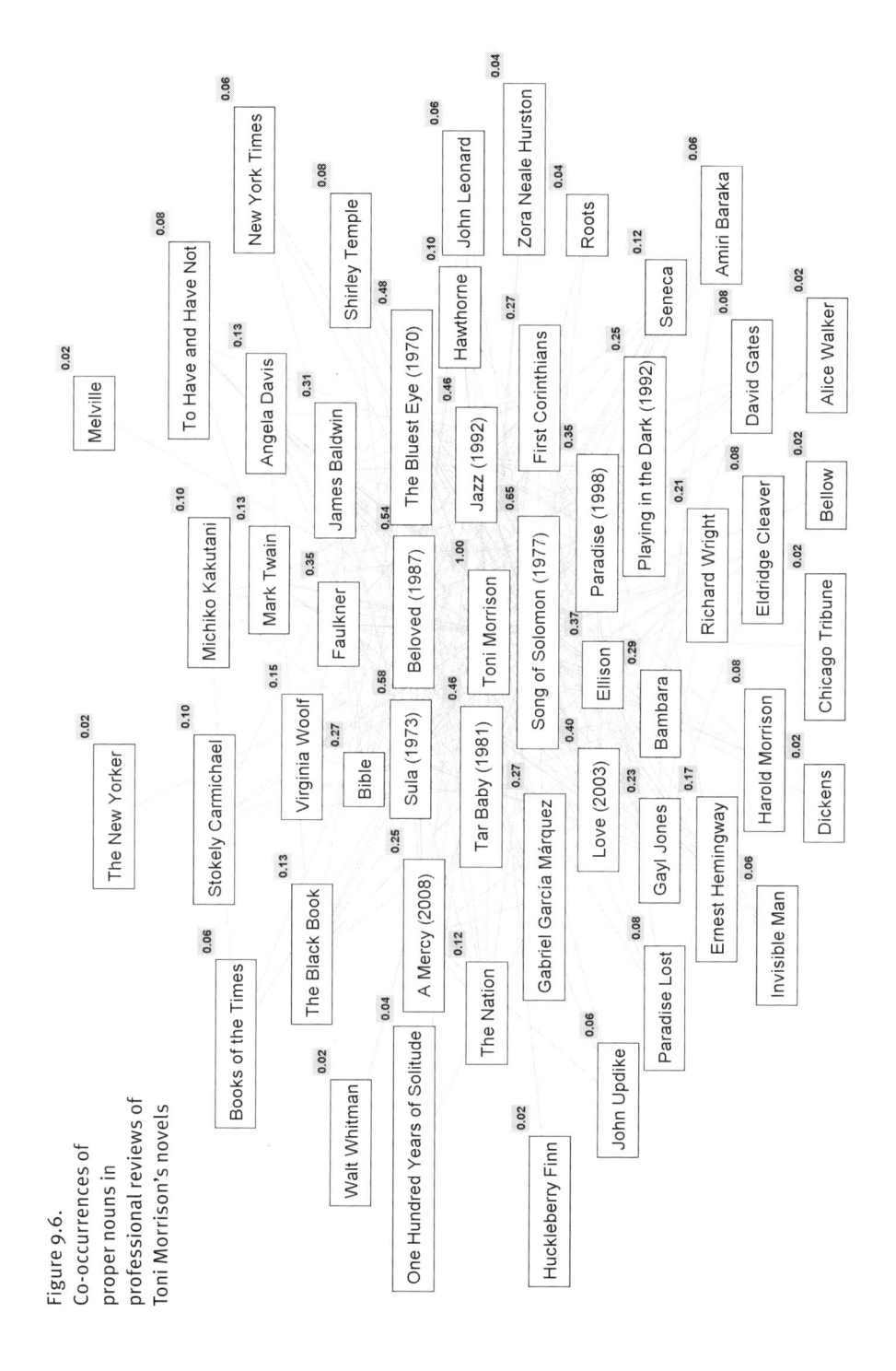

Figure 9.6.
Co-occurrences of
proper nouns in
professional reviews of
Toni Morrison's novels

set of signifiers (or, as Gates might put it, engages in complicated "signifyin'") around the heart of the diagram. These nouns effectively catalogue the process by which Morrison was inducted into the pantheon of American literary gods, and her connections to a close core of writers indicate the pathway to that apotheosis. A stylistic and thematic web of comparisons links Morrison, Richard Wright, Ellison, and Faulkner with the younger generation of Gayl Jones and Toni Cade Bambara. Separately, Morrison shares ties to Faulkner through several of her novels, and Faulkner strengthens her affiliation with modernism and Virginia Woolf as well as Hemingway and other "American classics" nodes. The most important part of this engine of literary ascendance is also the easiest to overlook: those nodes on the fringes of the network (less tightly connected than the writers just discussed, but still integral to the central core of Morrison's literary networks). Michiko Kakutani and John Leonard, the *Books of the Times,* and the *New Yorker:* these repeat critics and persistent reviewing platforms have played an important role in building Morrison's fame and, not incidentally, linking their evaluations and their publications to her affirmed brilliance.

The network also reveals some of the ways in which critics respond to the multiple valences of Morrison's work, the way she blends biblical allusion, modernist style, and African American themes, and the particular ways in which the predominantly white publishing industry "marks" African American texts.[25] Morrison successfully defined a distinctively, self-consciously black voice in American letters, addressing the challenging history and politics of that ethnic identity while nevertheless achieving wide popularity among a broad range of American readers. Whereas Wright was infamously asked to rewrite the closing of *Native Son* in a more positive light for the Book-of-the-Month Club, Morrison seems to pull no punches as she explores slavery, rape, and many kinds of social oppression in her work.[26] While they address these themes, the critics also identify Morrison as an American writer who crosses a number of boundaries, frequently mentioning her not only with Ellison and James Baldwin but also with Faulkner and Woolf. Gabriel García Márquez is almost as central here as Bambara, and Morrison is included in an American literary tradition that ranges from Twain to Hemingway.

Readers at Work: Amazon Reviews of Morrison's *Beloved*

In her conclusion to *Reading the Romance,* Janice Radway argues that the study of everyday literary consumption reinstates "active individuals and their creative, constructive activities at the heart of our interpretive enterprise [in which] the essential human practice of making meaning goes on."[27] Although Amazon is not a book group, the site fosters a sense of community around each book in its catalogue by allowing users to write reviews and vote on the reviews of others, implicitly endorsing this kind of self-expression as a form of literary evaluation just as useful as the other data presented on each book's page: its sales rank, category, recommendations, and so on. By conferring on users the entitlement to evaluate books and to see their words appear in essentially the same format as the judgments of professional critics, Amazon encourages emotional and intellectual investment. It also provides a virtual space for readers to, as Elizabeth Long puts it in her description of book clubs, "create a conversation that begins with the book each woman has read but moves beyond the book to include the personal connections and meanings each has found in the book. . . . At its best, this kind of discussion is profoundly transformative."[28] Unlike most professional critics, but like members of a traditional book club, these Amazon reviewers often share the emotional experience of reading a book, literally writing themselves into the narrative of the review.

Looking at the consumer reviews of *Beloved* reveals that the rules of the literary field change dramatically when the evaluators of a text are not professional critics. In fact, the economic equation is reversed: critics are paid to write book reviews, while everyday readers typically pay for the privilege by buying the books.[29] Both forms of review take place in complicated cultural spaces and defy simplistic analysis of reviewers' motivations. Professional critics address lofty ideals of literary culture while striving to maintain a consistent cultural product of their own, and their authority as critics rests on opaque assertions of class, employment, publication, and previous judgments. Amazon's consumers speak to a more commercial notion of the book as a product that is reviewed on a simple five-star scale with a box for comments. Their reviews, however, create an equally complex cultural space of motivations: Amazon provides architectures of prestige for reviewers to achieve status within the site, though some reviewers post their comments anonymously. The reviews themselves range from employing the language and implicit rhetorical claims of the professionals to reading diaries, educational narratives, testimonials, and many other sui generis forms.

Overall, the Amazon network (figure 9.7) presents a much more canonical version of Morrison, retaining her links to figures such as Dickens, Hemingway, Hurston, and Faulkner but minimizing her literary and editorial connections to younger black writers. In part this can be explained by our units of measurement: by defining co-occurrences as shared presence in a single review, we give the longer, more reference-packed professional reviews an advantage in terms

[194] Ed Finn

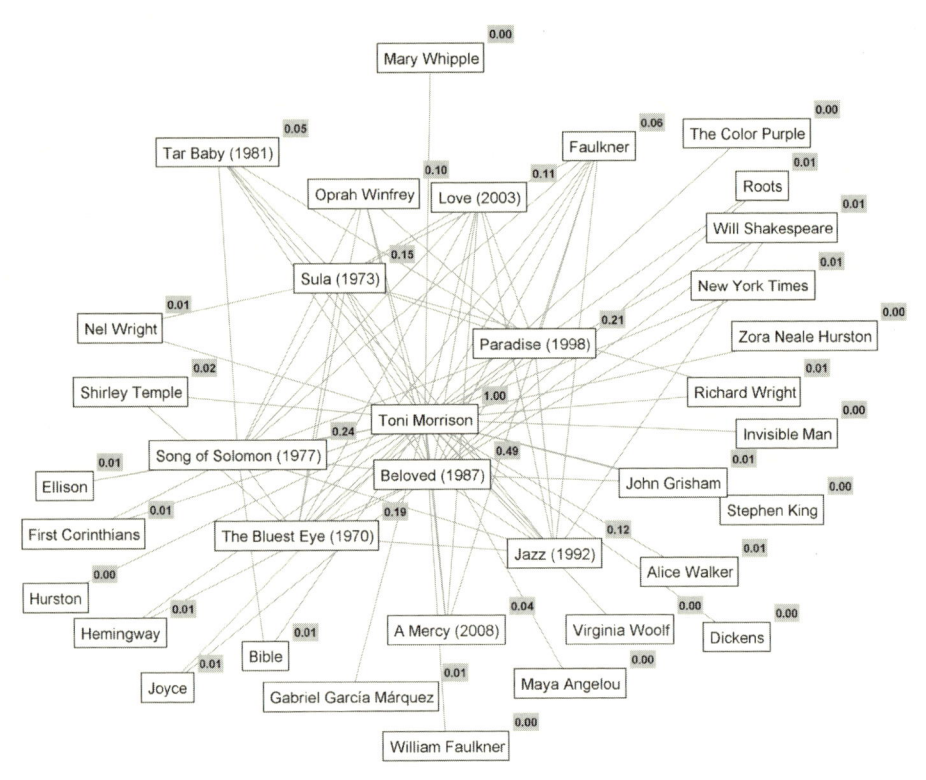

Figure 9.7. Co-occurrences of proper nouns in Amazon reviews of Toni Morrison's novels

of the number of links emanating from each node. In light of this diversity, it is surprising that Amazon reviews make as many connections as they do in such compact form, and once again the diversity of approaches within the Amazon reviewing community makes the analysis interesting. While some readers write very short reviews, nonreferential reviews, or evaluations of the book as an object and of Amazon's customer service, others take more involved and discursive approaches to reviewing, providing a wealth of critical forms.

We can make a closer comparison between critics and everyday readers by focusing on a particularly significant node in both networks, the word "Black."[30] Figures 9.8 and 9.9 produce the subnets around "Black" in professional and Amazon reviews of *Beloved*, a novel widely recognized for its meditations on race in the United States. Here, nodes that appeared together in at least three reviews of *Beloved* share a link.

While professional publications and Amazon reviewers alike vary in their

NEW LITERARY CULTURES [195]

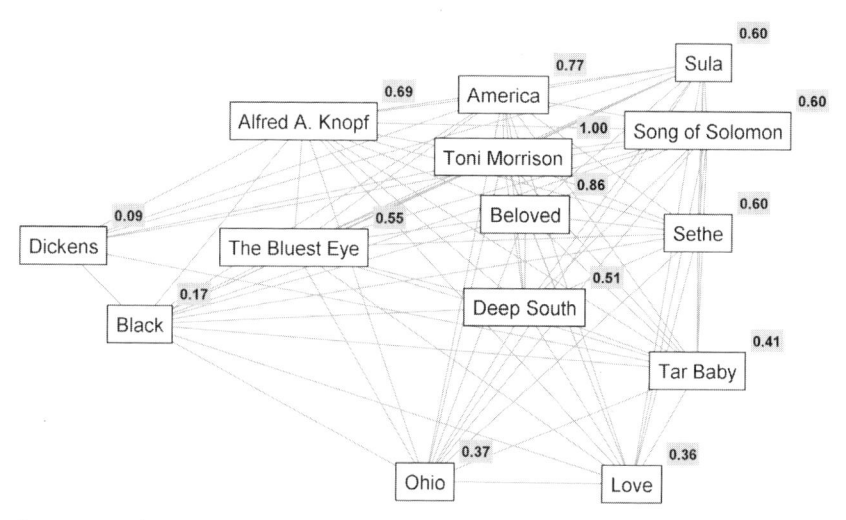

Figure 9.8. "Black" subnet in professional reviews of *Beloved*

capitalization of "Black," the word frequently appears capitalized in book and article titles. This particular use as an introductory signifier (for example, "America Means Black, Too," titling a review of *Jazz*) is pervasive within the corpus of professional reviews. In fact, the way "White" slips past copy editors is fascinating in its own strangely Freudian way.[31] In professional reviews it is mentioned most often in discussions of books by black writers: *Playing in the Dark: Whiteness and the Literary Imagination* by Morrison and *White Rat* by Gayl Jones (nine and three appearances respectively). Aside from references to those two books and instances in which "White" begins a sentence—again quite often in quoted dialogue from African American fiction—"White" makes three appearances in professional reviews: "Snow White," "White Castles" (plural of the fast food chain), and "Great White Narcissists." By contrast, in Amazon reviews "White" is almost always used as an explicit racial signifier, frequently in parallel with "Black": "anti-White language," "African American culture/literature . . . White culture/society," "Black People White People," "Blacks and Whites."[32]

The subnet generated from the corpus of Amazon reviews offers a very different understanding of "Black" as a literary concept, expanding this network through several additions. The only Morrison character in the professional subnet is Sethe (*Beloved*), but Amazon readers also link the term "Black" to First Corinthians, Pilate, Guitar, and Macon (all from *Song of Solomon*) as well as Pecola Breedlove (*The Bluest Eye*). As these Amazon readers make abun-

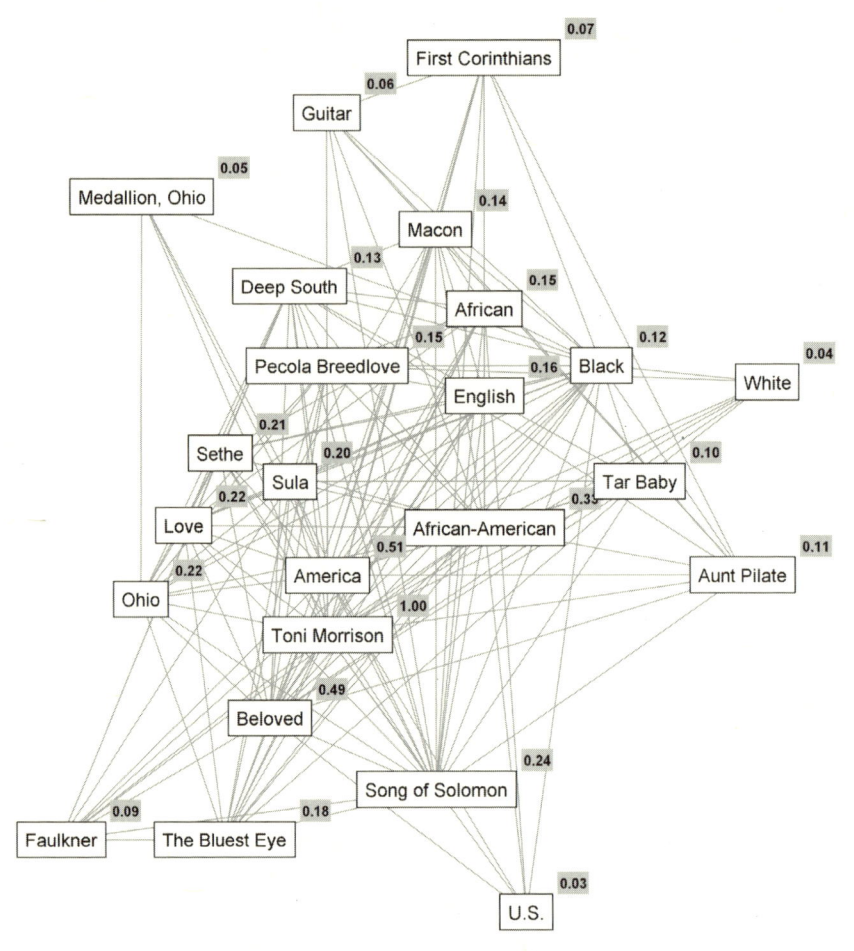

[Figure: network diagram with nodes including First Corinthians (0.07), Guitar (0.06), Medallion, Ohio (0.05), Macon (0.14), Deep South (0.13), African (0.15), Pecola Breedlove (0.15), Black (0.12), English (0.16), White (0.04), Sethe (0.21), Sula (0.20), Love (0.22), Tar Baby (0.10), African-American (0.35), Ohio (0.22), America (0.51), Aunt Pilate (0.11), Toni Morrison (1.00), Beloved (0.49), Song of Solomon (0.24), Faulkner (0.09), The Bluest Eye (0.18), U.S. (0.03)]

Figure 9.9. "Black" subnet in Amazon reviews of *Beloved*

dantly clear in their reviews, the details of characterization and plotting are extremely important to them, suggesting that identification and literary empathy play a major role in their evaluations. For these nonprofessional readers, "Black" is defined by Morrison's characters as much as it is by literary form or a book jacket photo of an African American author. In the place of Dickens we get Faulkner, along with "English," a node incorporating various references to English literature and language classes.[33] Faulkner plays a role similar to Dickens's, acting as a guide star from a more traditional Western canon, but he also represents the way in which Morrison is taught in "English" classes, as part of a distinctly American literary tradition. Finally, the presence of "White," as discussed earlier, represents these consumers' more explicit approach to the dialectical challenges (along with many others) of defining and even conceptualizing the language of race. "Black" links to "White," to "African," to "African American," and of course to every other node in the subnet, making it a cultural crossroads in these networks like Morrison herself, conveying many meanings to many readers. We see an inverse relationship between the nuance of the reviews themselves and the nuance present in these diagrams: the professional reviewers allow many things to go unsaid and unnamed.

Reinventing Prestige: Reading in the Twenty-first Century

At first glance it might seem as if the new networks on Amazon recapitulate the old systems of prestige Guillory identified in *Cultural Capital:* the heavy emphasis on "English" and the educational context suggest that the academy is still the primary site of cultural elevation, while the emergence of established canonical hierarchies implies that the marketplace is only following the rules set by other cultural powers. But there are some vital distinctions between the landscapes described by Guillory and Bourdieu and the digital spaces in which reading is increasingly occurring at the turn of the twenty-first century. First, while some of the topics are familiar, those discussing them disrupt the lines of power from traditional cultural structures. Here, students are the most active contributors to the aggregate node "English" I described earlier, as they discuss the Morrison books they have read in school assignments. The democratized commercial space of Amazon opens up a new arena for distinction in which students can reject or endorse the canons being imposed on them through syllabi and reading lists. This is, in a sense, the kind of "counterhegemonic public"[34] that allows a culturally marginalized group to develop a collective voice, continuously reasserting moments of individual autonomy within a capitalist system.

Second, websites such as Amazon, through their focus on ease of navigation for their customers, also make structures of prestige and canonicity more visible, often intentionally, for example, by highlighting prizewinning texts. Through linking algorithms like their recommendations engines, they have created and shared a new form of cultural context to join the implicit and explicit contextual cues presented in bookstores, critical reviews, and literary conversations. These webs of reference contain far more detail than influential taste-forming institutions such as the *New York Times* best-seller lists, and allow us to perceive clustering effects like single-author magnetism in Morrison or Bolaño. These clusters, particularly the pervasive CliffsNotes groups, trace out what we might think of as literary-economic feedback loops, wherein a particular author or editorial group has created a successful exchange with the market. The CliffsNotes network is the most transparent of these structures-made-visible, since its intention is to monetize and streamline the transfer of cultural capital, a process usually begun at school. By visualizing and even promoting these kinds of prestige structures, companies like Amazon grant them new powers to influence reading further, creating complex interactions among readers, critics, authors, and teachers.

Finally, the details of authorial style and persona "signify" more than ever in our networked age. Morrison continues to demonstrate her willingness to engage these new communities on their own terms, from her appearances on Oprah's Book Club to her willingness to abridge and record her own audiobook editions of her novels. A prolific editor and critic, Morrison has long been an intensely self-conscious and forthright commentator on her work, as her incisive forewords to trade reprints of her novels attest. As Amazon advertises its latest Kindle electronic readers, she is also one of the authors extolling the virtues of portability and near-instant access to millions of texts that it makes available.[35] The intersubjective, collaborative mission of intellectual sharing that Oprah's Book Club espouses is one example of how these books change lives, but the Amazon reviews of Morrison's books are also full of these moments of personal transformation: "I don't ever remember being so moved by a novel. When I was done [reading *Song of Solomon*], I knew myself better than I ever thought I could."[36] These reviews make explicit the anxieties and arguments that are unlikely to be aired in professional reviews, classrooms, or book clubs. One anonymous reviewer of *Beloved* described her book club's refusal to confront the novel and its emotional challenges, including "white guilt" and other varieties of emotional pain, asking, "Were readers dismissing the novel out of a need to dismiss a subject that makes people (both black & white) squirm, or were the claims legitimate?"[37] These are precisely the questions that Morrison has sought to inspire as she has continued to define writing that is "indisputably black," approaching the challenge of multiple audiences as an opportunity for powerful new kinds of dialogue.[38]

When Morrison's readers create new structures of connection and affiliation online, they leave behind individual records of their critical acts which, in their own polyvocal, collaborative forms, lend themselves naturally to being examined in aggregate with computational tools of the kind I have demonstrated in this chapter. By upending the chorus of critically and academically situated opinions on literature, digital media are expanding opportunities for collective consciousness about how and why we read. The networks of texts and reviews explored here demonstrate some of the ways in which readers are revising canons and defining their own fields of literary context. E-book readers and online tools will continue to encourage forms of sharing—from popular highlighted passages on electronic readers to real-time interactions with authors through services like Twitter—and expand the social sphere of literature to include more participants in these conversations. In qualitative terms, digital media amplify Morrison's call to "work *with* the author in the construction of the book,"[39] no longer singly or in scattered reading groups but in the thousands and millions. These new technologies are helping readers to reinvent the way authorial prestige coalesces and to reshape the structures of distinction through which we encounter new texts and new ideas.

Notes

1. Pierre Bourdieu, *The Field of Cultural Production,* ed. Randal Johnson (New York: Columbia University Press, 1993), 38; Pierre Bourdieu, *The Rules of Art: Genesis and Structure of the Literary Field* (Stanford: Stanford University Press, 1996), 347.
2. John Guillory, *Cultural Capital: The Problem of Literary Canon Formation* (Chicago: University of Chicago Press, 1995), 33.
3. John K. Young, *Black Writers, White Publishers: Marketplace Politics in Twentieth-Century African American Literature,* 1st ed. (Jackson: University Press of Mississippi, 2006), 120. For more on the growing importance of authorial fame in American letters, see Joe Moran, *Star Authors: Literary Celebrity in America* (London: Pluto Press, 2000).
4. James F. English, *The Economy of Prestige: Prizes, Awards, and the Circulation of Cultural Value* (Cambridge: Harvard University Press, 2005).
5. Quoted in Cecilia Konchar Farr, *Reading Oprah: How Oprah's Book Club Changed the Way America Reads* (Albany: State University of New York Press, 2005), 60.
6. Henry Louis Gates Jr., *The Signifying Monkey: A Theory of Afro-American Literary Criticism* (New York: Oxford University Press, 1988), 129.
7. Ibid., xxvi.
8. Toni Morrison, "The Nobel Lecture in Literature," in *What Moves at the Margin* (Jackson: University Press of Mississippi, 2008), 198–208.
9. I collected the data discussed in this paper between May and August 2010, using a script to emulate an anonymous browser on Amazon.com's U.S. book site. The data collected by this script from each book page (author, title, books recommended from this page, and so on) were then entered into a MySQL database and later exported into the GraphML format for visualization with yEd, an open-source graph editor created by yWorks, GmbH. Nodes in the figures have been shaded according to the number of customer reviews each text received (one rough measure of popular canonicity), with darker shading indicating more reviews. The number of reviews is also included in parentheses in the label of each node.

10. These links are unweighted, since Amazon does not allow a book to be recommended by another book multiple times. Each link represents a single "Customers Who Bought" item, with directionality corresponding to the following logic: customers who bought [source] also bought [target].
11. Guillory, *Cultural Capital*, 29.
12. Cf. Guillory on the pedagogic imaginary, ibid., 28–38.
13. Expanded and full-color images of the networks explored here are available at http://www.edfinn.net/publications.
14. For one basic definition of the term and some applications, see Stanley Wasserman and Katherine Faust, *Social Network Analysis: Methods and Applications* (Cambridge: Cambridge University Press, 1994), 174–75.
15. This is, of course, not always the case. Bourdieu's original formulation of a truly autonomous field of critical production still holds sway in certain fields where "a systematic inversion of the fundamental principles of all ordinary economies" reigns, and commercial obscurity is a prerequisite for critical fame. Bourdieu, *The Field of Cultural Production*, 39.
16. Wasserman and Faust, *Social Network Analysis*, 254–62. The software used for this analysis, CFinder, employs the Clique Percolation Method to identify closely linked sub-diagrams within each diagram. Essentially the program identifies all cliques in the network that are not part of any larger clique. It then calculates the overlaps and relationships among all of these cliques to give a complete picture of clustering in the network. See http://cfinder.org for further details.
17. Moran, *Star Authors*, 25.
18. These results include only items published from 1980 to 2010, in an effort to control for the much longer period of time scholars have had access to Faulkner's work. Using another metric (from fifty to seventy years after each author's birth) provides similar ratios: 2,244 for Faulkner from 1947 to 1977, and 1,281 for Morrison from 1981 to 2001. These searches were conducted by using EBSCO Host's MLA International Bibliography database. For a discussion of this kind of analysis, see Matt Jockers's online debate with Matthew Wilkins, Matt Jockers, "Is It the Joyce Industry or the Shakespeare Industry?" blog, July 1, 2009, www.stanford.edu/~mjockers/cgi-bin/drupal/node/29.
19. English argues that scandal (for instance, the cozy relationships between judges and contestants and the public tantrums thrown by writers who do not win) is not a distraction from literary prizes but actually central to their impact. Whatever tarnishing effect these events might have on prizes such as the Man Booker, they make up for it in increased publicity, thus creating a cycle of growing prestige. English, *The Economy of Prestige*, 203–16.
20. Pierre Bourdieu, *Distinction: A Social Critique of the Judgement of Taste*, trans. Richard Nice (Cambridge: Harvard University Press, 2007), 235.
21. Bourdieu's seminal studies of artistic production in *The Field of Cultural Production* have been joined more recently by work such as James Curran, "Literary Editors, Social Networks and Cultural Tradition," in *Media Organisations in Society* (New York: Oxford University Press, 2000), 215–39; and Grant Blank, *Critics, Ratings, and Society: The Sociology of Reviews* (Lanham, Md.: Rowman & Littlefield, 2006). As Blank notes, however, cultural reviews remain relatively unstudied in sociology.
22. On the social and critical influence reviewers bring to bear on one another, see Curran, "Literary Editors, Social Networks and Cultural Tradition," 230. For a discussion of

the consensus effect in reviewing, see Susanne Janssen, "Reviewing as Social Practice: Institutional Constraints on Critics' Attention for Contemporary Fiction," *Poetics* 24 (1997): 275–97.

23. A "co-occurrence" here means that the two proper nouns appeared in the same review together—not necessarily the same sentence or even paragraph. The corpus includes all reviews of Morrison's work (including a few substantive book release–related profiles) to appear in established, nationally recognized reviewing publications in the United States. These included both newspapers (*Los Angeles Times, New York Times, Chicago Tribune,* and *Washington Post*) and magazines (*Nation, Newsweek, Time, New Yorker,* and *New York Review of Books*). The goal was to identify widely read publications with consistent patterns of reviewing.
24. In a few cases I have chosen to aggregate related nouns into one node, in those instances in which the terms referred to the same cultural entity. Hence Ms. Morrison, Toni Morrison, Morrison, Chloe Wofford, and a number of other terms all resolve to the same node. These aggregations were done sparingly and in most cases reflected different abbreviations of a book title or a person's name.
25. Young, *Black Writers, White Publishers,* 5.
26. Janice A. Radway, *A Feeling for Books: The Book-of-The-Month Club, Literary Taste, and Middle-Class Desire* (Chapel Hill: University of North Carolina Press, 1997), 286–87.
27. Janice A. Radway, *Reading the Romance: Women, Patriarchy, and Popular Literature* (Chapel Hill: University of North Carolina Press, 1984), 221.
28. Elizabeth Long, *Book Clubs: Women and the Uses of Reading in Everyday Life,* 1st ed. (Chicago: University of Chicago Press, 2003), 144.
29. Note, however, that anyone can review a product on Amazon, whether or not it was purchased there. The extent to which Amazon and other social websites like it have become noncommercial or supracommercial spaces for literary exchange (that is, among book borrowers as opposed to consumers) is an intriguing, open question.
30. "Black" was lemmatized in a very limited way here to include "Blacks" and "Black Life" (the latter term occurring only once in each corpus). Reviewers used a number of other racial descriptors, including "African American" and "Negro," but I felt that each of these terms carried significant distinguishing connotations that it would be a mistake to ignore.
31. "White" and "Black" are both proscribed by the widely followed Associated Press style guide, which dictates that these words remain in lowercase when used as racial descriptors.
32. Intriguingly, Amazon users almost never begin a sentence with a capitalized "White"; only two of the thirty-three instances of the word started a sentence in the Amazon corpus. In professional reviews, by contrast, nine out of twenty-five appearances of "White" started a sentence.
33. Some of the terms I aggregated into the node "English" were "AP English," "English Lit," "American Lit," "Lit," and "International Baccalaureate Advanced Lit Studies."
34. Elizabeth Long uses this term from Nancy Fraser to advance a similar possibility among book clubs in *Book Clubs,* 219–20.
35. Toni Morrison, "Toni Morrison Discusses Amazon Kindle," www.amazon.com/gp/mpd /permalink/m1SMOFDCLT5DMB.
36. Earl Hazell, "Unparalleled Lyricism, A Black Symphony of the Human Soul," August 28, 2000, www.amazon.com/review/RKD4EJAM1QJWS.

37. "Powerful, Wonderfully 'Uncomfortable,' and Sadly Avoided," October 17, 1998, www.amazon.com/review/RQPAM1F6DXJC4/ref=cm_srch_res_rtr_alt_1.
38. Toni Morrison, *The Bluest Eye* (New York: Vintage, 2007), xii.
39. Toni Morrison, *What Moves at the Margin: Selected Nonfiction* (Jackson: University Press of Mississippi, 2008), 59.

10

CONFOUNDING THE LITERARY
Temporal Problems in Hypertext

David S. Miall

A number of authors and critics have claimed that hypertext supersedes conventional printed literature. Moreover, theorists of hypertext have typically deprecated literary reading in print form in the belief that hypertext empowers readers, liberating them from the constraints of linear reading.[1] This theoretical challenge to the qualities of traditional print-based literary reading has never been properly answered. In this chapter I consider in what ways hypertext reading differs from the literary effects of print reading. I argue that what hypertext sacrifices, through promoting the machinery of reader choice, is the absorption of the literary reader and its invitation to develop the feelings and self of the reader. A hypertext reader, in contrast, must be active in moving about the screen, clicking links, making decisions. The subtle and varying flow of attention typical of literary reading is likely to be thwarted from the outset by the disjunctive structure of the hypertext, with its emphasis on the manipulation of screen objects. In this and other ways the computer has been described as a writing *space* by theorists of hypertext, notably by Jay David Bolter.[2] What are the implications of this claim for the reader of hyperfiction? If hypertext represents a turn to the visual, what might we expect readers to see? In seeking to answer these questions, I focus in particular on the relative claims of space and time as these differentiate hypertext from traditional literary reading.

If hypertext is intended to transcend the powers of the literary text, as authors such as Marku Eskelinen and N. Katherine Hayles maintain, this is to claim that hypertext enlivens or replaces the qualities for which we value literary reading. This could be assessed by empirical methods, as I will mention, by examining the responses of actual readers, but for this to be informative, for findings to be interpretable, we must first formulate our theoretical understanding. What should we expect? What hypotheses does our theory suggest might test the distinctions between the different kinds of reading,

[203]

and in particular enable us to elaborate a perspective embracing both literary and hypertext modes of reading? In this chapter I advance several theoretical considerations toward this goal. Bearing in mind how literary reading (itself a contentious topic) has typically been understood, we will see that such considerations include the nature of literary or poetic language (as studied in stylistics), narrative perspective, empathy for characters, the relation to a narrator, the imaginary worlds of fiction, the absorption of the reader, and the impact of reading on the self-concept and feelings of the reader, each to be assessed for its comparative contributions to the effectiveness of both literary and hypertext forms of reading. I begin with the question of space.

Space or Time?

The design of a hypertext screen is spatial, yet the experience of reading text is primarily temporal. On a printed page containing a narrative, nothing spatial about the page layout influences reading except paragraph breaks and chapter headings; once the reader is immersed in a narrative, even turning the page occurs unnoticed. Book designers might, perhaps, disagree with this claim; yet the better designed the book, the more effectively it enables us to engage with the meaning on the page, like a window open to a landscape, unless the writer explicitly introduces devices that draw our attention to the page. On a hypertext screen, in contrast, the spatial features impose a disciplinary constraint of their own on reading which cannot be ignored. I may need to click the mouse to scroll down the current text window; I must choose a link or click a button to move from this window to the next; the menu of options at the top of the screen provides other actions; the hypertext may open up a graphic: either I examine then dismiss it in order to proceed, or the graphic provides a site for interaction. These are among the ways in which spatial elements intrude on the temporal act of reading in a hypertext. What issues does this raise for the reader? In particular, is reading as a temporal process changed by the spatial elements that hypertext imposes?[3]

Reading from the printed page constitutes a temporal unfolding. The flux of time is shaped by the experience of reading a text such as a novel or a poem; temporal patterns are created by shifts and variations in the directions taken by the text, since successive phases of a text differ in the demands they make on a reader's attention, and in the calls made on her concepts, feelings, and memories, or on her experience with similar texts. As critics such as T. E. Hulme have noted,[4] this experience of time shaped through reading corresponds to

Henri Bergson's concept of *durée* (usually translated as "duration"), which is opposed to the spatial, clock-driven view of time.[5] In the latter conception, the moments of time are imagined as laid out on a line, on which one moment is equivalent to any other moment. Although literary texts evoke places or spaces, we tend to treat these impressionistically, absorbing them into the temporal flow of reading. Readers will only vaguely specify dimensions such as movement or the relative disposition of features of a setting, unless strong local reasons exist for building a spatial model.[6] In traditional literary reading, space thus appears to play only a limited and subsidiary role in the imaginary world we enter while reading.

Claims about the nature of hypertext, however, typically reverse the priority of time and space, as in accounts such as Bolter's.[7] The organization of hypertext into links and nodes tends to result in text being treated iconically, a tendency strengthened by the presence of other media (graphics, animations) in more recent hyperfictions. Thus, at the extreme, hypertext is read not for the experience it offers but for its affordances in invoking the surrounding mechanism, or the *hypotext,* as Stuart Moulthrop has termed it.[8] In this view hypertext writing becomes a continuous and unstable dance of screen objects whose principle of variation is driven not by a reader but by the underlying structures of the hypertext system itself. The privileging of space as the medium of text thus seems to confront literary reading with a major problem. Most or all of what we understand by literary reading, as I outlined it earlier, is disabled. The short lexias of hypertext (a series of single windows usually containing text) and the need to choose one from several links may disrupt the reader's own unfolding dynamic of reading or forestall its development. Rather than hypertext liberating the reader, as its advocates have argued, a common response to hypertext is to feel trapped within its machinery. The hypertext reader is liable to become restless, to become a surfer looking for satisfaction down an endless chain of links, rather than finding it in the window opened up by the text itself.[9]

If reading spatially is not sustainable—and turns into surfing—we may find the reader becoming haunted by the sense of lost time. The mode of time constituted by hypertext is signified by the flashing cursor, the imperative to click links, and the machine-imposed events (movements, graphic transformations) embedded in many hypertexts with Flash or Javascripts. Produced by the order of the machine, this mode manifests Bergson's mathematical time, the succession of moments on a line. For the hypertext reader, however, a drift takes place into another mode of time that possesses elements of the uncanny. Given the repetitive and often recursive nature of the linking structure of hypertext, a reader can become ensnared, struggling inside a web that may seem to have no ending and no means of exit. Like the protagonist of a gothic novel, the reader is immersed in a dreamlike world whose laws of operation are obscure, confounding agency.

Moreover, the recurring requirement to choose among hypertext links imposes a template of self-awareness over the act of reading. This also forms part of the temporal structure of hypertext reading. In the suspension of reading, the reader is returned to the self: unless choice is arbitrary, each act of choice helps define the self as it pauses to choose. I must consider my interests as these are reflected in the choices available: How do I wish to invest myself as I move forward? To what will I commit myself by selecting this link rather than that? And as I move beyond the opening lexias and become familiar with the design and tendencies of the hypertext, I may also be asking other questions: Does my choice make any difference? What kind of commitment is it that can be reversed by clicking on the "back" button? Our literary experience with books does not pose such questions every half page. This self-conscious mode of engagement suggests that literary reading confronts some significant and novel disruptions in the new hypertext forms of fiction.[10] Whether hypertext fiction necessarily incurs these liabilities is a question I return to at the end of this essay; more immediately, the issue I take up is that posed by the proponents of hypertext who celebrate it precisely on these grounds—that it is an innovation on the conventional fixity and dullness of print-based reading.

In what follows, then, I consider some conceptions of time as these help us understand the process of reading in both conventional and hypertext media. I focus in particular on Bergson's account, as this provides a valuable perspective on two kinds of time at issue in reading hypertext. I also consider the reading experience as it impacts the reader's sense of narrative engagement and awareness of self, drawing on psychological studies of reading as well as the neuropsychological basis for the self proposed by the neuropsychologist Antonio Damasio. In this way, in contrast to the views promoting hypertext that I have mentioned, I propose a different approach to framing the question. Instead of taking hypertext itself and its novel components as my starting point, I ask what we know about reading. Given the psychological processes that support it, how effectively does hypertext interact with or engage those processes?

The Primacy of Time

"Time," Hans Meyerhoff notes, "is the most characteristic mode of our experience. It is more general than space, because it applies to the inner world of impressions, emotion, and ideas for which no spatial order can be given."[11] In the postmodern dispensation, however, the time-space relation is reversed: space is the governing medium, directing how we understand time. For example, in an essay published in 1980, W. J. T. Mitchell undertakes to extend Joseph Frank's arguments about spatial form (first published in 1945) by contending that the spatial is an essential component of all literature, not merely what we call modernist. Spatiality is not opposed to temporality but is its condition. Mitchell observes that "spatial form is the perceptual basis of our notion of time, that we literally cannot 'tell time' without the mediation of space. All our temporal language is contaminated with spatial imagery."[12] He finds our notions of continuity and sequence in literature explicable spatially: they are simply "spatial images based in the schema of the unbroken line or surface."[13]

Recourse to the spatial, then, is one way to call into question presence, that is, presentness of time, or presentness *in* time. The evoking of the line, however, is a reminder of the founding principle of Bergson's philosophy of time, which is intended to elaborate the sense of presence. Only by going beyond spatial models of time can we grasp the self and imagine the possibility of change and growth. We forestall this by representing time spatially, by "placing side by side in space phenomena which do not occupy space," by the "illegitimate translation of the unextended into the extended."[14] Such a homogeneous and uniform view of time, Bergson claims, "by introducing space into our perception of duration . . . corrupts at its very source our feeling of outer and inner change, of movement, and of freedom."[15] It constitutes a "reaction against that heterogeneity which is the very ground of our experience."[16]

The locating of time as a series in space is consistent with the associationist views that pervade accounts of hypertext, suggesting the regressive nature of such views.[17] As Bergson explains, "The associationist reduces the self to an aggregate of conscious states: sensations, feelings, and ideas"; but these "he may set . . . side by side for ever without getting anything but a phantom self, the shadow of the ego projecting itself into space."[18] The separateness of lexias seems to impose on us the view that they are located in space rather than time, or at least in a spatialized succession of moments. In striking contrast, a note by Coleridge provides a vivid image of the temporal moment comparable to Bergson's concept of duration: "What a swarm of Thoughts & Feelings, endlessly minute fragments & as it were representations of all preceding & embryos of all future Thought lie . . . compact in any one moment."[19] It is this continuousness of thought that hypertext segmentation by lexias and links seems designed to truncate, thwarting the development of the representations that exist potentially in thought and reducing the self to a phantom—an outcome embraced by

Moulthrop in his concept of *breakdown*. In Moulthrop's words, "hypertext is a technology of trauma, reflexively figuring its own assault on the textual corpus in terms of insults to the physical body."[20]

Tracing the spatial sequence of lexias does not emancipate the reader from time, however. Rather, the abortion of the embryos of future thought, cut off at the link, seems likely to wear away and negate the reader's process of conception with each lexia.[21] We might regard reading that frustrates the birth of new forms as entropic: it absorbs energies, exercises the will, and modifies agency in ways that systematically deplete the reader's functions in comparison with literary reading. In effect it wastes the self of the reader.

This view of the self as dependent on temporal flow is reflected in the account of Damasio, who argues for the presence of the self in the "convergence zones" that support each moment of conscious activity.[22] This view echoes Bergson's argument for the heterogeneity of duration. Since there is no single convergence zone at which all experience is integrated, the brain can be seen as an interlocking set of partly independent, shifting convergence zones that allows for local integration. The subjective experience of coherence in experience, Damasio suggests, is "a trick of timing."[23] What Damasio calls the "autobiographical self" is continually active in the form of dispositions recalled from memory, thus ensuring that working memory holds in mind "*both* a particular object *and* the autobiographical self."[24] Additionally, convergence zones "can blend responses, that is, produce reactivation of fragments that did not originally belong to the same experiential set."[25] While Damasio argues that this feature is responsible for learning, his account also provides a basis for the modifications that can occur during literary reading, as readers' feelings or memories are evoked in settings in which they have not previously occurred. This suggests that reading is dependent in particular on memory, the self, and the possibility of shifts between convergence zones, that is, the heterogeneous experience that occurs when we gain insights about ourselves or others.

In literary reading the effects of memory appear to be intermittent. They may take time to be manifested to the degree that the act of reading speaks to what is individual in the reader, generating the sense that the self is implicated in the events and outcomes of a narrative.[26] But the hypertext reader is increasingly distanced from the memory that imbues duration. The short lexias of hypertext tend to forestall the contributions of memory—that personal memory which is, in the end, perhaps the most significant context for locating a literary text. Excluded from this central current flowing through duration, the reader is likely to treat the lexias of hypertext as counters in a game, an intellectualized game of perception. How can the lexias be made to reveal the pattern behind them? Is it possible to second-guess the author who designed this machinery?

Being rooted in memory and the self, literary response requires a degree of textual underdetermination by the text or deliberate ambiguity for the possibility of insight, that is, for registering effectively the implications of the shifts in feeling and understanding that insight brings. The uncertainty of literary meaning, whether on the large scale (does Tolstoy's novel invite us to empathize with Anna Karenina's feelings?) or the small (what can Emily Dickinson mean by "The Brain – is wider than the Sky"?), invites the reader to construe some significant aspect of the world anew—a construal that may have not only conceptual but also emotional, cultural, or ethical implications for the reader's sense of self. The reduction of this possibility is perhaps the main liability of hypertext, in which the diminishing reflection of the reader's self in the difference of each lexia, its entropic exhaustion of the reader's commitment, argues for a homogeneous view of hypertext lexias; they are able to manifest only differences in degree, not in kind. In other words, for the reader the lexias of hyperfiction are liable to constitute a series on the same plane, regardless of how they are presented or what they contain.

Moreover, as lexias vary arbitrarily in their relation to one another, so they lose their integrity as self-defining sequences with clear boundaries. The space of hypertext, to borrow Gilles Deleuze's words, "appears as the schema of an indefinite divisibility,"[27] if in principle it may be constituted at this moment by several paragraphs or at that by a single letter. The hypertext reader may become indifferent to the length of a lexia if no internal signs of difference mark out why it should not be longer or shorter.[28] This seems to enforce the arbitrariness not just of the design of lexias but of language itself, further removing us from duration. Only through duration, Bergson suggests, can we overcome the rough approximations of language, "the word with well-defined outlines, the rough and ready word, which stores up the stable, common, and consequently impersonal element in the impressions of mankind."[29] This is particularly apparent in the poverty of language for capturing feeling. In literature, language tricks us into sensing the feelings that are interwoven with duration. The author manages to overcome in part the abstraction and enumeration of feelings by showing how they interweave and permeate one another. "Encouraged by him," says Bergson, "we have put aside for an instant the veil which we interposed between our consciousness and ourselves. He has brought us back into our own presence."[30]

Anticipation and Feeling

As Raimonda Modiano explains, commenting on a remark of Coleridge's, art imitates nature "only in so far as the object of imitation is the spiritual essence of nature (*natura naturans*) and not its external appearance (*natura naturata*)." Merely to copy nature is to produce "lifeless masks" or "empty forms devoid of reality."[31] In Deleuze's words, echoing Bergson's similar conception, "duration is like a naturing nature (*nature naturante*), and matter a natured nature (*nature naturée*)."[32] The former contains differences in kind, the latter only differences in degree. In other words, the literary experience embodies processes that it invites the reader to represent through shifts and changes in feelings, whereas hypertext has already encoded the allowable steps of narrative experience, specifying in advance the set of equivalent objects that is to determine the reader's attention.

In this (Coleridgean) perspective, it is likely that the mechanism that is hypertext fails to correspond to the "nature" that is the object of the narrative; its structure of lexias predetermines a limited set of forms for the narrative that is being shaped. Obligatory link choices cut across—or cut off—the feelings that the reader would, in another context, have been able to develop in a moment of duration. Feeling "natures" us as literary readers, whereas hypertext lexias already bear the marks of their nature, as preshaped, determinate matter, tied to mechanism. The link mechanism segments time according to mechanical rules, multiplying isolated moments of experience. Duration, in contrast, to borrow Bergson's concept of lived experience again, is characterized not by isolatable constituents but by the rhythm of successive episodes that bear within them both traces of the past and intimations of the future.

The loss of rhythm in hypertext is suggested by our frequent failure to anticipate what will be revealed by clicking on a particular link.[33] Bergson's characterization of two kinds of movement is apropos here: "If jerky movements are wanting in grace, the reason is that each of them is self-sufficient and does not announce those which are to follow." In contrast, in movement that is smooth (Bergson provides the example of a dancer), the grace we recognize results because each movement prepares the way for the next: "We are led to find a superior ease in the movements which can be foreseen, in the present attitudes in which future attitudes are pointed out and, as it were, prefigured."[34] Bergson points to the anticipatory role of feeling in this respect, describing our pleasure in such movements as a "moral sympathy" due to their "attractiveness," while the aesthetic pleasure resolves into a flux of many different feelings.[35] We rely frequently on feeling in this respect, although we may not make explicit to ourselves what outcome a particular feeling has projected. It is present as a "gut feeling," to use Damasio's term, that signals "the merits of a given response" by promoting attention to its positive or negative aspects.[36] Damasio points in particular to the bodily components of feeling; hence his term for the anticipatory property of feeling is the "somatic marker."

Feeling thus provides a key temporal orienting process, promoting the salience of the issues at various levels of our engagement with a text and keeping them active.[37] Among the many possibilities, this relates us to the stylistic variations in the text that signal mood, context, or attitude. Feeling monitors the evolving plot, manages our recognition of the personality of characters and our empathy with their situations, and signals the ethical issues at stake. Given the shifts and conflicts in feeling that occur during reading, it is also obvious that the complement of anticipation is surprise—since literary texts often exceed our expectations or thwart them in some significant way. Through feeling, the reader is invited to entertain altered states of being. As an experience in duration, then, reading can also be an experiment in self-making, as alternative feelings project shifts in identity.

In this light, hypertext—as it has been characterized by some of its proponents—is less likely to offer the complexity of feelings that makes literature compelling, as it may disrupt the anticipatory element of our feelings as we pass from one lexia to the next. Movement in hypertext is, in this respect, illusory, since it is merely tracing a pathway across a preexisting network; it is not the movement of the reader that forges new structures of thought and feeling (the personal network of response). To the extent that we recognize the mechanism underlying and determining the possible choices, we derogate from the feelings that would shape our reading—since to examine and to participate are mutually exclusive states.[38] Hypertext thus reduces to a pattern; it ceases to challenge the reader, except as a puzzle, by coming to exist in space rather than time.

To offer a choice between links suggests that our sensations are multiple and separable, and can be placed side by side. Hypertext theory proposes that the branching point of links promotes a free choice, liberating the reader, but this picture is misleading.[39] Freedom lies not here, in the hesitation between two pathways, but prior to this, in the anticipatory qualities of different feelings: "I pass in review my different affections: it seems to me that each of them contains, after its kind, an invitation to act, with at the same time leave to wait and even to do nothing."[40] The freedom bestowed by hypertext is limited to operating the machinery below the lexias; the freedom of literary reading lies in the feelings that solicit the shaping and redirecting of response at each moment.

Owing to this indifference of the links to readers' feelings, the world of hypertext has a curiously weightless, inconsequential quality. Its formal design, which makes its narrative into mere surface, designates it a mechanism in Deleuze's terms, involving "closed systems, actions of contact, immobile instantaneous sections."[41] Though the reader may never visit all the links, the hypertext is visibly a closed world, already determined: "One misses the movement because one constructs a Whole, one assumes that 'all is given,' whilst movement only occurs if the whole is neither given nor giveable."[42] Thus hypertext returns us to the problem of space. As a medium for representing the flux of feeling and thought, hypertext undermines the sense of change, as spatializing time does for Bergson: "By invading the series of our psychic states, by introducing space into our perception of duration, it corrupts at its very source our feeling of outer and inner change, of movement, and of freedom."[43] By demarcating text sections into separate lexias, hypertext forestalls the permeation of feelings, sensations, and thoughts that constitutes duration. The lexias as spatialized entities are imposed on "an empty homogeneous medium."[44]

I have mentioned some of the alterations of perception that occur within hyperfiction reading. Once we are within its boundaries, one change that becomes possible can be characterized as a kind of gothic entrapment. For example, many hypertexts from Michael Joyce's *Afternoon*[45] onwards unfold such that after an initial fifty or sixty lexias have been read, sequences of lexias begin to repeat. The reader becomes caught in a loop, which at first seems short and easy to escape. But further into the reading, as the ratio of repetitions to new lexias increases, such loops may become more intrusive. Like a phobic patient for whom some trivial daily action has assumed enormous importance, the reader is obliged to carry out motions, clicking from one link to the next, which have no obvious function, yet which cannot be avoided each time the loop repeats. In this situation, agency becomes confused. Is it the reader choosing to click through the loop, or has the reader become the agent of the author who designed the hypertext? The hypertext author, after all, is present yet not present, just as a ghost is neither alive nor definitively dead, but a *revenant* (one who has returned). The author, moreover, is the reverse of the one criticized by Plato in *Phaedrus* for creating texts that go out into the world with no control: the hypertext author will continue to intervene.[46]

Thus, as duration does not cease when we become readers of hypertext, our entrapment changes the sense of time. As each action becomes a repetition, or meets with frustration, the meaning of time begins to evacuate; if time no longer sustains choice or change, and to stand still is impossible, then time begins to deconstruct the reader. Hypertext becomes the space that time devours. It might seem from the writings of hypertext theorists that the reverse must be the case, that hypertext, like the Cerberus of postmodernism, is the revenge of space on time. But time is not so readily defeated: what time does not serve to create, it will destroy.

I have suggested that hypertext reading considered within a temporal perspective is subject to a number of liabilities. Let me emphasize again that I aim not to dismiss hypertext per se as a vehicle for reading but to call into question its suitability as a new medium for literary experience, basing my approach on the rhetoric of hypertext theorists and on my reading of hypertext fictions, early and recent. My approach has depended on two kinds of argument: first, that the case for a new type of literary experience made possible by hypertext has not yet been demonstrated by its proponents, and second, that on intrinsic grounds, the properties of hypertext, as these have been proposed and celebrated by George Landow, Bolter, and their followers, provide an inhospitable context for literary reading. In this respect, I have focused in this chapter on the psychological processes that appear to be integral and probably distinctive to literary experience, and suggested that these processes are systematically disrupted by the hypertext machinery for reading. I have focused on time, with Bergson's help, since these processes are to a major degree time sensitive, and for their development require a temporal framework of the kind that hypertext appears to negate. Bergson's concept of duration, while not an aesthetic theory as such, enables several key components of literary response to be identified and situated in relation to the spatializing tendencies that would depreciate them—among which hypertext, as it is conceived by its theorists, is a notable example. Thus the literary reader anticipates a complex, changing, and continuous experience from a literary text of any length, such as a narrative. In hypertext, in contrast, the segmented lexias and link structure instead enforce repetition, discontinuity, and reductiveness. The literary reader experiences the self as an enlarged consciousness of the themes and predicaments of the narrative; in hypertext the reader's self-consciousness is evoked by operating the hypertext machinery.

Whether these liabilities become a permanent feature of hypertext design remains to be seen.[47] Whether creative writers can overcome them, whether new forms will emerge that effectively relocate or reinvent the literary, whether the stylistic and narrative qualities that sustain literary reading can be more effectively exploited by hypertext—these are eventualities that no one can rule out.[48] Whether such new hypertexts will be read as commonly and with as much pleasure as the average novel is read now—this will be a powerful test of their literary value.

Notes

1. This problem dates back to the first hypertext theorists such as Jay David Bolter. More recent deprecatory commentators include Marku Eskelinen, who states that "all the knowledge we can gain from traditional literary studies is based on literary objects that are static, intransient, determinate, impersonal, random access, solely interpretative and without links" ("Cybertext Theory and Literary Studies, A User's Manual," *ebr* 12 [Fall 2001], www.altx.com/ebr/ebr12/eskel.htm); and N. Katherine Hayles, who claims that "print is flat" and that literary scholars have been "lulled into somnolence by five hundred years of print" ("Print Is Flat, Code Is Deep: The Importance of Media-Specific Analysis," *Poetics Today* 25.1 [2004]: 68).
2. As the title of his influential book suggests: see Jay David Bolter, *Writing Space: The Computer, Hypertext, and the History of Writing* (Hillsdale, N.J.: Erlbaum, 1991).
3. The claims made for literary reading here are based on narrative. Similar evidence for reading processes is, however, available from studies of readers of poetry. While poetry readers tend to be more self-aware and more challenged by the medium, they form similar expectations of stylistic features and a productive role for feeling-based anticipation. For an empirical study bearing on these issues, see Don Kuiken, David S. Miall, and Shelley Sikora, "Forms of Self-Implication in Literary Reading," *Poetics Today* 25.2 (2004): 171–203.
4. T. E. Hulme, *Speculations: Essays on Humanism and the Philosophy of Art*, ed. Herbert Read (London: Routledge & Kegan Paul, 1936), 181.
5. "Pure duration is the form which the succession of our conscious states assumes when our ego lets itself *live*, when it refrains from separating its present state from its former states," as "clock time" tends to enforce. In duration "both the past and the present states [form] into an organic whole, as happens when we recall the notes of a tune, melting, so to speak, into one another." Henri Bergson, *Time and Free Will*, trans. F. L. Pogson (London: Allen and Unwin, 1910), 100.
6. Rolf A. Zwaan and Herre Van Oostendorp, "Do Readers Construct Spatial Representations in Naturalistic Story Comprehension?" *Discourse Processes* 16.1–2 (January–June 1993): 125–43.
7. For further discussion of the spatial issue, see David S. Miall, "Trivializing or Liberating: The Limitations of Hypertext Theorizing," *Mosaic* 32.2 (1999): 157–71.
8. Stuart Moulthrop, "You Say You Want a Revolution? Hypertext and the Laws of Media," in *Essays in Postmodern Culture*, ed. Eyal Amiran and John Unsworth (New York: Oxford University Press, 1994), 69–97.
9. For empirical evidence of this and several other claims made in this chapter, see David S. Miall and Teresa Dobson, "Reading Hypertext and the Experience of Literature," *Journal of Digital Information* 2.1 (2001), http://jodi.tamu.edu/Articles/v02/i01/Miall/; and Ed Tan and Sarita Dev, "Bypassing the Author: Two Examples of Reading Interactive Stories," in *The Psychology and Sociology of Literature: In Honor of Elrud Ibsch*, ed. Gerard Steen and Dick H. Schram (Amsterdam: John Benjamins, 2001), 289–313. For a critical review of these issues in the light of cognitive narratology, see Ralf Schneider, "Hypertext

Narrative and the Reader: A View from Cognitive Theory," *European Journal of English Studies* 9.2 (2005): 197–208.
10. Although disruptions of various kinds also characterize some postmodern novels, for example, Italo Calvino, *If on a Winter's Night a Traveler,* trans. William Weaver (London: Secker & Warburg, 1981).
11. Hans Meyerhoff, *Time in Literature* (Berkeley: University of California Press, 1955), 1.
12. W. J. T. Mitchell, "Spatial Form in Literature: Toward a General Theory," *Critical Inquiry* 6.3 (Spring 1980): 541–42. The essay Mitchell draws on is Joseph Frank, "Spatial Form in Modern Literature (Revised Version)," in *The Widening Gyre: Crisis and Mastery in Modern Literature* (Bloomington: Indiana University Press, 1968), 3–62.
13. Mitchell, "Spatial Form in Literature," 542.
14. Bergson, *Time and Free Will,* xix.
15. Ibid., 74.
16. Ibid., 97.
17. See, for example, Ilana Snyder, *Hypertext: The Electronic Labyrinth* (New York: New York University Press, 1996), 25.
18. Bergson, *Time and Free Will,* 165.
19. Samuel Taylor Coleridge, *The Notebooks of Samuel Taylor Coleridge,* ed. Kathleen Coburn, 5 vols. (London: Routledge, 2002), 3:4057. See also William James on the stream of thought: how "in our feeling of each word there chimes an echo or foretaste of every other" (*The Principles of Psychology,* vol. 1 [New York: Henry Holt, 1890], 281).
20. Stuart Moulthrop, "Traveling in the Breakdown Lane: A Principle of Resistance for Hypertext," *Mosaic* 28.4 (1995): 70.
21. For examples of analyses, see Tan and Dev, "Bypassing the Author," 293–308; David S. Miall, "Reading Hypertext: Theoretical Ambitions and Empirical Studies," *Jahrbuch für Computerphilologie* 5 (2003): 161–78; and David S. Miall and Teresa Dobson, "Reading Hypertext and the Experience of Literature," *Journal of Digital Information* 2.1 (2001), http://journals.tdl.org/jodi/article/viewArticle/35/37.
22. In this concept, neural impulses co-occur in temporary, shifting assemblies based on relations of similarity and placement in space and time. Impulses are likely to include the early association cortex which undertakes feature detection, the amygdala for feeling registration, and the frontal cortex. The stream of experience recruits autobiographical memory as well as promoting appropriate perceptual or affective elements by feedback mechanisms.
23. Antonio R. Damasio, "Time-Locked Multiregional Retroactivation: A Systems-Level Proposal for the Neural Substrates of Recall and Recognition," *Cognition* 33.1–2 (1989): 28.
24. Antonio R. Damasio, *The Feeling of What Happens: Body, Emotion, and the Making of Consciousness* (New York: Harcourt Brace, 1999), 161, 222.
25. Damasio, "Time-Locked Multiregional Retroactivation," 47.
26. For detailed discussion of this issue in the context of an empirical study of reading, see Kuiken, Miall and Sikora, "Forms of Self-Implication in Literary Reading," esp. 176, 182–83.
27. Gilles Deleuze, *Bergsonism,* trans. Hugh Tomlinson and Barbara Habberjam (New York: Zone, 1988), 92–93.
28. The lexias become cumulative rather than constitutive. For example, if three lexias link only one to the next, why should this not consist of only one lexia (constituting an episode), or, alternatively, why not six lexias, or ten?

29. Bergson, *Time and Free Will*, 132.
30. Ibid., 134.
31. Raimonda Modiano, *Coleridge and the Concept of Nature* (London: Macmillan, 1985), 54. Cf. Samuel Taylor Coleridge, "On Poesy or Art," in *Lectures, 1808–1819: On Literature,* vol. 2, ed. R. A. Foakes (London: Routledge & Kegan Paul, 1987), 220–21.
32. Deleuze, *Bergsonism*, 93.
33. For empirical evidence of this point, showing that hypertext readers' expectations were disappointed in comparison with those of linear readers, see Tan and Dev, "Bypassing the Author," 306–7.
34. Bergson, *Time and Free Will*, 11–12.
35. Ibid., 13.
36. Antonio R. Damasio, Daniel Tranel, and Hannah Damasio, "Somatic Markers and the Guidance of Behavior: Theory and Preliminary Testing," in *Frontal Lobe Function and Dysfunction,* ed. Harvey S. Levin, Howard M. Eisenberg, and Arthur L. Benton (New York: Oxford University Press, 1991), 220–21.
37. For some of the theoretical and empirical evidence behind these claims and those that follow, see David S. Miall, "Feeling from the Perspective of the Empirical Study of Literature," *Journal of Literary Theory* 1.2 (2008): 377–93.
38. For an important discussion of this issue, see Marie-Laure Ryan, *Narrative as Virtual Reality: Immersion and Interactivity in Literature and Electronic Media* (Baltimore: Johns Hopkins University Press, 2001).
39. Bergson, *Time and Free Will*, 175–83. Cf. F. C. T. Moore, *Bergson: Thinking Backwards* (Cambridge: Cambridge University Press, 1996), 110.
40. Henri Bergson, *Matter and Memory,* trans. Nancy Margaret Paul and W. Scott Palmer (London: Allen & Unwin, 1911), 2.
41. Gilles Deleuze, *Cinema 1: The Movement-Image,* trans. Barbara Habberjam and Hugh Tomlinson (Minneapolis: University of Minnesota Press, 1986), 59.
42. Ibid., 7.
43. Bergson, *Time and Free Will*, 74.
44. Ibid., 95.
45. Michael Joyce, *Afternoon: A Story* (Watertown, Mass.: Eastgate Systems, 1987), diskette.
46. For a more positive view of the loop as a poetic feature, see Bronwen Thomas, "Stuck in a Loop? Dialogue in Hypertext Fiction," *Narrative* 15.3 (2007): 357–72.
47. As Michel Chaouli points out, the readership for hypertext remains small and confined largely to academic circles and the writers who create it. It seems that readers with a taste for contemporary fiction are not interested in seeking out interactive hyperfiction. Michel Chaouli, "How Interactive Can Fiction Be?" *Critical Inquiry* 31.3 (2005): 599–617.
48. For some detailed analysis of these qualities, see Miall, "Reading Hypertext"; and Schneider, "Hypertext Narrative."

11

READING THE READING EXPERIENCE
An Ethnomethodological Approach to "Booktalk"

Daniel Allington and Bethan Benwell

Interviews and focus groups have long been employed to research the ways in which literary and televisual texts are understood by their contemporary consumers,[1] and the historical study of reading and of reception has often taken the same approach to written descriptions of reading experiences.[2] The appeal of this kind of information is obvious: where better to learn about readers than straight from the horse's mouth?

Nonetheless, there are problems with treating such data, whether researcher-elicited or spontaneous, as transparent. Acknowledgment of this has led to an emerging "crisis of representation"[3] within the fields of cultural and reception studies, whereby researchers have begun to question their ability to represent social reality with any objectivity. Whether we are interested in acts of reading past or acts of reading and viewing present, this apparently leaves us with a choice of closing our eyes to obvious difficulties or restricting ourselves to only such topics of investigation as can be approached by the powerful but impersonal methods of quantitative sociology, book history, and economics.[4] In this chapter we propose an alternative approach whose roots lie in ethnomethodology. Ethnomethodology is the study of the ways in which people display their understandings of the world around them to others, negotiating those understandings with one another and in this way producing social order as an achieved phenomenon. These displays and negotiations are referred to as "accounting practices" which are "contingent, ongoing accomplishments of organized artful practices of everyday life" and "are carried on under the auspices of, and . . . made to happen as events in, the same ordinary affairs that in organizing they describe."[5] Many reception data can be seen as the residue of such accounting practices: when people talk or write about reading and about texts, they are collaborating—cooperatively or antagonistically—in the production of the (local) social order of reading and of texts. Statements describing a reader's experiences in reading a particular book may appear to be literal *reports* of events taking place in a preexisting reality, but to an ethnomethodologist, these must be seen as *accounts* constructing reality.

In common with the ethnomethodologically inspired research tradition known as discursive psychology (discussed later in this chapter), our approach to the analysis of readers' discourse involves recording spoken interactions, examining the sequential organization of "turns" within those interactions, and assuming that this discourse is "constitutive of, performative of, and pervasively oriented to, the social interactional contingencies of whatever setting it is produced in."[6] As Jonathan Potter explains,[7] this means that the researcher does not have to make inferences from the "data collection arena" (that is, the situation in which reading is discussed) to the object of research (that is, reading), since the two are identical: if we study the members of a book group talking about their private reading experiences, for example, this is because we are interested in what the study of their talk reveals about the constructions of their own reading practices. Far from making private reading experiences inaccessible, this involves analyzing the ways in which such talkers construct those experiences as accessible or inaccessible to one another.[8] In this manner we attempt to fulfill Janice Radway's plea for attention to "the ever-shifting nature of subjectivity produced through the articulation of discourses,"[9] and to come closer to an understanding of why an individual's responses to a text—and descriptions of his or her prior responses to that text—may be as myriad as the occasions on which his or her views are elicited.[10]

Other approaches to verbal representations of reading are of course possible. For example, reception researchers working in other traditions might seek to explain statements about reading experiences by relating them to the context in which those experiences took place (or are supposed to have taken place) and to the identities of the participants. Thus Megan Sweeney treats statements by female prisoners as indicative of their "general sense of frustration" with aspects of Gayl Jones's novel *Eva's Man,* and then explains this frustration by reference to the those readers' "first-hand experience with a justice system that leaves little room for accommodating ambiguity or complex and partial notions of agency, responsibility, guilt, and innocence."[11] In chapter 12 of this volume, Danielle Fuller and DeNel Rehberg Sedo offer a "mixed research method" approach to reception data which involves the synthesis of quantitative survey data with qualitative micro-observations of sampled details of participants' talk about books, in pursuit of their objective of describing reading as a "situated social practice." These are valid and useful methods, but they do not appear to take into account the rhetorical or performative character of the speakers' statements within the interactional context in which they were made. Our purpose here, by contrast, is to show how one particular group of readers negotiates the interpretation and evaluation of a poetic work by producing accounts of reading experiences. By contextualizing accounts in relation to the sequential structure of the interaction in which they were produced, we are able to analyze what a given reader may have been *doing* in producing a given account.

Attempts have been made elsewhere to relate accounts of reading experiences to an "objective" sociohistorical context *as well as* to their immediate narrative or sequential context—a move that is acknowledged to be problematic, but which may permit a halfway house between the social constructionist position associated with ethnomethodology and the critical realism of studies such as Sweeney's.[12] In this chapter, however, we present a relatively "pure" form of discourse analysis, focusing exclusively on the micro-processes of verbal interaction as context for the represented reading experience.[13] In this way we fulfill our commitment to explicating a particular *kind* of contextual reading, one that retrieves its interpretation from the participants' talk itself within the local situation in which the talk occurs. This may, of course, include participants' *own* articulations of how their readings may be connected to broader social or historical events, but avoids speculation about what these connections may be.

The Social Accountability of Reading: The Structure of a Book Group Discussion Sequence

Here we analyze a reading group discussion, employing the discourse analytical procedures and ethnomethodological assumptions outlined in the introductory sections in order to provide insight into how the subjective experience of reading has to be carefully managed and negotiated within a specific social environment. An important principle of ethnomethodological inquiry is the notion of "members' methods" for conducting social life in an orderly fashion, the analysis of which involves seeking "to explicate rational grounds for the collaborative production of courses of action."[14] Such a focus in the context of the analysis of our reading group data enables us to form some insights into the "social order" of a particular book group, its shared norms, implicit values, and systems of accountability.

We focus on a thirty-minute segment of a book group session at a public library in Edinburgh, in which the group members discuss Jackie Kay's long narrative poem *The Adoption Papers*.[15] This poem deals with adoption and ethnicity, offering the perspectives of three characters: the birth mother, the adoptive mother, and the daughter, who, like Kay herself, is of mixed race and is adopted by a white Scottish couple. The work's autobiographical nature, its emotional impact, and its "authenticity" are made relevant throughout.

Our particular interest is the detail of how certain responses get "validated" in the context of the discussion. Using a turn-by-turn discourse analytical approach, we demonstrate how reader response is collaboratively worked up in the course of a situated discussion. At issue is the way in which particular opinions are ratified, taken up, and endorsed by the group. While a number of sometimes conflicting interpretations may be voiced in a session, not all of these utterances gain the status of consensus. We are interested in examining which interpretations *are* taken up by other members, how this is achieved discursively, and how utterances that do not chime with the collective will of the group are not developed. This kind of analysis thus demonstrates the way in which accounts of past reading experiences can be occasioned by the immediate interactional context.

A key means of securing consensus and accomplishing an accountable reading identity in the sequence we present is by the invocation of *emotion*. Our analysis of the construction of the subjective experience of reading is partly informed by the preoccupations and rationale of discursive psychology, a school of social psychology rooted in the principles of ethnomethodology that investigates the everyday discussion of psychological topics such as memory and emotion. The original aim of discursive psychology was to challenge the tenets of cognitive psychology, particularly the assumption that psychological states operate *behind* talk, causing us to say what we do. It is concerned with the way such states are *performed*, and how references to phenomena such as attitudes, memory, emotions, and motivations are deployed rhetorically and strategically as resources in talk.

In our first sequence of data (extract 1) we use "S" and a number to identify speakers, so as to keep our participants anonymous and to avoid the class, age, and gender connotations that attach to pseudonyms. No number is used where it has been impossible to identify the speaker. A bracket in line with one in the next turn denotes simultaneous speech; underlining denotes emphasis; pauses are denoted in parentheses as timed—for example, "(0.2)" is two-tenths of a second, "(1.0)" is one second. A single period in parentheses denotes a micro pause. Asterisks denote indecipherable speech; quotation marks indicate that the speaker is quoting or affecting to quote; and question marks denote utterances hearable as questions. Other notes are given in parentheses, and equal signs are used to denote that one turn follows directly from another without pause (see extract 2).

Extract 1

S9: I did find it a bit confusing though in the *se*cond chapter when (1.0) th- i- y'know there was a sort of um "on the second night I'll suffocate her with a feather *pi*llow on the third nigh-" (0.8) er I I was a bit confused about the the images of her killing and and burying this child (.) um cuz quite clearly that hadn't *ha*ppened

(1.0)

S3: "the first night second night third night" [thing?

S9: [yes the first night well first night's okay I can't um and then (1.5) um "on the second night I'll suffocate her with a feather *pi*llow bury her under a weeping *wi*llow or take her far out to sea (.) and watch her tiny uh body sink to shells and reshape her[self"

S2: [no no I I I quite understood that that's the (.) birth *mo*ther

S9: aha

S2: struggling with the the relationship with the *child* and what (0.2) she's *know*ing that she can't keep this child and struggling with th the thoughts about (.) how how to part with this child what's the best (.) what to do and and this is the process in *her* head of starting to reject the child which she *has* to do in order to part with the child so I I saw that as very (0.8) much the thought processes

	of someone who's just given birth (0.2) initially (0.2) wants desperately wants the child uh and then second realizing "no I'm not going to take this baby home"
S9:	mm hmm
S2	and then having to deal with that in a way that says says these things in her head she's not gonna *do* it
S9:	mm
S2:	but it's just her way of dealing with (.) where she's at at that point (.) and I felt that was that was actually (.) that was quite re*veal*ing because don't think many (0.3) people would give voice to those *really* negative feelings
S9:	mm-hmm
S2:	although I think that process of parting with (.) the newly born baby that was (.) conceived out of what would have *seemed* to have been described as a a loving (1.0) l– a *short* but loving relationship (0.5) to part with the child (0.5) that was that was what was going (0.5)um going on (1.0) and then the child wasn't well and then there's all this about "are you going to die? Or are you
S4:	[mm yes
S6:	[yes
S2:	[going to live?" ["and do I want you to die?=
S5:	[that's right
S2:	=[or do I want you to live?" [and I thought=
S6:	[that's right * * [mm yes * *
S3:	[that was * *
S2:	=that was quite poignant that that particular it actually I almost was was crying as I thought about (0.5) that mother in the hospital
S5:	yes I thought it was very moving because even

READING THE READING EXPERIENCE [223]

               at the end actually (0.4) she's she's very
               much wanting a child cuz she wants to feed the
               baby [that's what I read
S2:   [yes (0.5)
               yes "and push my [nipples through"
S5:   [* * * yes and she's actually
S2:   [her her her
S5:   [* * * she's wanting [* *
S2:   [but her body her body's
               coming in with the milk [and she's thinking=
S5:   [exactly
S2:   ="I want to feed my baby" (2.0) so I thought
               that was really very moving chap- um (0.5)
               chapter

In this sequence, S9 expresses confusion about chapter 2 of the poem, in which a sequence occurs where the birth mother narrates a series of poetic yet violent images involving suffocating and burying her child, whom she has decided to give up for adoption. S9 says: "I I was a bit confused about the the images of her killing and and burying this child um cuz quite clearly that hadn't *hap*pened." S3 supports her point by locating the "problem" sequence more precisely within the poem: "the first night second night third night." At this point S2 reveals a different and more positive interpretation of this part of the poem, seeing the sequence as an extended metaphor for the birth mother's ambivalence about her newborn child: "that's the birth mother struggling with the the relationship with the child." S2's point is arguably challenging, since it rejects S9's interpretation; she says "no" and uses emphatic language to express the certitude of her understanding: "I quite understood." She also makes explicit that S9 has misread the birth mother's words as being literal rather than metaphorical ("having to deal with that in a way that says says these things in her head she's not gonna *do* it"). Nonetheless, the potential threat of this challenge is arguably mitigated by her judicious attribution of this opinion to herself rather than as a universal truth or fact ("I quite understood," "I I saw that as"), demonstrating an orientation to the group's avoidance of overt disagreement or criticism of others' opinions. Initially S2's metaphorical reading of this sequence is simply expressed as a relational process: "that's the birth mother struggling with the the relationship with the child." As her turn progresses, and arguably as she receives little feedback from her fellow members, this explanation is reformulated as something that takes place in the mother's head, a thought process rather than a poetic metaphor: "this is the process in *her* head of starting to reject the child which she *has* to do in order to part with the child." This then transforms the explanation of the sequence into a psychological one rather than a literary one, and arguably accommodates S9's earlier ontological conundrum that "quite clearly that hadn't *hap*pened."

Despite this shift of explanation, there continues to be a noticeable absence of take-up from other participants. Despite opportunities to support S2's interpretation at the end of turn units, the only response is from S9—two minimal "mm-hmm" tokens. This arguably prompts an extended turn by S2 in which she adopts a series of different responses to this part of the poem before alighting on a strategy that elicits a take-up from another member. First, S2 discusses the unusual and possibly brave choice the poet makes to voice negative feelings about a baby: "don't think many people would give voice to those *really* negative feelings." This also suggests a value attached to the invocation of "authentic" responses or emotions (which arguably paves the way for further appeals to "authentic responses" later in this particular sequence). The birth mother is represented as expressing ("giving voice to") an authentic emotion, even if this is conventionally unpopular or taboo (or usually merely thought, and thus concealed). This observation, however, also receives no explicit endorsement, merely another "mm-hmm" token from S9. At this point, S2 partially counters her reading of the "negative," non-maternal—albeit authentic—impulses of the birth mother by stressing the difficulty of parting from the product of a "loving relationship." This slight volte-face (indexed by "although") may be in response to a perceived disapproval on the part of the rest of the group of the birth mother's lack of maternal feeling; or it may simply reflect S2's attempts to convey the genuine ambivalence of this particular narrative sequence in the poem. This contribution is marked by hesitation and falling intonation ("that was that was what was going . um going on") suggestive of the desire to close the topic and relinquish the conversational floor.[16] Nevertheless, no take-up from other members is forthcoming.

S2 then animates her response with a form of direct reported thought or speech, voicing the birth mother's probable perspective—"are you going to die? Or are you going to live?"—a strategy that finally prompts agreement. There is a well-established literature on the conversational effects of reported speech and thought (both direct and indirect) in talk and narratives,[17] which can be summarized under the heading "the linguistics of affect."[18] Direct reported speech has been shown to occur at the climax of storytelling, usually as a way of animating and dramatizing a narrative.[19] It is also a narrative method associated with authenticity: "RS provides a method for giving veracity and authenticity to a descriptive account."[20] In our example, S2 offers a more directly emotional appeal to her listeners by her use of a form of direct reporting, which then prompts more positive affirmation from S4, S5, and S6 ("mm yes," "that's right," "yes") and ultimately leads to a disclosure of the emotional response to the poem which she claims to have experienced at the time of reading ("it actually I almost was crying as I thought about that mother in the hospital"). S5 agrees, providing further textual details as a warrant ("because even at the end"), and the conversation becomes highly animated, with S2 and S5 not only agreeing with each other ("yes," "exactly") but speaking simultaneously as they interpret the text, performing empathy with the mother as they co-construct her.

Derek Edwards has described the way in which emotion descriptions are deployed in the situated rhetoric of description and narrative. He argues that "emotions" may, in narratives or accounts, become a superordinate and explanatory category: "Emotion categories provide for rational . . . accountability, though they can also be worked up in contrast to rational thought, to label behavior as spontaneous."[21] Similarly, Edwards and Potter describe the function of such emotion discourse as a kind of "warrant" or document of experiential recall "that bolsters the validity of all kinds of stories and descriptions when they are in danger of being countered."[22]

We can see this deployment of emotion discourse in S2's response to the poem. Having gained little support for her series of observations about this particular metaphorical sequence in the poem, S2 describes an "authentic" response to the reading process, which she claims was experienced spontaneously at the moment of reading: "it actually I almost was crying as I thought about that mother in the hospital." The tense here is also interesting—the past progressive arguably lends a greater immediacy than does the simple past (I almost cried), as the sense is that of a speaker re-creating the moment for the listener. In response to this invocation of emotion discourse, S5 offers a response that supports the emotional reading of this part of the poem: "yes I thought it was very moving." Her use of emphatics ("very," "very much," "actually") strengthens her agreement, and her attribution of this "emotional reading" to her *own* perception ("I thought," "that's what I read") develops this response as one that is similarly "authentic" and not simply a polite agreement with S2's reading. Her response is supportively echoed later in the exchange by S2, but as a way of providing a warrant for her original counter to S9's initial "problem" with the chapter: "well I thought that was really very moving chapter." In other words, once framed in the rhetoric of "an authentic emotional response," her positive interpretation of this chapter has been endorsed by S5, and she confidently closes this sequence with a restatement of her position. In this context, the expression or invocation of emotion does not simply index a specific subjective or bodily experience. Rather, it indexes a kind of moral accountability, an account of the subjective experience of reading that is compatible with the social and moral "order" of the group as it is performatively and continuously worked out. In the context of this interaction, emotion is endorsed as an appropriate and valid currency of interpretation.

This analysis suggests that book group opinions are partly constructed in response to evidence of approval or support from the other members: S2 tries out a series of responses before alighting on one that seems to galvanize other members of the group. An appeal both to the authentic moment of reception as well as to the authentic response of emotion gains a kind of collective approval and status within the group and is thus implicitly validated as the "right" kind of response. In using emotion discourse, this reader is not reading from the script of her past experiences but accounting for her present response as emotionally authentic and therefore valid within this group's norms. It is important to recognize that in making this analysis, we are not denying that S2 is "telling the truth"; that is hardly the issue. For us, the issue is how this reader came to tell this particular "truth," and not one of any number of other things she could have said with potentially equal truthfulness.

The significance of readerly negotiation of responses can be more clearly seen in longer sequences, so we now turn to two more extracts. The first occurs at the beginning of the discussion.

Extract 2

S7: it was quite effective in a way (0.2) though
it was very basic and simple (.) I mean a lot
of it (.) it says says poetry but a lot of
it's just prose (.) written out
[like (draws lines with finger) poetic lines=

S3: [broken up

S7: =isn't it? (0.2) it was very very weak (.)
short of imagery and things like that but

READING THE READING EXPERIENCE [227]

	(0.8) I suppose a lot of the repetitions began
	to (1.0) hammer home y'know (.) what it felt
	like to be (0.8) in her situation adopted (.)
	but (1.0) subtle I *don't* think it was y'know
S:	(cough)
S7:	mm (1.0) I couldn't work out too much about
	the (.) the natural mother (0.8) never really
	sort of (1.0) it never really y'know (0.5)
	gave reasons why she would've just abandoned
	the the child so easily but then (.) of course
	the child * * * * the child (.) didn't have
	much chance to make contact did she? (.) um
	(1.0) I don't know but it was [it was okay=
S:	[(cough)
S7:	=but I didn't didn't think it was very subtle
	and very developed

In this extract, S7 (the only male member of the group) uses the idea that the poem is "short of imagery and things like that" and is "just prose written out like poetic lines" (our emphases) to justify his evaluation of the poem as "very very weak." The judgment "subtle I don't think it was" is supported by textual analysis in which the potentially positive claim that it makes the reader aware of "what it felt like to be in her situation" is mitigated by the claim that this is achieved by the crude means of "repetitions" and "hammer[ing] home." The complaint about the poem not being "very developed" may relate to S7's professed inability to "work out too much about the natural mother," presented as a fault with the poem: "it never really y'know gave reasons why."

This expansion on "quite effective in a way though . . . very basic and simple" could be viewed as self-defense: having committed himself to a position, S7 must now construct an unassailably rational basis for that position lest he become subject to criticism. But accounting practices do not (as in a crude reading of discursive psychology) function solely to present the speaker in the best possible light by any means necessary; they are an attempt to co-construct a social order to which participants will be committed. This has interesting consequences when speakers' positions change. Half an hour after this exchange, S7's opinion is different:

Extract 3

S6:	shall we move on to the short story? (0.3) has anyone got anything else to say about (.) the book?
S7:	well once you start (.) looking at it instead of rushing through it it is more subtle than I thought at first actually
S6:	ye[ah
S7:	[quite powerful
S:	mm-hmm
S:	mm
S7:	it's economical I mean it's uh (1.0)
S3:	it's [* * * *
S7:	[quite touching
S3:	it's (0.7) not easy to keep going to try and get a clue (.) in fact it's probably best to stop isn't it
S:	[yes
S:	[mm
S3:	and say "I didn't get that"
S:	mm
S:	yes
S3:	with with the frustration of it (0.7) you keep going on thinking it'll clear (0.5) it'll get clearer and it doesn't
S7:	at the very end she's wondering if she'll (.) if her mother's writing'll be like hers isn't she?
S:	mm
S7:	but then I mean there's * * anyway because the mother gets up before the birds get up (.) and she's up before the birds so maybe they've got (0.5) traits in common
S:	mm
S:	mm
S7:	maybe she will connect with her mother (0.5)

if she writes like the mother she'll feel
she's (.) connected with her which (1.0) the
kind couple that adopted her just fade (.)
into the background don't they?
S: mm
S: yes

S7's self-contradiction is systematic. Having called the poem "very very weak," now he refers to it as "quite powerful"; having talked in terms of its brutal "hammer[ing] home" of a point, now he calls it "quite touching"; having said "subtle I don't think it was," now he calls it "more subtle than I thought at first." He attributes this to "looking at it" rather than "rushing through it." David Peplow argues that reading group members often stress "that their opinion of [a] text altered on subsequent readings" in order "to proof themselves against claims that they have a stake in their particular interpretation";[23] here, S7 appeals to the idea that a hasty first reading may be mistaken in order to account for his departure from an opinion expressed earlier.

So, how did this volte-face take place? S7 was isolated by his early negative judgment, since subsequent comments from the other members of the group were much more positive about the poem, creating a strong social reason for S7 to change position. There is more to it than that, however. In the earlier and the later judgments, S7 follows more general comments with specific reference to the "natural mother." In the first case, this comprises the complaint that he "couldn't work out too much" about her, but in the second case, it comprises two things that he *has* worked out.

This can be related to two intervening exchanges in which the same character is discussed. Constraints of space prevent us from including transcripts of these; we beg the reader's forgiveness in this regard. The first of these is initiated by S7's identification of a contrast between the adoptive mother's *social* awareness of the daughter's skin color and the natural mother's *sensual* awareness of this. As in his initial comments, S7 presents this textual characteristic as compromised by a perceived problem: the natural mother's apparent lack of motivation. S3, S5, S8, and S9 respond by jointly constructing plausible emotional motivations, principally guilt and the fear of rejection. This is resumed when the group returns to an earlier-discussed problem: the natural mother throwing away her only photo of her daughter. S5 suggests that the natural mother has "been healed of her" (the daughter) and now "can move on." When S6 subsequently uses direct speech to speak for the birth mother ("it's now a twenty-six-year-old that I've got to write to and I can't write to her thinking y'know she's a three-day-old baby"), prompting enthusiastic agreement, S5 links this back to her own interpretation by rephrasing it as "moving on." Group satisfaction with this interpretation is clear: once questions about the pages on which the relevant details are printed have been resolved, there is a very long (twenty-four-second) pause and a change of subject.

In this way, points that explained S7's dislike of the poem become problems to be solved through discussion, both prompting reevaluation and providing a means by which to account for S7's subsequently changed opinion. The reasons S7 initially gave for his opinion can be seen not only as attempts to persuade the others but also as invitations for his own dissuasion. Simply by accounting for one's assessment of a text—the action that is arguably most characteristic of reading group interaction—one rejects the dictum *de gustibus non est disputandum*,[24] and in doing so provides for the possibility that one's opinion may reasonably be changed.

Reading and Opinion in Sequential Context

Analyzed as an *accounting* activity, reading and reception involve the negotiation of social norms and the articulation of group-acceptable interpretations. The social dimension of reading does more than intrude on readers' accounts of their private responses; it provides the occasion for those accounts, and is the medium in which they are constructed. The contextualization of utterances within a sequential organization of turns should be of relevance to any study of the discursive uses to which groups of readers put texts.

An approach viewing reception data as a situated and performative account might be thought to have limited ability to re-create both the "original," private context of reading and indeed the "nomadic" range of reading experiences. Nonetheless, it provides insight into reading as a performative, interactional, and collaborative activity. For some, reading group data might be a substitute for reception; for others it is one step removed—a *report* of reception. For us it is a situated *account* occasioned by the specific conditions in which it is produced.

Attention to the situated contingencies of accounting contributes to our understanding of reading, groups, and experiences as social constructions. Thus a discursive psychological or ethnomethodological approach might help us gain a more nuanced understanding of the context for reading (by looking at how readers invoke the relevance of context in their accounts of reading experiences) and of the nature of the reading group (by looking at how group members accept or resist shared understandings of what a reading group is in the course of their discussions). Moreover, as we have seen in this chapter, an emphasis on sequentiality is of particular help in researching changes of expressed opinion. This phenomenon is not specific to the twenty-first century. Katie Halsey shows that Virginia Woolf revised her assessment of James Joyce's *Ulysses* not while reading the novel but afterwards, when she encountered Gilbert Seldes's review.[25] But with its reading groups and mass reading events, "lit blogs" and book rating sites, twenty-first-century literary culture arguably provides readers with more opportunities than ever before to persuade one another, and to be persuaded in turn.[26]

Notes

1. See, for example, Norman Norwood Holland, *Five Readers Reading* (New Haven: Yale University Press, 1975); Tamar Liebes and Elihu Katz, *The Export of Meaning: Cross-Cultural Readings of* Dallas (Cambridge: Polity Press, 1993); Dave Morley, *The "Nationwide" Audience: Structure and Decoding* (London: British Film Institute, 1980); and Janice Radway, *Reading the Romance: Women, Patriarchy, and Popular Literature* (Chapel Hill: University of North Carolina Press, 1984).
2. See, for example, Robert Darnton, "Readers Respond to Rousseau: The Fabrication of Romantic Sensitivity," in *The Great Cat Massacre and Other Episodes in French Cultural History* (London: Allen Lane, 1984), 215–56; and Jonathan Rose, *The Intellectual Life of the British Working Classes* (New Haven: Yale University Press, 2001). A major project to catalogue such documents systematically is the Reading Experience Database, www.open.ac.uk/Arts/RED/.
3. Shaun Moores, *Interpreting Audiences: The Ethnography of Media Consumption* (London: Sage, 1993), 62.
4. See, for example, Tony Bennett et al., *Culture, Class, Distinction* (London: Routledge, 2009); Robert Darnton, *The Business of Enlightenment: A Publishing History of the Encyclopédie, 1775–1800* (Cambridge: Belknap Press, 1979); and William St. Clair, *The Reading Nation in the Romantic Period* (Cambridge: Cambridge University Press, 2004).
5. Harold Garfinkel, *Studies in Ethnomethodology* (Cambridge: Polity, 1984), 1, 11.
6. Derek Edwards and Elizabeth Stokoe, "Discursive Psychology, Focus Group Interviews, and Participants' Categories," *British Journal of Developmental Psychology* 22 (2004): 505.
7. Jonathan Potter, "Two Kinds of Natural," *Discourse Studies* 4.4 (2002): 540.
8. See Daniel Allington, "'How Come They Don't See It?' Slashing *The Lord of the Rings*," *Social Semiotics* 17.1 (2007): 43–62, for a study of ways in which such representations of shareable and unshareable private experience are employed in online discussion of a popular Hollywood film trilogy.
9. Janice Radway, "Reception Study: Ethnography and the Problems of Dispersed Audiences and Nomadic Subjects," *Cultural Studies* 2.3 (1988): 368.
10. See also research that explores similar issues in interview or focus group data, for

example, Greg Myers, "Displaying Opinions: Topics and Disagreement in Focus Groups," *Language and Society* 27 (1998): 85–111; Greg Myers, "Functions of Reported Speech in Group Discussions," *Applied Linguistics* 20.3 (1999): 376–401; Greg Myers, "Becoming a Group: Face and Sociability in Moderated Discussions," in *Discourse and Social Life*, ed. Srikant Sarangi and Malcolm Coulthard (Harlow, UK: Longman, 2000), 121–37; Phil Macnaghten and Greg Myers, "Focus Groups: The Moderator's View and the Analyst's View," in *Qualitative Research Practice*, ed. Clive Seale et al. (London: Sage, 2004), 65–79; Claudia Puchta and Jonathan Potter, "Asking Elaborate Questions: Focus Groups and the Management of Spontaneity," *Journal of Sociolinguistics* 3.3 (1999): 314–35; Timothy John Rapley, "The Art(fulness) of Open-Ended Interviewing: Some Considerations on Analysing Interviews," *Qualitative Research* 1.3 (2001): 303–23; and David Silverman, *Interpreting Qualitative Data: Methods for Analysing Talk, Text and Interaction* (London: Sage, 1993).

11. Megan Sweeney, "Prison Narratives, Narrative Prisons: Incarcerated Women Reading Gayl Jones's *Eva's Man*," *Feminist Studies* 30.2 (2004): 460.
12. Daniel Allington, "Distinction, Intentions, and the Consumption of Fiction: Negotiating Cultural Legitimacy in a Gay Reading Group," *European Journal of Cultural Studies* 14.2 (2011): 129–46.
13. See Bethan Benwell, "'A pathetic and racist and awful character': Ethnomethodological Approaches to the Reception of Diasporic Fiction," *Language and Literature* 18.3 (2009): 300–315; and David Peplow, "'Oh, I've known a lot of Irish people': Reading Groups and the Negotiation of Literary Interpretation," *Language and Literature* 20.4 (2011): 295–315, for further examples of such analysis.
14. Maria T. Wowk, "Kitzinger's Feminist Conversation Analysis: Critical Observations," *Human Studies* 30.2 (June 2007): 137.
15. Jackie Kay, *The Adoption Papers* (Newcastle upon Tyne: Bloodaxe, 1991).
16. Emanuel A. Schegloff and Harvey Sacks, "Opening up Closings," *Semiotica* 8.4 (1973): 289–327.
17. For a useful summary, see Elizabeth Holt and Rebecca Clift, eds., *Reporting Talk: Reported Speech in Interaction* (Cambridge: Cambridge University Press, 2007).
18. Maarit Niemelä, "Voiced Direct Reported Speech in Conversational Storytelling: Sequential Patterns of Stance Taking," *SKY Journal of Linguistics* 18 (2005): 197.
19. See, for example, Paul Drew, "Complaints about Transgressions and Misconduct," *Research on Language and Social Interaction* 31.3–4 (1998): 295–325; Patricia Mayes, "Quotation in Spoken English," *Studies in Languages* 14.2 (1990): 325–63; Elizabeth Holt, "Reporting on Talk: The Use of Direct Reported Speech in Conversation," *Research on Language and Social Interaction* 29.3 (1996): 219–45; Elizabeth Holt, "Reporting and Reacting: Concurrent Responses to Reported Speech," *Research on Language and Social Interaction* 33.4 (January 2000): 425–54; and William Labov, *Language in the Inner City: Studies in the Black English Vernacular* (Philadelphia: University of Pennsylvania Press, 1972).
20. Elizabeth Stokoe and Derek Edwards, "'Black This, Black That': Racial Insults and Reported Speech in Neighbour Complaints and Police Interrogations," *Discourse & Society* 18.3 (2007): 339.
21. Derek Edwards, "Emotion Discourse," *Culture and Society* 5.3 (1999): 277.
22. Derek Edwards and Jonathan Potter, *Discursive Psychology* (London: Sage, 1992), 281.
23. Peplow, "'Oh, I've known a lot of Irish people,'" 308, 307.

24. Translated as "there is no disputing about tastes" and meaning that disagreements about likes and dislikes cannot be objectively resolved.
25. Katie Halsey, "'Folk Stylistics' and the History of Reading: A Discussion of Method," *Language & Literature* 18.3 (2009): 241–42.
26. See Kathryn Grafton, *Paying Attention to Public Readers of Canadian Literature: Popular Genre Systems, Publics, and Canons* (PhD diss., University of British Columbia, 2010) for analysis of how bloggers and mass media celebrities have collectively contributed to the canonizing of Canadian literature.

12

MIXING IT UP
Using Mixed Methods Research to Investigate Contemporary Cultures of Reading

Danielle Fuller and DeNel Rehberg Sedo

Understanding complex cultural phenomena such as the widely adopted "One Book, One Community" (OBOC) model demands a methodology that can generate a series of standpoints on the social, ideological, material, economic, and political aspects of what we might term "formally organized" shared reading, or mass reading events (MREs). How, then, might reading studies researchers attend to these standpoints and the relations between different agents—readers, event organizers, institutions including libraries and schools, publishers, and the media—to produce a nuanced account of contemporary shared reading as a situated social practice? The investigative methods we used for the Beyond the Book project help us to understand what happens when people come together to share reading, and can be categorized as mixed methods research. This chapter examines our use of mixed methods in our multisite project, including an intentional mixing of language and concepts from realist and interpretative paradigms,[1] and a combination of quantitative survey methods alongside qualitative focus group and individual interviews, participant observation of mass reading events, and textual and content analysis of promotional materials and event ephemera. We make a case for the employment of similar methodologies within reading studies scholarship, particularly in the study of shared reading as a situated social practice in the northern industrialized countries of the early twenty-first century.[2]

After contextualizing our study within recent scholarship about reading, we examine three significant aspects of our research design and process by focusing on a question that recurs across several of our methods, and the responses to it that we gathered: "What type of book is the best choice for an MRE?" We consider, first, the identity-work evidenced by research participants in some answers to this question, alongside their articulations of knowledge about taste hierarchies, notions of literary value, and the intended purpose of MREs. Second, we illustrate how the interactive use of qualitative and quantitative methods, combined with paradigm clashes within an interdisciplinary research team, created epistemological problems in coding and understanding the questionnaire responses to our book choice question. Third, we discuss the extent to which our mixed methods research captures the ideological, structural, institutional, and discursive complexities that inflect the ways readers and event organizers make sense of the books chosen for mass reading events. Finally, we reflect on some of the benefits and limitations of our methodology.

Reading as a Social Practice

In 2005 the National Endowment for the Arts (NEA) announced "The Big Read," its OBOC-modeled "solution" to the findings of *Reading at Risk*.[3] Though at least one scholarly electronic listserv (Society for the History of Authorship, Reading, and Publishing) debated the merits of this report, its coverage in the mass media reflected the anxious tone of the NEA's press release. "The NEA's landmark 2004 study, *Reading at Risk,* showed that literary reading in the U.S. is in steep decline," NEA chair Dana Gioia stated in a press release. "No single program can entirely reverse this trend. But if cities nationally unite to adopt The Big Read, our community-wide reading program, together we can restore reading to its essential place in American culture."[4] Gioia's plan to "unite" the nation illuminates some of the reasons why we consider reading to be a social activity. When people read, not only do they do so with and within themselves, but also they come to the reading, in part, as members of an audience. As Virginia Nightingale and Karen Ross argue, readers are themselves reflections of the complex social and cultural nature of the audiences they help to constitute.[5] Readers as a group, however, are not homogeneous. While Catherine Ross, Lynne McKechnie, and Paulette Rothbauer's meta-analysis of reading studies illustrates how the NEA study and other quantitative projects link readers to active social engagement through correlation of responses, they also warn that taken alone, large-scale quantitative studies are unable to elicit nuanced details of individual reading practices.[6] Furthermore, such large-scale studies also fail to recognize how reading and discussing a text with others influences individual readers as social and interpretative subjects.

Attention to the social aspects of reading is most evident in scholarship focusing on communities of readers, such as research into Oprah's Book Club and face-to-face and online reading groups.[7] These studies tell us a great deal about ideology- and identity-work. Particularly relevant to our own study of shared reading are the processes of acquiring, representing, and articulating cultural capital, cultural literacies, and cultural tastes—processes influenced by social and educational structures as well as by the media and publishing industries. To access these, we combined quantitative and qualitative methods, including participant observation and textual analysis, to reveal examples of individual and collective agency, and to determine levels of access to texts and events. We also explored readers' own narratives about social and cultural factors—such as gender, ethnicity, and age—inflecting interpretative practices. Each of these methods brings a degree of insight to our analysis of contemporary cultures of reading.

Readers, Books, and Identity-Work

Gathering quantitative data about readers' involvement in MREs enabled comparison within and across our ten selected case studies in Canada, the United States, and the UK.[8] One striking consistency across many of our fieldwork sites was the way readers articulated their attachment to place and locale, and the consequent pleasures to be had in reading and sharing a book that refers to one's own city, region, or nation. Nevertheless, quantitative data from our online survey revealed a significant difference between those who identified themselves as participants in Canada Reads (CR) and Richard & Judy's Book Club (R & J) in the UK, with regard to their perception of the national, regional, or cultural relevance of the books chosen for these broadcast MREs. Questionnaire respondents were asked: "What type of book/s is/are the best choice for [name of MRE]? Why? (feel free to write up to 50 words)." While 25 percent of the CR participants cited national, regional, or cultural relevance as their first mention (that is, in the initial part of their textual response to the question), fewer than 1 percent of the R & J participants did so in their first mention. Instead, 30 percent stated that the chosen book should be accessible to a wide range of readers. Accessibility was also cited as one of the top two desirable qualities for an MRE book by participants in Canada Reads (21 percent). These figures are suggestive about readers' preferences for the type of books chosen for these events, but additional data of a more qualitative nature are required in order to expand on these preferences and to further nuance the ways that readers understand their relationship to the books and the events.

The responses to this particular survey question indicated various forms of reader engagement with—and motivations for preferring—a local book selection. Across all research sites (excepting R & J) the question yielded responses that illustrated readers' desire for mimetic identification between their own experiences of daily life within a place and the selected book. One Huntsville, Alabama, reader, for example, preferred "books about life, and living here in the South" (May 2007), while a Liverpool respondent thought that a good book choice was "something that a community can relate to where they can see something of themselves or a family member" (February 2007). Other survey respondents indicated that reader identification with a local connection could take various forms or operate through different factors including themes, setting, or authorship, for example, "a Chicago author, a regional book, urbanism" (October 2005). Usually respondents did not elaborate on their answers, and indeed, not all survey respondents chose to answer this question, but a few readers offered rationales for their preferences and tantalizing insights into their reading lives. One Vancouver reader, expressing what she understood as the potential social and educational function of a local book choice for One Book, One Vancouver (OBOV), articulated a preference for "books that have a strong local connection . . . that 'introduce' different sections of the population to each other" (June 2006). Meanwhile, in Huntsville, another respondent approved of the 2007 program's selection, Harper Lee's *To Kill a Mockingbird*, on ideological grounds, because of its proximity to living memory and familiar places, and also because of the people she encountered through the library's event program: "[It] didn't hurt that people here know Alabama, even some knew the author, and her town. The book was an edifying, thoughtful experience towards tolerance and being tuned into community. One person I met went to school with Nelle [Harper Lee] and Truman [Capote]—we had an amazing conversation. I also enjoyed talking to Mary Badham's [the actress who played Scout in the film adaptation] brother—I think he lives around New Hope area" (May 2007).

This necessarily brief set of examples offers a series of analytic clues that can be considered alongside data gathered through qualitative methods, such as the research team's participant observation of events and focus groups with both event participants and nonparticipants. Through this cross-referencing, we sought not only to "confirm, cross-validate, or corroborate findings arrived at through another method,"[9] but also to enrich and complicate the themes and issues nominated by survey respondents. Such an approach is broadly accepted by proponents of mixed methods research, even while it enacts a slippage between the triangulation and synthesis of data. As Ravi Kanbur notes, using qualitative and quantitative methods in conjunction can generate findings through "examining, explaining, confirming, refuting, and/or enriching information from one approach with that from the other."[10] In Huntsville, for example, when we attended book discussions and formal talks about the film adaptation and Harper Lee's life, we repeatedly observed senior participants recalling their initial encounters with both the book (published in 1960) and the film (released in 1962). Such memory-work frequently involved speakers locating themselves geographically, sometimes citing familial connections to Lee's family, offering commentary on aspects of the social context such as race relations, describing their enjoyment of the text, and then reflecting on how a recent rereading had differed from earlier readings. An older man at the last presentation and discussion of the film recalled for the audience the omnipresence of heat in the book. He said he felt the hot southern sun as he read. Yet he did not remember having felt, as a young person growing up in the South, the intensity of the heat that Lee was able to evoke in the book and that, he believed, the film also represented effectively. Other participants explored what had and had not changed about small-town life in Alabama in the intervening years since their first encounter with the novel. The organizers of the Huntsville events created an interactive format, allowing plenty of time for questions and discussion, serving refreshments, and providing a space for the audience to meet and talk together beforehand and afterwards. The combination of this hospitable atmosphere, a much-loved "modern classic" book choice, and an Alabama setting and author encouraged readers to engage in personal storytelling. Their articulations resonated with, and expanded on, the comments provided by the survey respondents quoted earlier.

During the participant observation work in Huntsville, then, the social dynamics of one type of shared reading practice became visible. Various forms of individual and place-based identification were articulated, validated, and made collective through the exchange of stories. Some narratives were conservatively nostalgic or even sentimental in tenor and content (participants recalled being able to play outside safely as children, or the simplicity of life in the 1930s and 1940s), while others hinted at painful experiences such as racial segregation, poverty, and the isolation of rural living. Most reminiscences, whether they were personal histories or related to a first reading of the novel, tended to prompt reflection on how economic and social circumstances in Alabama had changed for the better, although several participants in our focus groups lamented the fact that the public discussions had not led to any real debate about contemporary racism. One middle-aged white man felt that the book afforded a real opportunity for such a discussion, given how effectively, in his words, "Harper Lee really captures something about the South: the way that kindness sits alongside violence" (May 2007). Huntsville librarian Cleareaser Bone, who runs an African American book club, reflected on the reasons why the events attracted a predominantly white audience:

> So . . . as far as the blacks go, like I said, "What's in it for me?" It's not a great ending. And I think the attitude is, "Well, not that much has changed." And I think the take on [*To Kill a Mockingbird*] is a bit different than whites, who feel that "yes, it [civil rights issues and racial equality] is better." And I'm not saying it's not, but it's not where it could be, or not where it should be. And even in Huntsville, it's not where it could be. So I think that was why there was a little less involvement, I think, on the part of blacks participating in this [program].

This comment complicates the notion that a book with local relevance will generate reader engagement, for it demonstrates that forms of identification produced by such a book can also result in a lack of engagement. Such commentaries, offered in the smaller, more intimate setting of interviews and focus groups, not only enrich and deepen data from surveys and participant observation work but also problematize the key themes emerging from other material. Cross-validating with material from other sites adds a further challenge, because the social and political contexts within which other MREs take place are necessarily different. Cross-validation, however, a concept borrowed from a realist paradigm, is important because it compels us to situate the specificities of the local site within the wider social structures that are constitutive of MREs.

When Problems Are Productive: Paradigm Clashes and Generative Consequences

Thus far we have illustrated how our employment of multiple research methods has "serve[d] the dual purpose of confirmation *and* elaboration of results."[11] The multisite aspect of our research design enabled us to attend to criteria within both quantitative and qualitative traditions. Listening for repeated responses from readers on key themes such as book choice, we found that this repetition (or what the qualitative tradition of grounded theory might term "saturation") allowed us to identify consistencies and discrepancies across different national contexts (which could be seen in terms of the realist concept of "reliability") as readers expressed their experiences of shared reading. These responses, gathered through different methods of data collection, enrich and complicate our knowledge of readers' engagement with the books selected for MREs. In this part of our discussion we move toward a more nuanced account of our version of mixed methods research, while demonstrating the generative potential of such an approach for reading studies through the example of a "paradigm clash."

The process of interpreting the textual responses to the book choice question in our online survey produced an interdisciplinary moment of philosophical difference within our research team, as well as a recognition that we were, in DeNel Rehberg Sedo's words, "slamming the qualitative up against the quantitative." Our questionnaire consisted of thirty-nine quantitative (check-box) and fifteen qualitative (open-ended textual) questions. Rehberg Sedo, the social scientist on the team, requested that these textual responses be coded to facilitate quantitative analysis using statistical software. Consulting the textual responses to the book choice question, she initially suggested thirty-three provisional coding categories, while the humanists on the team (Danielle Fuller and Anouk Lang) generated a longer list of forty-six categories. Our statistical consultant then requested that this be reduced to fifteen categories in order to facilitate the running of valid queries. Not surprisingly, given their training in textual analysis within literary studies, Fuller and Lang approached the task by employing close reading skills. Their impulse was to add more and more categories in order to account for the various interpretations produced as they attended to variations in language use and narrative strategies across the range of respondents.

Here is a small sample of these string responses drawn from different research sites. The annotations in brackets indicate how Fuller and Lang interpreted such responses in order to generate the coding categories listed in the middle column of table 12.1:

1. Canada Reads respondent: "Something that challenges popular visions of literature, like *Green Grass Running Water, Beautiful Losers.*" [formally and stylistically complex; taste hierarchies and notions of "high" and "low" literary culture]

2. One Book, One Chicago respondent: "A book that stimulates the reader's intellect and imagination and can appeal to many different kinds of people." [content/ideas complex; accessible]

3. One Book, One Vancouver respondent: "Important, well-written pieces that stand to move large groups of people. Anything that takes the reader beyond a 'normal' novel into the realm of 'extraordinary.'"

[canonical? "quality" literature; writing with affective impact on reader; formally and stylistically complex; educates readers; notions of "high"/"low" literature]

4. Great Reading Adventure, Bristol, respondent: "A book which provides challenge for readers of different abilities, one which is not too difficult or too simple." [challenges readers in an unspecified way; accessible book; not too formally complex]

Table 12.1 shows how the humanists' and the social scientist's coding categories were eventually condensed into a single category. To the humanities scholars, the textual responses suggested some intriguing—and recurring—ideological connections between what the respondents considered to be the best kind of book for an MRE and what they perceived to be the cultural work achieved by shared reading. This included bridging social divides, improving individuals morally and educationally, and encouraging people to read books they would not ordinarily choose. The kind of book capable of challenging a diverse group of readers thus became entangled in ideas about "quality" literature, and hence in negotiations about high and low culture. These analytic insights depended in part, however, on extratextual and expert knowledge. For example, as Canadian literature specialists, Fuller and Lang were familiar with the novels cited in the Canada Reads response (1) and the type of formal challenges they frequently pose to students in the classroom. By contrast, from Rehberg Sedo's perspective as a communications scholar, the discipline of literary studies accords a great deal of authority to analysts and their interpretative abilities, which is in contrast to some approaches within the social sciences that encourage a realist rather than an interpretative approach to researching the social world. For her, the humanists were overinterpreting the data and—in line with the insights of feminist standpoint theory—needed to surrender some of their interpretative authority in order to respect the respondents' voices. Working to code the book choice responses thus highlighted the different notions of interpretation and evidence within the research team.[12]

As we have argued elsewhere, differing concepts of evidence and practices of interpretation are not merely seen in the employment of different methods to gather and interpret data.[13] They are also underwritten by ontological assumptions about the nature of the social world and epistemological differences about whose knowledge counts, the researcher's or the respondent's. It is beyond the scope of this essay to discuss these philosophical differences in detail, but our point here is to demonstrate how this "interdisciplinary

Table 12.1. Process of generating coding categories

SOCIAL SCIENTIST'S CATEGORIES	HUMANISTS' CATEGORIES	FINAL CATEGORY
challenging instructional	formally or stylistically complex complex content/ideas challenging subject matter challenges readers in an unspecified way educates readers	→ Improving/edifying/challenging

moment" of paradigm clash, and our attempt to resolve it—one outcome of which was the categories in the third column of table 12.1—became in its turn a generative aspect of our mixed methods process. The final coding categories for the book choice question were inflected not only by the exigencies of statistical analysis but also by discussions about the meanings and significance of categories such as "improving/edifying/challenging." While "challenging" was a term used frequently by the readers themselves, and "improving" can be induced from the Chicago (2), Vancouver (3), and Bristol (4) responses, "edifying" captures the more ideologically freighted notion of moral uplift that the humanities-trained members of the research team interpreted as underwriting statements such as the Canada Reads (1) and Vancouver (3) responses. The final categories for the book choice question were thus the product of both interdisciplinary collaboration and mixing methods of qualitative, quantitative, and textual analysis. The research team worked to address the problems posed by the clash in order to reach a coding solution that retained contextual nuance alongside quantitative parsimony. The solution also represents and honors two different views of the social world underpinning two conceptualizations of interpretation.

The integration of mixed methods at the analytic stage is evident from the foregoing account, but these methods were also integrated within the design of our data-gathering processes, an approach described by Jennifer Greene as "intent of development (using one method to inform the development of another)."[14] Figure 12.2 demonstrates how responses from earlier stages of the study were used to inform survey and focus group questions posed during later stages.

MIXING IT UP

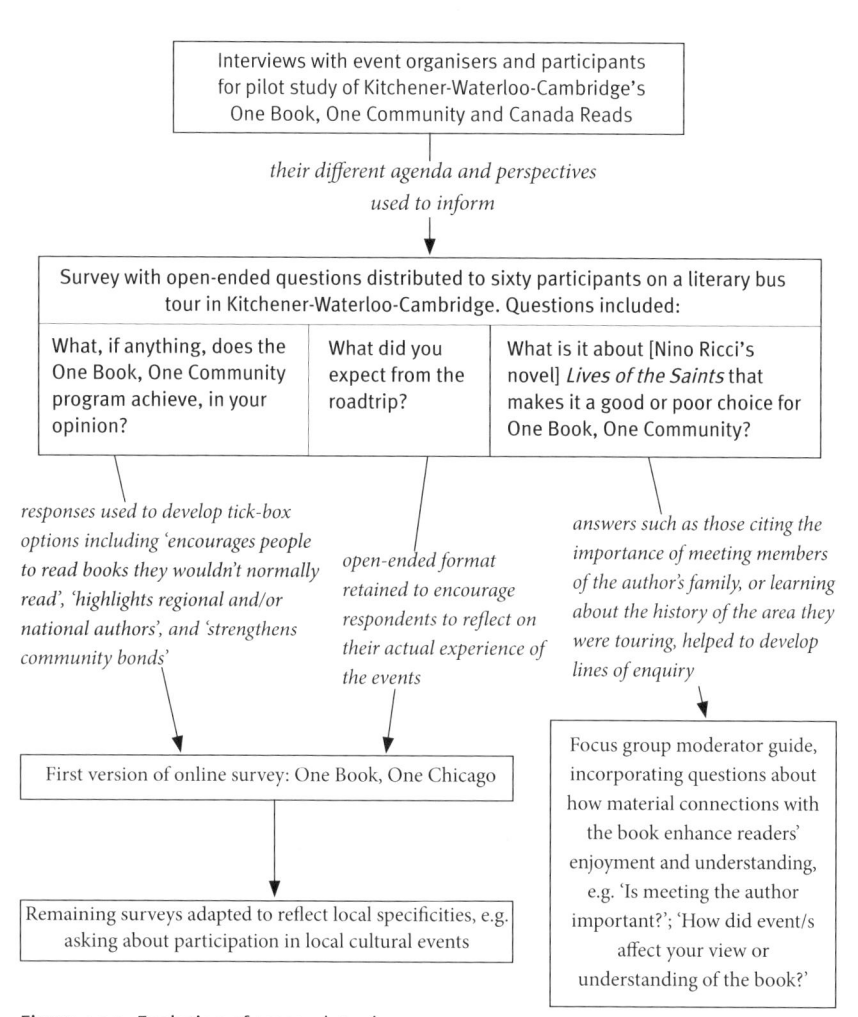

```
┌─────────────────────────────────────────────────────────┐
│ Interviews with event organisers and participants       │
│ for pilot study of Kitchener-Waterloo-Cambridge's       │
│ One Book, One Community and Canada Reads                │
└─────────────────────────────────────────────────────────┘
                           │
              *their different agenda and perspectives*
                       *used to inform*
                           ↓
┌─────────────────────────────────────────────────────────┐
│ Survey with open-ended questions distributed to sixty   │
│ participants on a literary bus tour in Kitchener-       │
│ Waterloo-Cambridge. Questions included:                 │
├──────────────────┬──────────────────┬───────────────────┤
│ What, if anything│ What did you     │ What is it about  │
│ does the One     │ expect from the  │ [Nino Ricci's     │
│ Book, One        │ roadtrip?        │ novel] *Lives of  │
│ Community        │                  │ the Saints* that  │
│ program achieve, │                  │ makes it a good   │
│ in your opinion? │                  │ or poor choice    │
│                  │                  │ for One Book,     │
│                  │                  │ One Community?    │
└──────────────────┴──────────────────┴───────────────────┘
```

responses used to develop tick-box options including 'encourages people to read books they wouldn't normally read', 'highlights regional and/or national authors', and 'strengthens community bonds'

open-ended format retained to encourage respondents to reflect on their actual experience of the events

answers such as those citing the importance of meeting members of the author's family, or learning about the history of the area they were touring, helped to develop lines of enquiry

```
┌──────────────────────────────────────────────────┐
│ First version of online survey: One Book, One    │
│ Chicago                                          │
└──────────────────────────────────────────────────┘
                        ↓
┌──────────────────────────────────────────────────┐
│ Remaining surveys adapted to reflect local       │
│ specificities, e.g. asking about participation   │
│ in local cultural events                         │
└──────────────────────────────────────────────────┘

┌──────────────────────────────────────────────────┐
│ Focus group moderator guide, incorporating       │
│ questions about how material connections with    │
│ the book enhance readers' enjoyment and          │
│ understanding, e.g. 'Is meeting the author       │
│ important?'; 'How did event/s affect your view   │
│ or understanding of the book?'                   │
└──────────────────────────────────────────────────┘
```

Figure 12.2. Evolution of research tools.

For the literary bus tour survey, which we conceived as a second-phase design stage, we deliberately used one method and its resultant data to inform and change another method, as well as to improve and refine our questionnaire. As we did so, we were aware of the imperatives of feminist standpoint epistemology to attend to the knowledge being articulated through the analyses performed by our research subjects, to move back and forth between theory and practice in ways that integrate some of the clues those analyses produced,[15] and to explore how our research subjects were variously situated within ruling and nonruling relations of power.[16] The next section of this chapter illustrates how mixed methods research facilitates this last practice, thereby enabling a situated analysis that accounts for the position of particular kinds of shared reading within economic and institutional power structures.

Elucidating the Power Dynamics of MREs

Returning to the examples of readers' responses to the book choice question, we find that an interesting tension emerges between the notion of a "challenging" book and an "accessible" book. This tension can be expanded on and complicated by data from focus groups and event organizer interviews, both of which reveal diverse knowledge of these terms and ideological negotiations taking place around taste hierarchies, literary value, and understandings of genres. Different standpoints about the meanings of reading and the cultural work that MREs perform thus become visible within the material collected through these focus groups and interviews. Readers in one Bristol focus group, for example, discussed their experiences of reading the 2006 Great Reading Adventure (GRA) selection, Jules Verne's *Around the World in Eighty Days* (1873). One woman in her early forties enjoyed the book because it was "well-researched," while another woman felt that "old books" were "difficult" to read because of the language used and the unfamiliar social and cultural contexts they depict. In addition to these stylistic, linguistic, and temporal obstacles to accessibility, another reader in this focus group described Verne's novel as "a blokey book" because of the engineering details it includes, while another complained that the narrative was too slow. Significantly for a project investigating shared reading, the participants agreed that "difficult" books can become easier—and even "fun"—when shared with others in discussion, a view we heard articulated across several fieldwork sites.

While recalling their earlier reading experiences of the novel, this Bristol group reflected on the fact that the GRA book choice needed to appeal to young people as well as older adults:

> GLYNIS: I didn't think it was very meaty. You know, if that was your introduction to reading, I don't know whether that would be the spur to do more of it really. It's very of its time.
>
> LAURA: I think that it's quite good, that it's a sort of easy read, adventure story, because I think, like *Treasure Island*, it's not necessarily a book I would choose and say, "Oh wow, I must read this!" But it's quite easy reading and

it's quite fun and keeps you going, and it gets you involved a little bit, which wouldn't necessarily . . .

CATHY: . . . Don't you think as well that it will appeal to [different] ages? So that if you were ten and you read that, it's not really controversial. Whereas if you were fifty and you read it—you know, not every book is suitable for younger people and older people. Like *The Curious Incident of the Dog in the Night Time* was a book that was meant to be suitable for adults and children, and yet there was quite a lot [of] swearing in there. And if I was a parent I would say, oh you know, there's the f-word on the first few pages and I don't really think I want my kids to read this, so I think maybe it's probably quite hard to choose a book that's going to appeal across . . . And then parents and children perhaps talking about them—no doubt my mother will talk about them . . . [laughter] . . . Do you know what I mean? So maybe you're right, it's not that meaty, but . . .

The Bristol women perform a series of interesting negotiations in this extract. They identify what they believe to be the aims of the GRA (introducing individuals to reading, prompting people to read books they would not normally choose, motivating those of different ages to read and discuss a book together). They demonstrate different opinions about how "readable" they consider *Around the World* to be and why. They also consider what type of book choice makes for an "accessible" and suitable selection for the GRA: an uncontroversial book, one that is "fun" and an "easy read," and one that tells a good story, even if it is not "meaty." In discussing these matters, they engage with issues of genre classification (adventure stories and crossover books), with Cathy rejecting the marketing and packaging of Mark Haddon's novel as "suitable for adults and children" by drawing on her own reading of the book. Here, the interactive and dialogic processes that occur in a focus group context illustrate how readers can work together to establish their own understandings of book genres as well as MREs themselves. Moreover, these Bristol readers demonstrate their capacity to recontextualize their own literary tastes, preferences, and definitions of genre within what they understand to be the goals of an MRE.

Certainly focus group participants were aware that we were academics investigating the GRA, and thus their discussions were in part framed by our own research imperatives as well as by our questions and physical presence. Nevertheless, the focus group method offered a cognate context for the types of shared reading experience—book groups, or book discussions with friends and family—with which many of our research participants were familiar. For a project investigating reading as a social practice, it was instructive to observe, and participate in, social interactions around reading such as focus groups and MRE programming. Without making these "live" social encounters part of our mixed methods, we would have been reliant on statistics combined with textual and content analysis of open-ended questionnaire responses and publicity materials. These latter methods are valuable for analyzing the rhetoric of organizing agencies and for identifying dominant knowledge about, for example, high and low culture or the "civilizing" intent that is frequently attached to reading in northern industrialized countries. Nevertheless, given the feminist imperative to analyze these categories as lived experience, methods foregrounding social interaction among readers were vital to the research process.

The final layer of our mixed methods investigation involved a top-down approach that combined the analysis of publicity materials—including websites, reading guides, advertisements, and ephemera—with interviews of event organizers and participating agencies. These agents varied from site to site but typically included booksellers, schoolteachers, city council employees working in the cultural sector, cultural workers within partnership organizations, and publishers. The aim of these interviews was not only to elucidate the meanings of reading that organizers attached to a particular MRE model but also to reach some understanding of how ideological standpoints on the significance of shared reading and the material practicalities involved in staging MREs are situated within ruling relations of power (such as governmental structures, educational systems, and capitalist economies).[17]

Concluding Reflections

In order to produce a nuanced analysis of this transnational cultural formation focused around shared reading, it is necessary to gather data by using a multilayered, multisite approach that honors the standpoints of differently positioned actors. The cultural workers who organize OBOC programs, for example, often invest in the model because they believe it can engender learning, social bonding, and even some of kind of transformation within their local communities. Their optimism about the capacity of shared reading events to build community or to facilitate cross-cultural dialogue derives in part from the ethics they developed through their professional training as librarians or arts administrators. But the ideological investment in reading as a social good also has a long history in all three nation-states of our study, and this history inflects the desires articulated by event organizers about the aims and outcomes of OBOC programs. The same, often unquestioned belief in the value of reading books informs cultural policy and influences the cultural agenda set by the grant-awarding organizations and supporting institutions that help to finance mass reading events. Nevertheless, the potential for some degree of social change can be realized through the OBOC model, especially when organizers engage with different cultural groups and generations through already established social networks. Although the core audience for OBOC programs is often the same demographic of white, middle-class, educated women who participate in other arts events and belong to book clubs, the flexibility of the model enables organizers and readers alike to adapt it to fit local, community, or personal concerns. In this respect, our study has encountered examples of readers engaging with activities variously focused on addiction and recovery, immigration, local histories of "race" relations, and access to ethically produced food. As this small and by no means all-inclusive sample suggests, OBOC enables readers to have a literary experience that is social—in terms of its publicly staged medium—and perhaps political in its import. The model can occasionally afford locations of affective belonging. As we have explored elsewhere, it can even generate an understanding of citizenship aside from institutionally sanctioned ideas of belonging.[18]

In sum, our mixed methods enabled us to produce an analysis of a particular set of shared reading formations that, in turn, has informed our reconceptualization of reading as a social practice.[19] Still, a brief outline of the benefits and constraints of our version of mixed methods is useful in highlighting areas for future development, as well as the limitations of our own knowledge and practice. First, despite attempts to vary our focus group recruitment techniques, some communities of readers were difficult to access, and our methods resulted in a data set with limited demographics. Second, it should be noted that focus group dynamics are inherently reflective of small-group dynamics more generally: inevitably, some people will speak more loudly, confidently, or frequently than others. One benefit of focus groups is that once comfortable with the setting and one another, participants often develop ideas together without reference to the moderator. As Daniel Allington and Bethan Benwell point out in chapter 11 of this volume with reference to book group talk, readers' discursive negotiations about interpretation provide insights into reading "as a performative, interactional, and collaborative activity," supporting our view that a focus group is a particularly appropriate medium through which to investigate the interactive aspects of shared reading as an enacted social practice. Third, as other scholars of reading have noted, talking about a book is one of the ways in which a reader's thoughts about it become accessible to investigators.[20] If researchers conceptualize this as a form of rereading, as we do, it is necessary to bring into visibility the frames within which this mediated interpretation occurs. Fourth, since we did not employ representative or random sampling for the survey, our findings are not generalizable, and this may limit their use for cultural policymakers who prefer statistical analyses. Nevertheless, our study draws on a large sample of readers who participate in MREs and those who do not, and our research has proved useful to event organizers who have combined it with their own knowledge to inform future program planning and reader advisory work. Often, organizers keep statistics of attendance but hear only infrequently from participating readers in any depth.

The mixed methods we employed moved us toward a more complex account of the dominant and emergent meanings of shared reading at the turn of the twenty-first century. They are especially useful for investigating the ideological aspects of shared reading and the material factors shaping the events. These include a series of commercial relationships with agents working within the contemporary book publishing industry, local economic realities such as the availability of public and corporate sponsors, and the nature of formal and informal collaborations with a variety of actors. More broadly conceived, our methods help us elaborate the role played by mass reading events in the contemporary field of literary production in an era when new technologies are impacting the ways that books are produced, disseminated, and received. The quantitative data generate a profile of keen readers, suggesting, for example, how the possession of higher education, time, and monetary resources informs motivations for participation and/or perceptions about what mass reading events might achieve. Combined with the various types of qualitative methods we selected, then, our attempt to "mix it up" was well suited to answering questions about who participates in mass reading events, who does not, and why.

While only offering glimpses into the shared reading practices of textual interpretation, our methods helped us build a critical account of some specific spaces, habits, and acts of shared reading. The same methods allowed us to investigate the cultural work that shared reading events perform for the readers, organizers, agencies, and institutions involved in them. In other words, our methods were oriented toward an interrogation of the structures and relationships among the agents who produce, disseminate, and participate in a dynamic contemporary formation of reading that crosses nation-state borders. Our study thus falls within the tradition of cultural studies research that aims to elucidate "*all* the relations among *all* the elements in a whole way of life."[21] The scale of our study meant that we could identify interesting continuities and differences in social attitudes toward the role that book reading is believed to play in people's lives. By contrast, the methods employed by linguistics specialists often operate on a micro-level, providing, for example, a fine-grained analysis of the collaborative meaning-making processes and performative gestures undertaken by readers sharing a specific book in a reading group.[22]

We are not claiming that our version of mixed methods offers a whole, true, or complete picture of reading as a social practice. Rather, we advocate mixed methods research as an approach that can benefit reading studies while avoiding the positivism of social science and the relativism that can characterize text-based humanities disciplines. Moreover, the ways that readers participating in MREs evaluate books and articulate the meanings of reading exhibit both complicity with and resistance to dominant knowledge. A mixed methods approach also, occasionally, enables the articulation of subordinate knowledge, something that may, for example, be seen in readers' analyses of their pleasure in reading genre fiction such as romance novels or science fiction. Our methodology enables researchers to attend to the voices of readers, and facilitates the delicate analytic task of teasing out the constraints of their structural positioning and the type of agency they may exercise. Mixed methods can also challenge commonly held ideas about reading, for instance, by encouraging the sharing of stories about books, and by providing readers with an opportunity to examine the role of various media within their own reading experiences.[23] Within ongoing methodological discussions around mixed methods, Jennifer Greene's assessment of this approach as an epistemology as well as a practice echoes our own feminist politics of research: "A mixed methods way of thinking . . . generates questions, alongside possible answers; it generates results that are both smooth and jagged, full of relative certainties alongside possibilities and even surprises, offering some stories not yet told. In these ways, a mixed methods way of thinking actively engages us with difference and diversity in service of both better understanding and greater equity of voice."[24] For scholars of reading who wish to engage with the fast-changing dynamics of reading cultures at the turn of the twenty-first century, and to attend to the voices of readers outside the academy, mixed methods research offers a very useful and flexible set of strategies.

Notes

1. In this essay, "realist" and "interpretative" refer to two of the dominant traditions of thought and practice within the social sciences. The "realist" paradigm, which, broadly speaking, underpins the employment of quantitative methods, conceptualizes the social world as knowable via the verifiable investigation of its properties and relations (as in the

scientific investigation of the natural world). The "interpretative" paradigm, traditionally associated with the employment of qualitative methods, operates from the assumption that the social world is accessed via its (mediated) representations. Knowledge is thus contingent on and constitutive of particular contextual and discursive factors.
2. The main investigative phase of the Beyond the Book project ran from 2005 to 2008; the core team consisted of Danielle Fuller (principal investigator/director), DeNel Rehberg Sedo (co-applicant/co-director, Mount Saint Vincent University, Canada), Anouk Lang (postdoctoral research fellow), and Anna Burrells (part-time administrative assistant). Our primary funder was the Arts and Humanities Research Council in the UK (grant number 121166).
3. Tom Bradshaw and Bonnie Nichols, *Reading at Risk: A Survey of Literary Reading in America: Research Division Report #46* (Washington, D.C.: National Endowment for the Arts, 2004). This report is based on four questions gleaned from the 2002 U.S. Census Bureau's Survey of Public Participation in the Arts.
4. National Endowment for the Arts, *National Endowment for the Arts Announces The Big Read: Ten Communities to Participate in Pilot Program to Promote Reading*, December 20, 2005, www.nea.gov/news/news05/bigreadannounce.html.
5. Virginia Nightingale and Karen Ross, *Critical Readings: Media and Audiences* (Maidenhead, UK: Open University Press, 2003), 2.
6. Catherine Sheldrick Ross, Lynne McKechnie, and Paulette M. Rothbauer, *Reading Matters: What the Research Reveals about Reading, Libraries, and Community* (Westport, Conn.: Libraries Unlimited, 2006), 24.
7. See, for example, Cecilia Konchar Farr, *Reading Oprah: How Oprah's Book Club Changed the Way America Reads* (Albany: State University of New York Press, 2005); Elizabeth Long, *Book Clubs: Women and the Uses of Reading in Everyday Life* (Chicago: University of Chicago Press, 2003); DeNel Rehberg Sedo, "Readers in Reading Groups: An On-line Survey of Face-to-Face and Virtual Book Clubs," *Convergence: The Journal of Research into New Media Technologies* 9.1 (Spring 2003): 66–90.
8. Our research sites and mass reading events were One Book, One Community (Kitchener, Waterloo, and Cambridge, Ontario); Canada Reads (nationwide radio); One Book, One Vancouver; One Book, One Chicago; One Book, One Huntsville (Huntsville, Alabama); Seattle Reads; The Great Reading Adventure (Bristol); The Birmingham Book Festival; Richard & Judy's Book Club (nationwide British TV); and Liverpool Reads.
9. John W. Creswell, *Research Design: Qualitative, Quantitative, and Mixed Methods Approaches* (London: Sage, 2003), 217.
10. Ravi Kanbur, "Q-Squared? A Commentary on Qualitative and Quantitative Poverty Appraisal," in *Q-Squared: Combining Qualitative and Quantitative Methods in Poverty Appraisal*, ed. Ravi Kanbur (Delhi: Permanent Black, 2001), 18.
11. Abbas Tashakkori and John W. Creswell, "Editorial: Developing Publishable Mixed Methods Manuscripts," *Journal of Mixed Methods Research* 1.2 (2007): 109.
12. For more on this distinction, see Linda Hutcheon and Michael Hutcheon, "A Convenience of Marriage: Collaboration and Interdisciplinarity," *PMLA* 116.5 (October 2001): 1364–76.
13. See Danielle Fuller, "Beyond CanLit(e): Reading. Interdisciplinarity. Trans-Atlantically," in *Shifting the Ground: Nation-State, Indigeneity, Culture*, ed. Smaro Kamboureli and Robert Zacharias (Waterloo, Ont.: Wilfrid Laurier University Press, 2012), 77–100.

14. Jennifer C. Greene, "Is Mixed Methods Social Inquiry a Distinctive Methodology?," *Journal of Mixed Methods Research* 2.1 (2008): 14.
15. Liz Stanley and Sue Wise, "Method, Methodology, and Epistemology in Feminist Research Processes," in *Feminist Praxis: Research, Theory and Epistemology in Feminist Sociology*, ed. Liz Stanley (London: Routledge, 1990), 25.
16. For an example of this kind of analysis in relation to Canada Reads, see Danielle Fuller and DeNel Rehberg Sedo, "A Reading Spectacle for the Nation: The CBC and 'Canada Reads,'" *Journal of Canadian Studies* 40.1 (Winter 2006): 5–36.
17. See, for example, the analysis provided in Danielle Fuller and James Procter, "Reading as 'Social Glue'? Book Groups, Multiculture, and Small Island Read 2007," *Moving Worlds: A Journal of Transcultural Writings* 9.2 (2009): 26–40.
18. Danielle Fuller, *Citizen Reader: Canadian Literature, Mass Reading Events, and the Promise of Belonging* (London: British Library, 2011).
19. Danielle Fuller and DeNel Rehberg Sedo, *Reading Beyond the Book: The Social Practices of Contemporary Literary Culture* (New York: Routledge, 2013).
20. See, for example, Elizabeth Long, "Textual Interpretation as Collective Action," in *The Ethnography of Reading*, ed. Jonathan Boyarin (Berkeley: University of California Press, 1993), 180–212; Lynne Pearce, *Feminism and the Politics of Reading* (London: Arnold, 1997).
21. Lawrence Grossberg, "Affect's Future: Rediscovering the Virtual in the Actual," in *The Affect Theory Reader*, ed. Melissa Gregg and Gregory J. Seigworth (Durham: Duke University Press), 323.
22. See, for example, chapter 11 by Allington and Benwell in this volume; and Kieran O'Halloran, "Investigating Argumentation in Reading Groups: Combining Manual Qualitative Coding and Automated Corpus Analysis Tools," *Applied Linguistics* 32.2 (2011): 172–96.
23. See, for example, DeNel Rehberg Sedo, "'Richard & Judy's Book Club' and 'Canada Reads': Readers, Books and Cultural Programming in a Digital Era," *Information, Communication & Society* 11.2 (March 2008): 188–206.
24. Jennifer C. Greene, "Is Mixed Methods Social Inquiry a Distinctive Methodology?" *Journal of Mixed Methods Research* 2.1 (2008): 20.

CONTRIBUTORS

DANIEL ALLINGTON is a lecturer in the Centre for Language and Communication at the Open University, UK.

BETHAN BENWELL is a senior lecturer in English Studies in the Division of Literature and Languages at the University of Stirling.

JIN FENG is a professor of Chinese in the Department of Chinese and Japanese, Grinnell College.

ED FINN is an assistant professor in the School of Arts, Media and Engineering and the Department of English at Arizona State University.

DANIELLE FULLER is a senior lecturer in the School of English, Drama, and American and Canadian Studies at the University of Birmingham.

ANOUK LANG is a lecturer in English Studies in the School of Humanities at the University of Strathclyde.

DAVID S. MIALL is a professor in the Department of English and Film Studies at the University of Alberta.

JULIAN PINDER completed his Ph.D. in the Department of English at the University of Sydney.

JANICE RADWAY is Walter Dill Scott Professor of Communication Studies and professor of American Studies and Gender Studies at Northwestern University.

JULIE RAK is a professor in the Department of English and Film Studies at the University of Alberta.

DENEL REHBERG SEDO is an associate professor in the Department of Communication Studies at Mount Saint Vincent University.

MEGAN SWEENEY is an associate professor at the University of Michigan with a joint appointment in the Department of English Language and Literatures and the Department of Afroamerican and African Studies.

JOAN BESSMAN TAYLOR is an assistant professor in the School of Library and Information Science at the University of Iowa.

MOLLY ABEL TRAVIS is an associate professor in the English Department at Tulane University.

DAVID WRIGHT is an assistant professor in the Centre for Cultural Policy Studies at the University of Warwick.

INDEX

2666 (Bolaño), 181, 182

AbeBooks, 10
Absalom, Absalom! (Faulkner), 187
academic critics. *See* critics
The Adoption Papers (Kay), 220
affinity, 80, 82; between readers on LibraryThing, 76–78
African American writing, 179, 180, 183, 192
Afternoon (Joyce), 212
agency of readers: 2, 120–21, 148, 236, 249; in hypertext reading, 205–6, 208, 210, 212; in resolving semiotic gaps, 16; in prison, 127
algorithms: and book purchases, 16, 113, 180, 189; role within LibraryThing, 73, 76, 83; used to match books to readers, 70–71, 83–84, 112–13, 120, 197; used to match books to reviewers, 15, 70–71
The Amazing Adventures of Kavalier and Clay (Chabon), 70 fig. 3.1, 77 fig. 3.2, 152–53
Amazon.com, 112–13, 178, 183, 184, 187; book reviews and reviewers, 7, 113, 190, 192–97, 198; connections with LibraryThing, 68; gathering data on user preferences, 109; identity-work on, 10, 19; making structures of prestige visible, 197–98; network diagrams of noun co-occurrences in reviews on, 194 fig. 9.7, 196 fig. 9.9; readers exchanging literary value on, 109, 113; recommendations generated by, 16, 83, 112–13, 120, 180, 188–89; visualizations of recommendation data generated by, 181 fig. 9.1, 182 fig. 9.2, fig 9.3, 186 fig. 9.5. *See also* Kindle
APIs (application programming interfaces), 69
Around the World in Eighty Days (Verne), 244
As I Lay Dying (Faulkner), 187
audiobooks, 5, 198
Austen, Jane, 116, 119
authors: boundaries between readers and, 63; as "brands", 187; managing relationships with readers, 62–63

Bad Girlz (Holmes), 128, 130, 132–33
Bambara, Toni Cade, 192
Bamboo Girl (zine), 33, 39–40
banned books. *See* censorship
Barthes, Roland, 84, 148–49, 156
BBC (British Broadcasting Corporation), 120; The BBC's Big Read, 7, 116, 118–20
being real and getting clean (zine), 33
Bergson, Henri, 205, 207–10, 212, 213
bestsellers, 99–100
The Big Read (NEA initiative), 235
Bikini Kill (zine), 33
Bitch (zine), 33
blogs, 68, 231; connections with LibraryThing, 69–71, 84; criticism of, 18, 73
Bolaño, Roberto, 185, 186 fig. 9.5, 187, 197
book choices, 108, 115, 143, 151; influences on, 16, 120, 188–89; relationship to lists, 120–21
book clubs. *See* book groups

[255]

book clubs, mail order, 111
book clubs, mass-mediated, 68. *See also* Oprah's Book Club
book discussion, 217–18; in book groups, 142, 143, 145–56, 219–31, 247; changes to readers' interpretations during, 227–30; of ethical issues, 155–56; at One Book, One Community events, 238, 244–45; resolution of interpretive gaps during, 147–49, 154–56, 223–24; validation of others' responses during, 220, 224–26, 229–30
book distribution, global, 100
book fairs: Cape Town, 97, 98, 99, 100, 103; Frankfurt, 98; Jozi, 99, 102; London, 98, 99, 102
book groups, 4, 142–58, 187, 230–31; guides for, 144–45; shared norms and values within, 219, 230–31; shortcomings of, 198. *See also* book discussion
book market, 117; global, 99, 100; in South Africa, 96, 97–98, 102, 103
book prices: in "best books" lists, 117; in South Africa compared to other nations, 96
book recommendations, 109–13; on LibraryThing, 76
book reviews, 164, 177, 178; embedded in institutions of book production, 111; on LibraryThing, 69, 70–71, 72, 84; of Toni Morrison by professional reviewers, 189–92, 191 fig. 9.6, 193–95, 195 fig. 9.8, 197; of Toni Morrison on Amazon.com, 192–97, 194 fig. 9.7, 196 fig. 9.9. *See also* reviewers
book swap sites, 69
books: as commodities, 72, 159, 189, 193, 194; covers of, 145; design of, 204; endings of, 153; length, 151–52; as material objects, 29, 145–47, 149, 151–54, 160; perceived as edifying, 240–41; as tools for identity-work, 136–38; treatment of characters in, 147, 150, 152, 153–55, 211
booksellers, 112, 145, 180, 246
bookstores, 113, 159–73, 163 fig. 8.1, 165 fig. 8.2, 188, 197; big-box, 162, 164, 166, 167, 169, 171; and book groups, 144, 166; Chapters Indigo (Canadian big-box store), 161, 162, 163, 167–71; connections with LibraryThing, 70; online (*see* AbeBooks; Amazon.com); relationships with customers, 111–12, 164, 166, 168, 171
Bourdieu, Pierre, 14, 19, 20, 21, 148, 189; distinction, 177–78, 197, 199; field of cultural production, 110, 115, 160; illusio, 110–11; legitimacy effect, 12; literary field, 110, 119, 120, 121, 189
Brick Lane (Ali), 154
Bristol's Great Reading Adventure, 240, 242, 244–45

canons, literary, 116, 178, 181, 196–97, 240–41; African American, 180, 183; American, 183, 184, 187, 188; challenges to, 83–84, 118, 119, 120, 197, 199; school reading lists and syllabi as, 116, 184; Toni Morrison's position in, 180, 193; Native American, 183, 185, 188; processes of canon-formation on Amazon.com, 177; policed by academics and critics, 110
The Catcher in the Rye (Salinger), 187
cell phones, publishing on, 103
censorship, 125, 127, 128; in South Africa, 90
Ceremony (Silko), 180–81, 182 fig. 9.2, 183, 184, 185, 188
Chautauqua movement, 89
Cheever, John, 187
China: Internet use in, 20; prominence of online literature in, 20, 48–49; relationship of Jinjiang to modernization in, 64
churches and religious institutions, 144; relationship to reading culture in South Africa, 89, 101, 103
classification of books, 111
CliffsNotes, 180, 183, 185, 186 fig. 9.5, 187–88, 197; used in book groups, 153
cliques (in networks of texts), 185, 186 fig. 9.5, 187, 188
Coetzee, J. M., 100, 101

INDEX

[257]

The Coldest Winter Ever (Sister Souljah), 128, 133–35
colleges. *See* universities
common book projects. *See* One Book, One Community (OBOC) projects
communities, 13, 79–80; on Amazon.com, 193; discursive, 170; formed through algorithmic recommendations on LibraryThing, 73; on LibraryThing, 68, 82, 84; potential for building through One Book, One Community projects, 246–47; virtual, 81–82. *See also* imagined communities; interpretive communities; online communities
computers. *See* Internet
consumers: blurring of line between producers and, 17, 112; relationship to producers, 117–18, 120–21
consumption: of texts, 82, 115; blurring of line between production and, 2–3, 30; structures mediating between production and, 113
convergence culture, 74, 75, 81; LibraryThing as example of, 72
critics, 116, 117, 178, 185; as cultural gatekeepers, 110, 112, 121, 140
cross-shelving books in bookstores, 162, 166, 167
Cry, the Beloved Country (Paton), 99–100, 101
cultural authority, 147, 178, 193; challenges posed by Internet to, 18, 109, 118, 177, 197
cultural capital, 10, 110, 114, 188, 198, 236
cultural exchange, 179
cultural studies, 248
curricula. *See* syllabi

danmei (Chinese male–male homoerotic fiction), 53–55, 57
data mining, gathering reader preference data on Amazon.com through, 109
"Data Mining the Amazon" (Waller), 113
The Da Vinci Code (Brown), 100
de Certeau, Michel, 7, 162
Death, Snow, and Mistletoe (Malmont), 151

Deleuze, Gilles, 209, 210, 212
detective fiction, 165
Dickens, Charles, 116, 119, 193, 195
digitization, 5, 20, 102
discursive psychology, 220, 230
discussability, 144–45, 151, 156
discussion. *See* book discussion
discussion forums, on LibraryThing, 77–78, 84, 85
Dostoevsky, Fyodor, 183

e-book readers, 199. *See also* Kindle
education, 178, 187, 236; literacies transmitted through, 8; reading lists as canons, 184–85, 196–97; relationship to reading culture in South Africa, 88, 89, 90, 91–94, 96, 101–3. *See also* syllabi; universities
Ellison, Ralph, 183, 187, 192
Erdrich, Louise, 184, 185, 186 fig. 9.5, 187, 188
ethnography, 9, 128
ethnomethodology, 217–18, 219–20, 230
evaluation of texts, 156, 192, 227
expert knowledge, 110, 111, 113, 120–21; challenges to, 73–75, 109, 118, 119
The Eye of the Dragon (King), 151

Facebook, connections with LibraryThing, 69, 72
fan communities, 8, 17, 32, 118, 165
fan fiction, 62, 63, 147
fantasy, 169
Faulkner, William, 183, 187; connections to Toni Morrison through Amazon data, 185, 186 fig. 9.5, 190, 192, 193, 196
field of cultural production. *See* Bourdieu, Pierre
Fitzgerald, F. Scott, 183
Flip Side of the Game (Whitaker), 128, 137–38
"Fools" (Ndebele), 91
Fools Crow (Welch), 188
Foucault, Michel, 161, 171
Four Souls (Erdrich), 188

Game Over (Whitaker), 128, 137–38

gatekeeping, cultural: challenges to, 73–74, 76; in relation to urban fiction, 125
gender: identity explored on Jinjiang, 49, 51–55, 57, 64. *See also* zines
genre, 159–71, 183, 185, 188, 244–45
genre fiction, 50, 165, 249. *See also* danmei; detective fiction; fantasy; horror; mystery novels; science fiction; time-travel fiction; time-travel romances; true crime; urban fiction
globalization, effects on reading in South Africa, 96, 99
Google, 7
Gordimer, Nadine, 100, 101
The Grapes of Wrath (Steinbeck), 187
Great Books Foundation. *See* Shared Inquiry model of book discussion
The Great Gatsby (Fitzgerald), 183
Grindin' (Santiago), 128, 132, 133, 134–36

Hamlet, 91
Hansberry, Lorraine, 188
Harry Potter series (Rowling), 100
Hawthorne, Nathaniel, 183
Hemingway, Ernest, 183, 192, 193
horror, 118
House Made of Dawn (Momaday), 188
Hurston, Zora Neale, 179, 183, 187, 193
hypertext, 203–16; and reader interactivity, 204, 206

identity: reading and, 10, 19, 236; relationship to networks, 84
imagined communities: invoked by zines, 34–35, 37; on Jinjiang, 49, 64; of readers, 18, 156, 158n26; of zinesters, 40
interdisciplinarity, needed for the study of reading, 10–13, 29–30, 240–43
Internet: changes posed to reading, 4; democratizing potential for reading, 6–7, 8; enhancing reader experiences on Jinjiang, 57; facilitating publication by Jinjiang authors, 15; providing a forum for identity-work, 20; putative threat to reading by, 5–6; reconfiguring elements in chain of book distribution, 15, 248; shared terminology with print culture, 4–5; textual construction of identity on, 9; use across different continents, 102; use in China, 48; use in South Africa and Africa, 102. *See also* Jinjiang; LibraryThing; websites
interpretive communities, 148–49; on LibraryThing, 78–79, 80
interpretive practices. *See* book discussion
Into Thin Air (Krakauer), 112
Invisible Man (Ellison), 180
Isiqalo–First Words in Print project (South Africa), 94–95, 103

Jinjiang (Chinese literature website), 49–64; construction of authorial identity on, 60; effects of user anonymity on, 57; genres on, 50–51; *fanwai* ("special features"), 62–3; fluidity of texts on, 62; interaction between readers and authors on, 60–63; overview of, 49–50; page layout of, 58–59, 58 fig. 2.1, 59 fig 2.2; reader bonds generated by, 62; role of moderators in shaping author and reader behavior on, 59; transgressive behavior enabled by, 57, 62; transition of online texts to print publication, 62; user demographics, 50. *See also* gender; pleasure
Jones, Gayl, 192; *Eva's Man*, 218; *White Rat,* 195
Joyce, James, 183
July's People (Gordimer), 91, 92

Kindle, 13, 197; alternative to existing systems of book production and distribution, 1
The Known World (Jones), 154

libraries: and book groups, 144, 220; connections with LibraryThing, 68, 69, 70; and One Book, One Community projects, 237, 239, 246; in prisons, 125, 126, 127; in South Africa, 88–90, 93–94, 96, 99, 102–3. *See also* zines

INDEX

Library and Information Association of South Africa (LIASA), 90
LibraryThing, 68–87; commercial interests' role within, 71; community on, 75, 84–85; connections with other readers through, 76–82; groups on, 77–78, 80, 82; identity-work done on, 71–72; mechanisms for participation in, 80; tags used in, 69, 70 fig. 3.1; users' book collections, 71–72
list culture, 108, 109, 114–21
lists, 114–21, 160; of "best books"/bestsellers, 16, 100, 113–18, 197; as forms of cultural guidance, 117; as mediating structures of value, 114, 118, 120; selection processes to determine, 114
litblogs. *See* blogs
literacy, 127; cultural, 236; relationship of lists to, 116, 117, 120; relationship to reading culture in South Africa, 88–90, 93–95, 99, 101–3
the "literary" (as category), 17, 84, 108, 110, 115, 118
literary critics. *See* critics
"literary" reading, 203–5, 209, 211, 213, 214n3, 241
literary value, 112, 113, 116, 213, 244; in Bourdieu's model of the literary field, 110; list culture facilitating democratization of, 118; new ways of determining, 18–19, 120–21; readers engaging with, 109
the "long tail" (Chris Anderson), 76, 109, 112–13, 116; LibraryThing as example of, 72–73
The Lord of the Rings (Tolkien), 100
Lost in a Good Book (Fforde), 147

The Magic Faraway Tree (Blyton), 101
Magopo Wa Rakgadi (Mehlape), 103
The Man in My Basement (Mosley), 146
marketing, 71, 114, 121, 166, 180, 245
Márquez, Gabriel Garcia, 192
Martin, Lauren, 37
mass culture, 120
mass media, 119, 236; Canada Reads (radio program), 164, 236, 240–42; radio and books, 5, 118; in South Africa, 94; television and books, 118–19, 164. *See also* BBC; *Oprah* (television show); Oprah's Book Club; Richard and Judy's Book Club
mass reading events. *See* One Book, One Community (OBOC) projects
Mda, Zakes, 101
media. *See* mass media
middlebrow culture, 117
mixed methods, 218, 234, 237–49, 243
MLA bibliography, 187
mobile phones. *See* cell phones
Morrison, Toni, 177–202; *Beloved,* 180–81, 183–87, 190, 193–96, 198; *The Bluest Eye,* 100, 189, 190, 195; *A Mercy,* 181, 182, 182 fig. 9.3; *Paradise,* 179; *Playing in the Dark,* 190; *Song of Solomon,* 184, 190, 195, 198; *Sula,* 190; data visualizations relating to, 181 fig. 9.1, 182 fig. 9.2, fig. 9.3, 186 fig. 9.5, 191 fig. 9.6, 194 fig. 9.7, 195 fig. 9.8, 196 fig. 9.9
multilingualism, relationship to reading culture in South Africa, 88, 89, 92–94
mystery novels, 169

National Endowment for the Arts (NEA), 235
National Home Reading Union (NHRU), 89
National Library of South Africa, 97; Centre for the Book, 88, 94–95, 96
nation-building: through reading, 235; relationship to reading culture in South Africa, 88, 89–90, 91, 92
Native American writing, 181, 183, 186 fig. 9.5, 188
neoliberalism, effects on reading culture in South Africa, 88–89, 95–96, 101–2
networks, 80–84; of lexias in hypertext fiction, 211; relationship to human subjectivity, 83–84; of texts, authors, and concepts associated with Morrison, 179–99; visualizations of Amazon.com data on Morrison, 181 fig. 9.1, 182 fig. 9.2, fig. 9.3, 194 fig. 9.7, 196 fig. 9.9; visualizations of data from

networks (*continued*)
  professional reviews of Morrison, 191 fig. 9.6, 195 fig. 9.8. *See also* social networks; zines

One Book, One Chicago, 240, 242
One Book, One Community (Kitchener, Waterloo, and Cambridge, Ontario), 243
One Book, One Community (OBOC) projects, 4, 231, 234–51; book clubs and, 247; choice of book for, 236–45; audience for, 247; cultural workers' involvement in, 246; ideological components of, 236–37, 240–42, 244, 246–48; importance of place to, 236–37; local government involvement in, 246; and publishing industry, 248; role of libraries and librarians in, 237, 239, 246; schoolteachers' involvement in, 246. *See also* BBC; The Big Read; Bristol's Great Reading Adventure; One Book, One Chicago; One Book, One Community (Kitchener, Waterloo, and Cambridge, Ontario); One Book, One Vancouver
One Book, One Vancouver, 237, 240, 242
One Mint Julep (zine), 33
online communities, connected through affinity, 73. *See also* Jinjiang; LibraryThing
Oprah (television show), 178, 179
Oprah's Book Club, 100, 119, 179, 187, 198, 235
orality, 83, 90

Parable of the Sower (Butler), 154
paratexts, 146, 153, 154
participant observation, 143
performativity: of book discussion, 219, 225, 226, 230–31, 247; of reading, 147, 148; of zine-ing, 35, 36, 40
perzines, 33
pleasure: centrality of evaluation to, 118; on Jinjiang, 53, 63; and reading, 153, 154, 210, 249; and urban fiction, 129–30, 132, 140; and zine-ing, 38, 41

poaching. *See* textual poaching
prestige, 177–78, 181, 183–85, 187–90, 193, 197–98; authorial, 199; of books as cultural objects, 10; rankings in Amazon network surrounding *Beloved*, 184 table 9.4. *See also* Bourdieu, Pierre
Princess Charming (zine), 33, 37
prizes, literary, 111, 112, 178, 200n19; in South Africa and Africa, 98
producers. *See* consumers
production, 115. *See also* consumption
Project Gutenberg, 6
Publishers' Association of South Africa (PASA), 97, 98
publishing industry, 180, 236, 246; growth over the twentieth century, 108; independent publishers, 161; multinational publishers, 100, 120, 161–62, 163, 166–68, 171; relationship between online and print publication, 50, 62; relationship to reading culture in South Africa, 88, 89, 95–99, 103; shifting to "publish then filter" model, 75–76
The Puttermesser Papers (Ozick), 146

Queer Punk Issue (zine), 33

"race" and ethnicity, 166–67, 170, 179, 194–97, 198, 220; in relation to One Book, One Community events, 238–39, 247; in relation to prisoners and urban fiction, 125, 126, 127, 130, 134; in South Africa, 89, 92–93; treatment in *Cry, the Beloved Country*, 106n55
radio. *See* mass media
ranking and rating systems, 111, 115; on Jinjiang, 59–60
readers: defying authorial authority, 61–62; desire for resolution, 153; emotions of, 193, 198, 209–12, 220, 224–26, 240; emotional support offered by Jinjiang to, 55, 60; expectations of, 150–51, 153; identity-work done on Jinjiang by, 63; pleasures available on Jinjiang to, 63; relationship with writers, 51, 139, 146, 149

reading: aloud, 147; as inherently social, 142–43, 154, 156; individuals' accounts of, 218–19, 230; memory and, 208–9, 220, 238; as process of creating an ideal text, 147–48, 154, 156; and social class, 7; social dimensions to, 148, 161, 230, 235; as social experience, 246–47. *See also* "literary" reading
reading groups. *See* book groups
reading practices, 13–14; in prisons, 126; outside formal education, 187
Reading the Romance (Radway), 12, 192
regimes of reading (Frow), 1–2
Restroom (zine), 33
reviewers: as cultural authorities, 147; as cultural intermediaries, 112. *See also* book reviews
Richard and Judy's Book Club (UK television show segment), 119, 236
Ringworld's Children (Niven), 150, 155
Riot Grrrl, 37; bands associated with, 38; connections to zine-ing, 32
Riot Grrrl [nyc] (zine), 33
romance novels, 118, 249. *See also* danmei; time-travel romances

The Satanic Verses (Rushdie), 90
The Scarlet Letter (Hawthorne), 187
schools. *See* education
science fiction, 118, 150, 155, 165, 169, 249
Shakespeare, William, 183
Shared Inquiry model of book discussion, 144, 147
Silko, Leslie Marmon, 184
Silver Rocket (zine), 33
snarla (zine), 33
social networks, creation through zines, 40
sourpuss (zine), 33, 37
South Africa: anti-apartheid movements, 90; culture of reading in, 88–107; effects of apartheid, 90, 91, 93, 94, 103; grassroots activism in, 90, 101–2, 103; indigenous African languages, 97, 101, 103; language rights in, 90, 93–94; role of government in building a culture of reading, 88–89, 91–93, 95, 97–98, 102–3; women's organizations in, 89–90
South African Home Reading Union (SAHRU), 89–90
space and spatiality: in hypertext reading, 204–5, 207, 212; in non-hypertext reading, 207
Steinbeck, John, 183
study guides. *See* CliffsNotes
subjectivity, 35, 218
syllabi, 178, 181, 183–85, 187–88; as nation-building tools in South Africa, 88, 90–93, 101

Tales from the Clit (zine), 33
Taormino, Tristan, 38–39
taste, 62, 83, 108, 110, 113, 236; attempts to shape, 147; institutions involved in forming, 197; Internet allowing readers to register own preferences, 7, 177–78; lists as structures embedded in, 120; popular, 100, 119, 120; preferences articulated by participants in mass reading events, 240–41, 244–45; producers following rather than shaping, 109lists offering insight into processes of formation of, 59, 115; readers redefining consumption habits as expressions of, 10, 19–20; shifts in, 51, 230
technology, anxieties over changes posed to reading by, 4; supporting rather than threatening reading, 5. *See also* Internet
Teeter Totter (zine), 33
television and books. *See* mass media
The Terminal Experiment (Sawyer), 155
textual consumption. *See* consumption
textual poaching, 82
textual production. *See* production
Things Fall Apart (Achebe), 101
time and temporality, 206–7, 214n5; in hypertext reading, 205–6, 209, 210, 212–13; in non-hypertext reading, 204–5, 211
The Time of Our Singing (Powers), 152–53
time-travel fiction, 65n19
time-travel romances: plots of, 52, 53, 56;

time-travel romances (*continued*)
sub-genres of, 50–51; treatment of gender in, 51–7
Tinuviel, zine collection and correspondence with zinesters, 38
To Kill a Mockingbird (Lee), 237–39
Touching the Void (Simpson), 112
Tracks (Erdrich), 183, 184, 188
true crime, 169
Twain, Mark, 183, 190, 192
Twitter, 103, 199; connection to LibraryThing, 69

universities, 116, 144, 178, 184, 187, 197; relationship to reading culture in South Africa, 88, 90
urban fiction, 4, 124–41; criticism of, 125, 128, 139, 140; focus on material wealth in, 129, 132–35, 138; in prisons, 124, 125; reinforcing ideologies underpinning inequality, 126, 131, 133–36, 140; sharing books, 125; thematic and narrative content, 124–25, 130–31, 133–35, 137; as tool for reflection, 128, 131, 132–38, 139. *See also* pleasure

value. *See* literary value
Velvet Grass (zine), 36–37

Web-based literature, 51. *See also* Jinjiang
websites, as paratextual contexts for reading, 100
The Western Canon (Bloom), 117
Whitman, Walt, 190
wikis, 76; used in LibraryThing, 69
Winfrey, Oprah, 189; *Oprah* (television show), 178, 179; Oprah's Book Club, 100, 119, 179, 187, 198, 235
Winnie the Pooh (Milne), 101
Woolf, Virginia, 192
Wright, Richard, 192

zines, 27–42; collected in libraries and archives, 31, 39, 43n3; defining, 27–28, 33; enabling exploration of gender identities, 33, 38, 39, 42; networks built through, 33, 36, 38; physical construction of, 28–29, 32, 34, 41, 46n22. *See also* performativity; pleasure